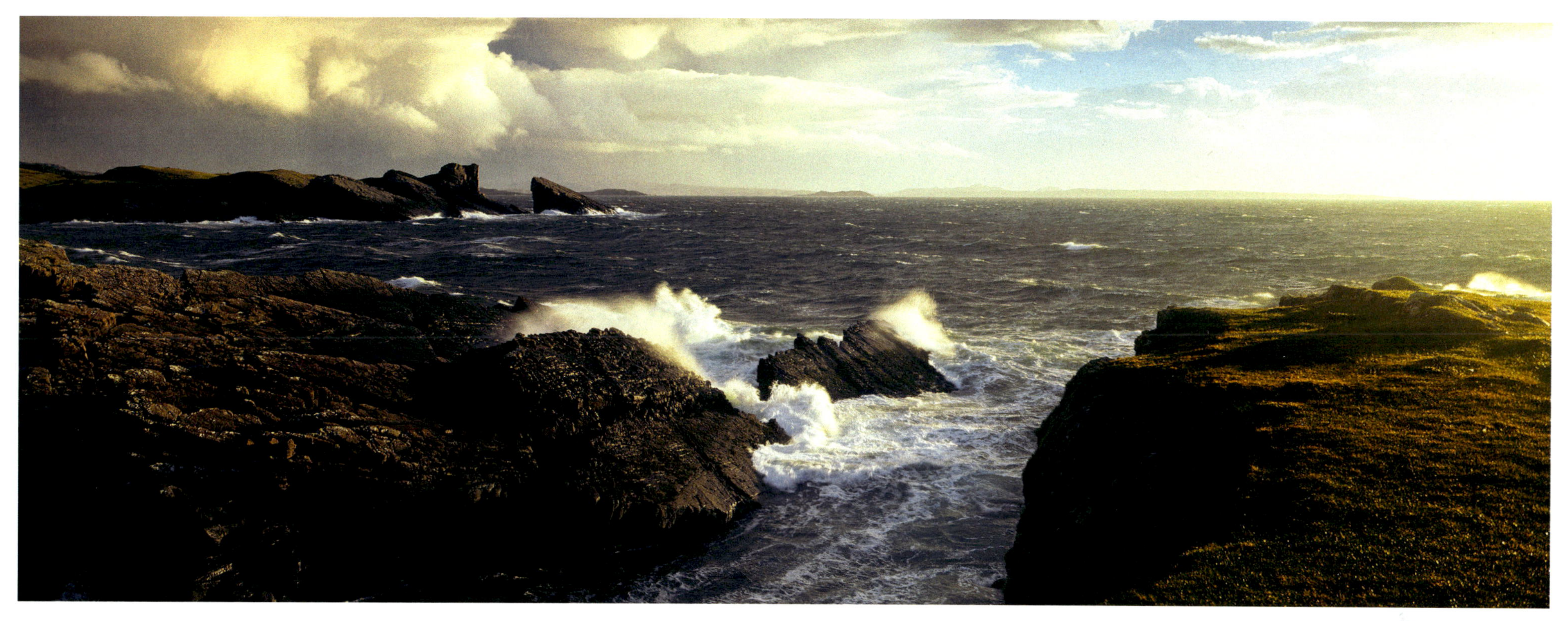

WILD LIGHT

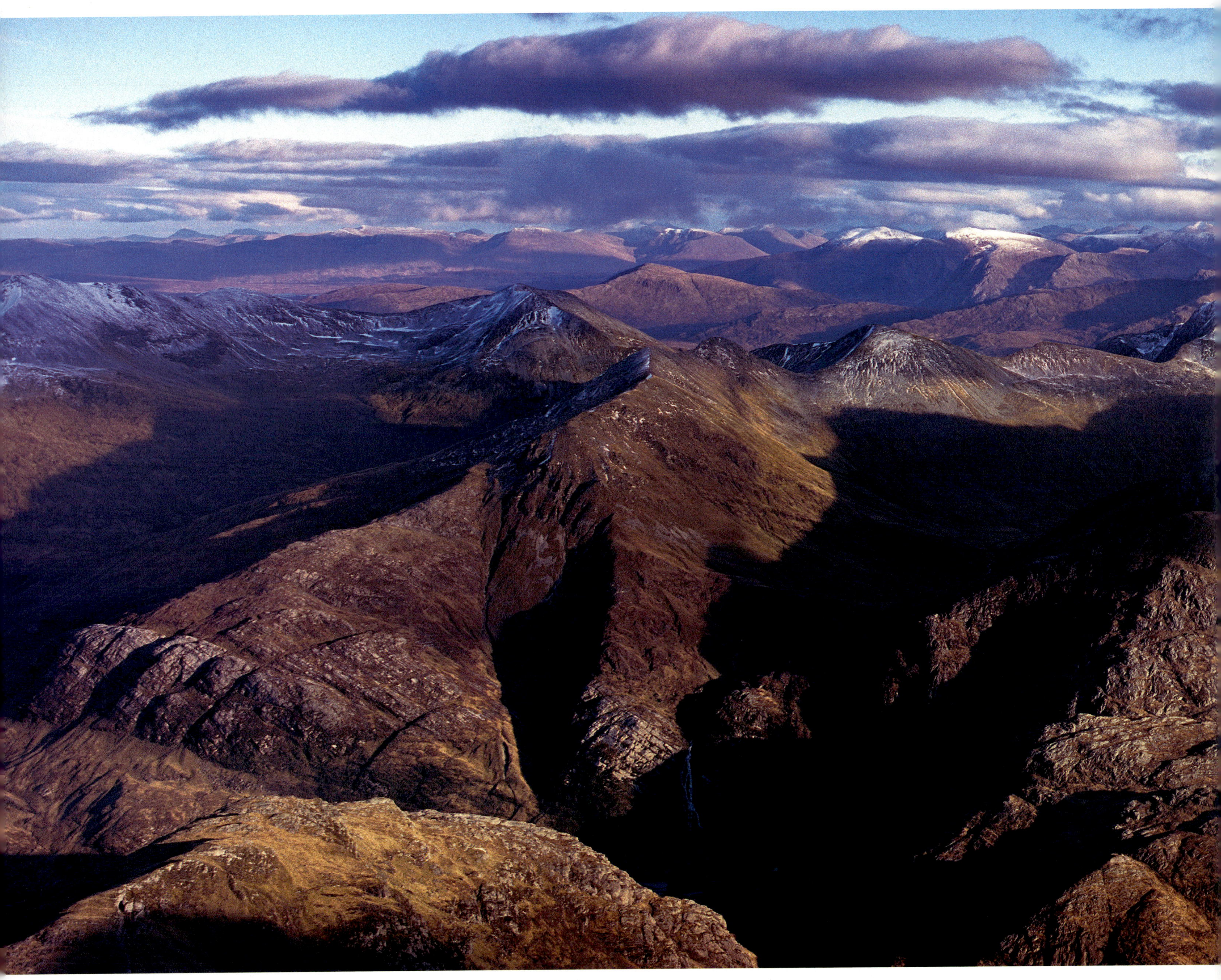

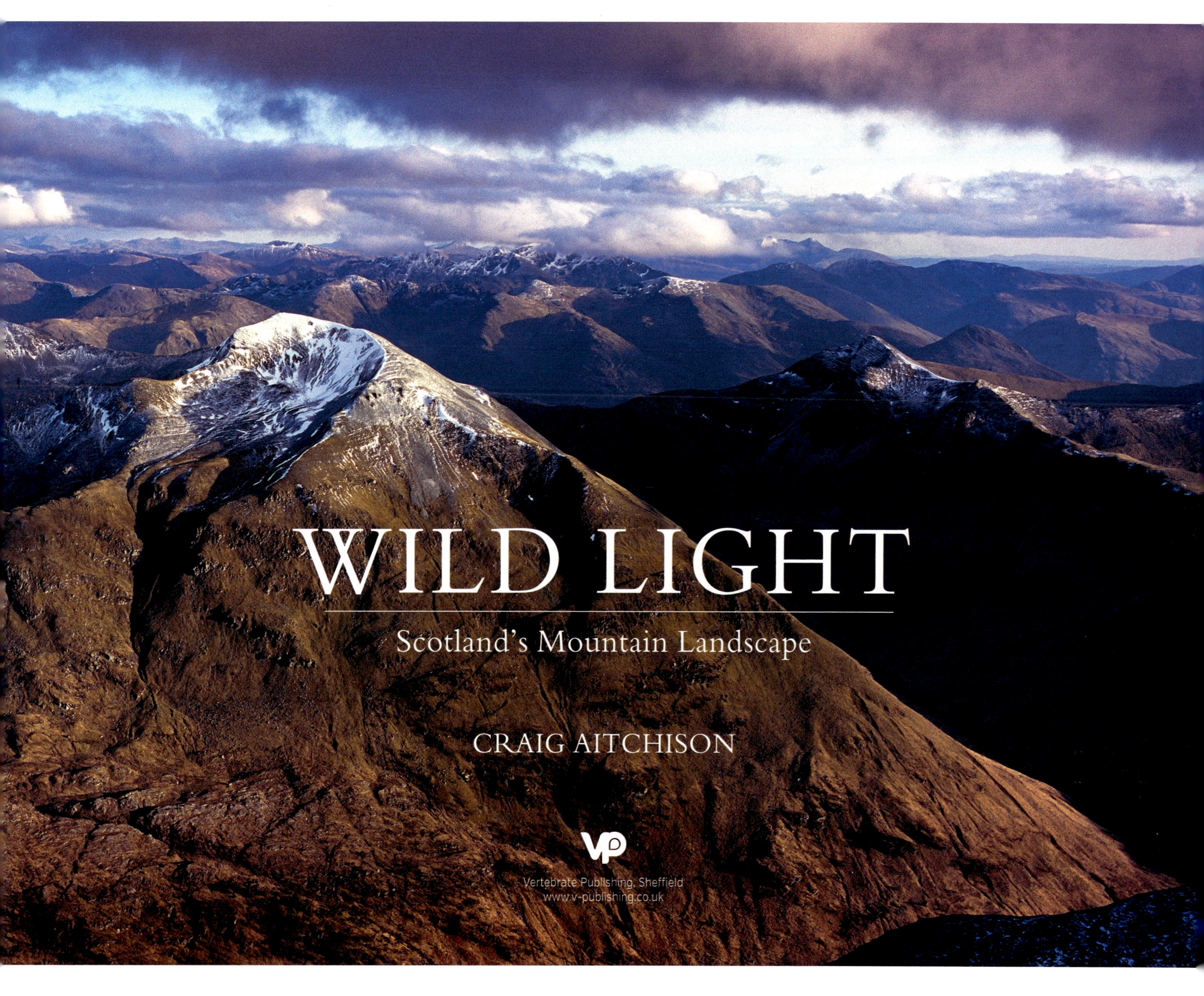

WILD LIGHT
Scotland's Mountain Landscape
CRAIG AITCHISON
Vertebrate Publishing, Sheffield
www.v-publishing.co.uk

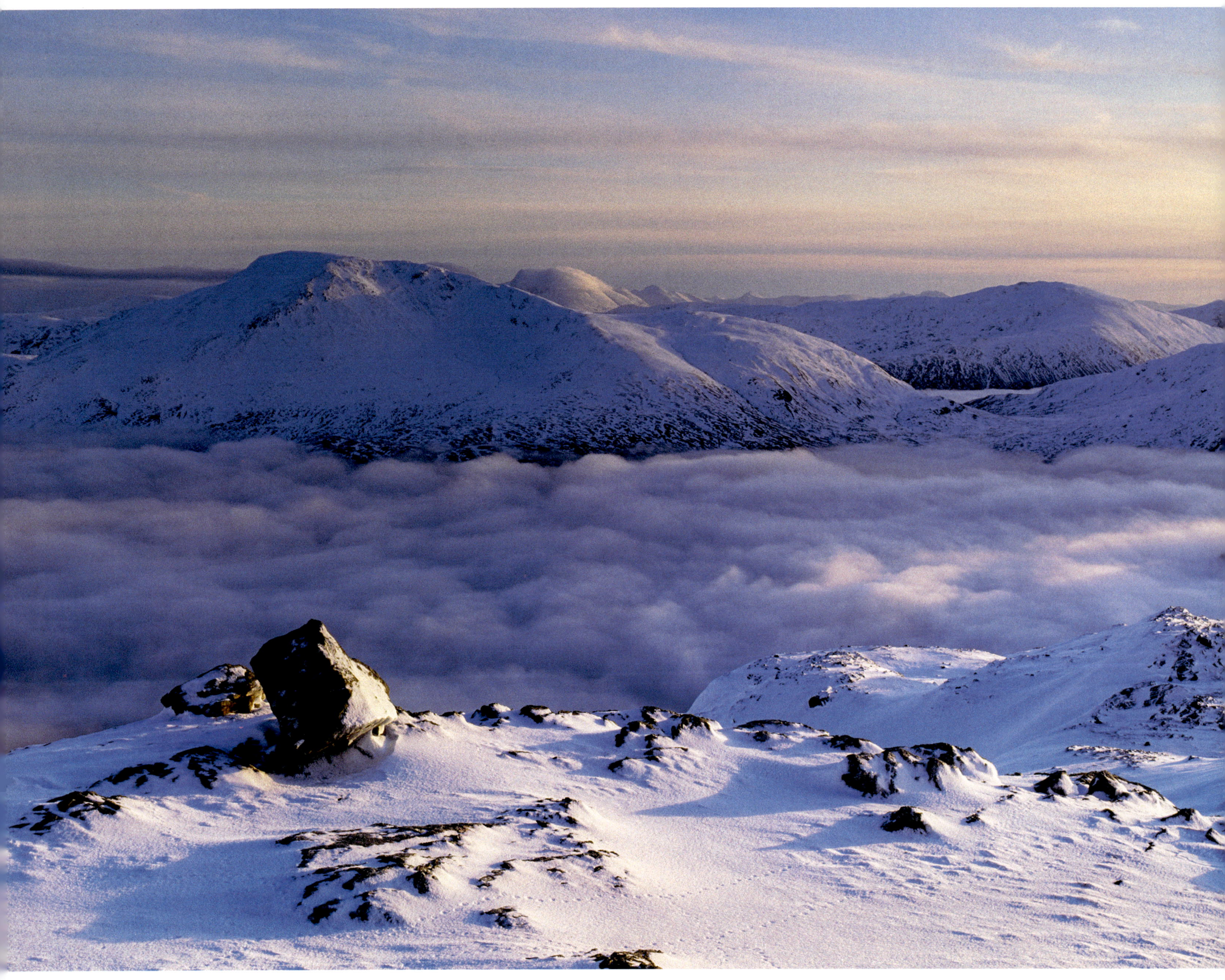

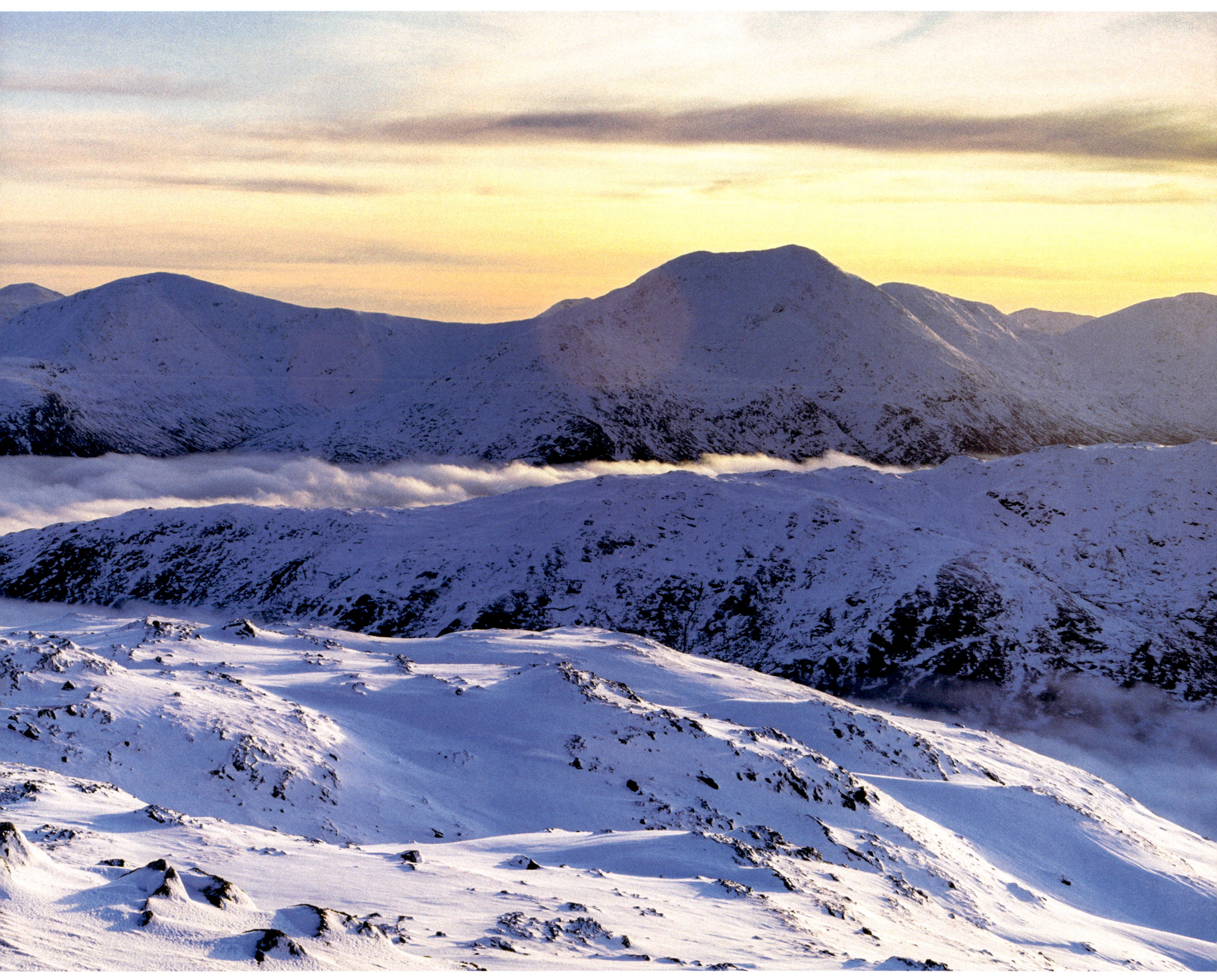

WILD LIGHT

CRAIG AITCHISON

First published in 2018 by Vertebrate Publishing. Reprinted in 2020 and 2022.

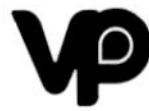 Vertebrate Publishing
Omega Court, 352 Cemetery Road, Sheffield, S11 8FT, United Kingdom.
www.v-publishing.co.uk

Front cover: Aonach Eagach, Glen Coe.

A CIP catalogue record for this book is available from the British Library.

ISBN: 978-1-911342-81-6 (Hardback)

10 9 8 7 6 5 4 3

Design and production by Jane Beagley.
www.v-publishing.co.uk

Vertebrate Publishing is committed to printing on paper from sustainable sources.

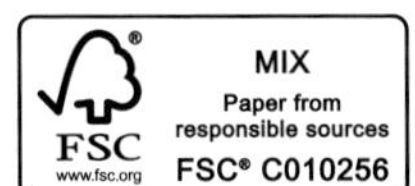

Printed and bound in China by Latitude Press Ltd.

Half-title Page
Split Rock, Clachtoll
October 2014

Autumn can generate some incredibly dynamic conditions for photography: very often huge storms come rolling in from the Atlantic, fully charged and battering Scotland's coast. On the Assynt peninsula overlooking The Minch, the Bay of Clachtoll is a spectacular location to visit in such conditions. The rugged bay is home to some world-renowned geology with the main feature being Split Rock, the remnants of a long-lost natural sea arch.

Title Page
The Ring of Steall, Mamores
April 2017

The Ring of Steall is a classic high-level ridge walk that traverses the tops of four Munros. Starting from Glen Nevis, the horseshoe route takes in (right to left) Sgùrr a' Mhàim, Am Bodach, Stob Choire a' Chàirn and An Gearanach, before finishing at the foot of the stunning 120-metre-tall Steall Falls.

Previous Page
Gairich and Sgùrr Mòr, Loch Quoich
December 2011

Descending from the summit of Sgùrr a' Mhaoraich, the high-level cloud that had blighted much of the day slowly began to disperse. When the late afternoon light eventually broke through I was still high enough above the cloud inversion to take advantage of some well-earned winter light across these remote hills.

For my daughter, Rowan
and in loving memory of my sister, Elaine.

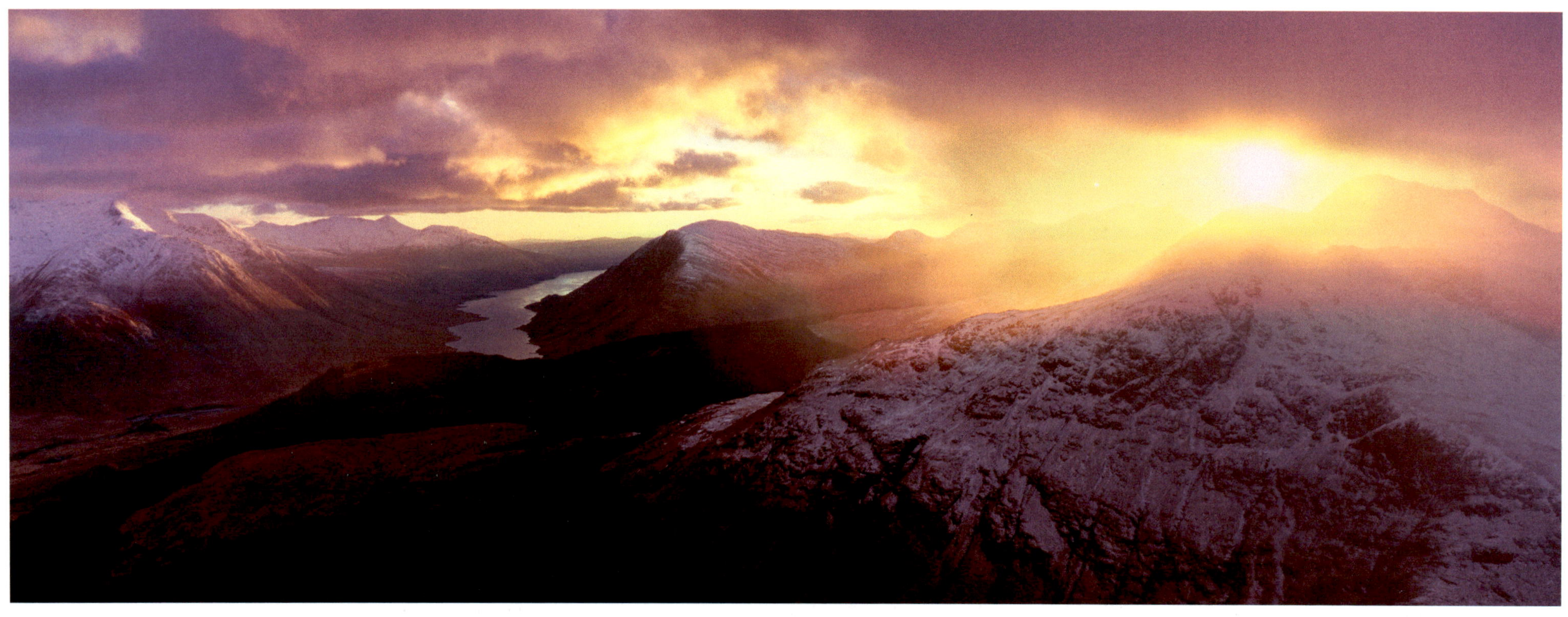

Glen Etive

INTRODUCTION

Silence. In an increasingly busy and turbulent world, it is the true, absolute quiet that is the exclusive preserve of the wild; a priceless attribute of nature. No traffic, no ringtones, no tapping of keyboards. Even the wind, normally a constant companion at Munro level, is absent as I survey the scene from Bidein a' Ghlas Thuill, An Teallach's highest summit. The light has an ethereal quality as the sun creeps above the eastern horizon, seemingly reluctant to disturb the peaceful morning as the dawn light begins its intricate dance across the landscape. Soon I will be busy with my camera as I attempt to capture an image of the beautiful, monumental lines of An Teallach. But for now I take a few minutes just to savour the moment, aware that I am fortunate and privileged to be alone on the mountain, with the light, the landscape and the silence around me.

It isn't always like this, of course. For every idyllic moment with a perfect confluence of timing and conditions, there will be many more that are born of frustration as the myriad of elements outwith my control conspire to ruin my best-laid plans. Scotland's dynamic and volatile weather means that flat light, poor visibility, an errant bank of clouds or many other variables can result in disappointing images of even this most exceptional of landscapes. It is those timeless moments however, like that magical early morning on An Teallach, that keep drawing me back to the wild, to attempt to create images that encapsulate Scotland's beautiful light.

Capturing this image marked the realisation of a long-held personal ambition. I was determined to portray the landscape at its very best: with the light and weather conditions at their peak, an image befitting a mountain of such storied beauty and grandeur. The path that led me to that moment is illustrative of the long and complex planning process involved in mountain photography and is characteristic of my workflow for almost all the images within this book. This process will normally begin with a visualisation or preconceived image that captures the imagination. This can be the result of my experience in a given area of the landscape and my perception of the interaction between the light and the terrain. Ultimately, it is this relationship that will best determine when I will plan and attempt to execute an image.

I was introduced to the Highlands as a child through day trips and some relatively modest hill walks with my parents. Having had a general introduction to this landscape my knowledge was still severely lacking, but gradually through hillwalking and other adventures my experience grew in places like Glen Coe, Rannoch Moor and around Argyll. I would document these trips using a first-generation digital SLR; it was the perfect cost-effective platform for learning the basic elements and principles of photography. The instant feedback it provided alongside the virtually limitless shooting potential helped me understand and determine a great deal in a short period of time. Scotland has

a plethora of well-known roadside locations offering easy access to stunning vistas, and initially these established landmarks served as an excellent playground for experimentation; they were the perfect foundation to my development as a photographer.

While I still had a lot to learn, this early groundwork provided a number of important lessons. Firstly, it gave me greater knowledge of the specific areas I was interested in. I recorded the rise and fall of the sun and how this angle and time varies throughout the year. I began to understand how this movement of light affects a specific location depending on the given geography, and I could assess when and where a particular photograph would be possible. I was fascinated by the way that this process altered the appearance of the landscape – how two images captured from the same spot a few months apart could be so dramatically different. This, combined with the movement of the seasons, means the nature and appearance of the landscape can radically change depending on when a photograph is taken. With the benefit of hindsight this now seems all too obvious, but learning how to take advantage of this was one of the most important lessons I learned early on, and is, of course, one of the keystones to successful landscape photography.

Increasingly, I began to venture further afield, away from the roadside, challenging myself with more ambitious adventures and slowly discovering new, lesser-known locations. This is where I found my real passion: exploring and photographing

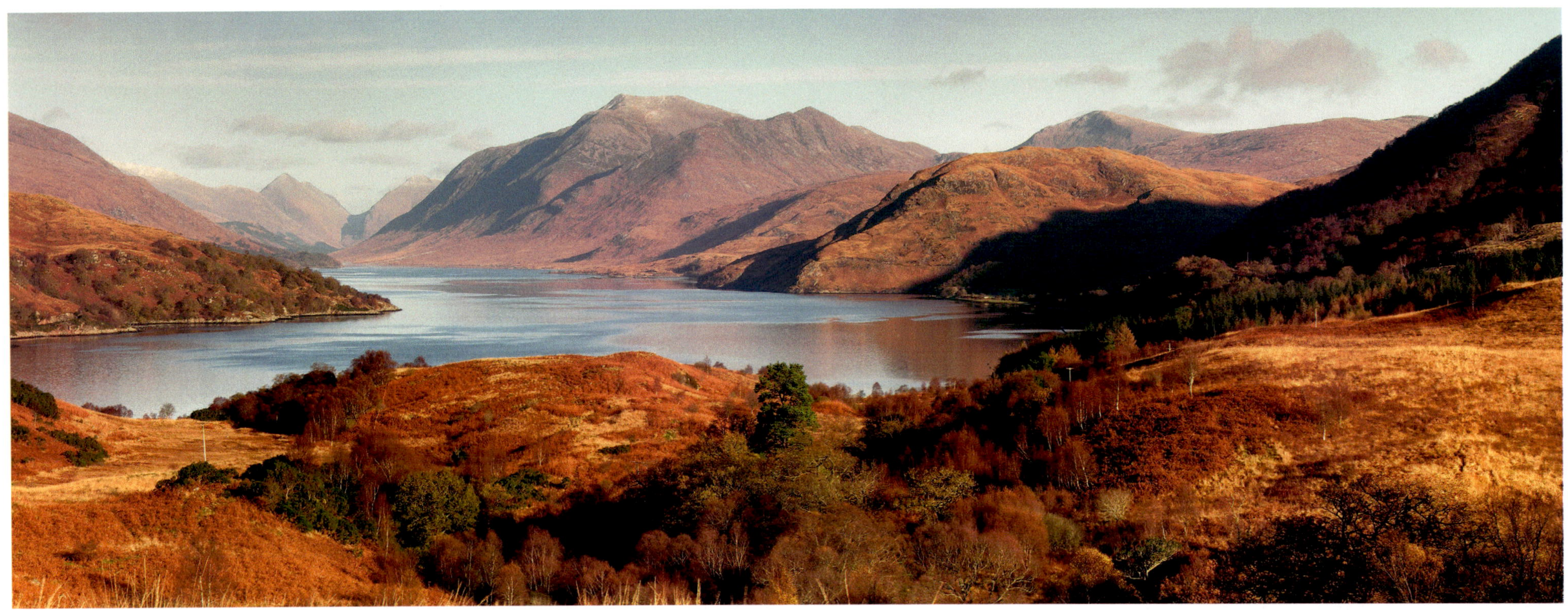

Loch Etive

the wild places, being immersed in an environment surrounded by mountain, loch and glen. It is where I nurtured a real affinity for the art of recording the ever-changing relationship between land and light, trying to convey the sense of belonging in the Scottish landscape that I had come to cherish. I thus embarked on a journey to capture what I felt was most important and produce images from places that mattered to me.

The first meaningful photograph I made was an early image of Loch Etive, taken from a quiet corner at the western end of the loch near Taynuilt. It was a place I inadvertently stumbled across on a fine autumn morning; there was no grand plan for what I wanted to shoot, I was simply out exploring with my camera. Revealed from this newly discovered foreland was a breathtaking, uninterrupted view I had never seen before. It held all the ingredients I had been searching for, epitomising all that is best about the Scottish

Highlands. It was here that I started to take photography seriously, getting to know the nuances of the art and beginning to understand how to plan and execute an image. As I dedicated more time to photography, I realised that as I travelled further into the wild I could not simply rely on stumbling across such beautiful locations by chance. Instead, I began to properly arrange my trips with the sole intention of visiting specific locations for a particular image.

With my new approach in mind, I set about exploring other areas of the Highlands that I had yet to encounter and soon found myself making the first of many trips into Knoydart. It was here that I began to experience true wilderness, Knoydart being one of the relatively few places remaining in the UK that can evoke such a feeling. With other commitments elsewhere, a two- or three-day trip into this region might only be possible a couple of times a year, with each

one being strictly limited by the supplies I could carry in my rucksack. With limited time and opportunity I therefore got used to the discipline of mentally composing an image, visualising how to portray a given landscape and understanding the impact that factors such as season and time of day may have on that image. It is of little use simply to arrive somewhere like Knoydart and then try to decide what to photograph. A shoot might well be planned several months in advance, depending on exactly what I wanted to capture. I would therefore journey into Knoydart with a specific goal in mind, knowing exactly where I wanted to be and when I wanted to be there, purely to capture the image I had planned. Some people may see this approach as somewhat clinical given the extent of planning that is involved, but I firmly believe that this level of commitment and planning is absolutely essential to successful mountain photography. Each image

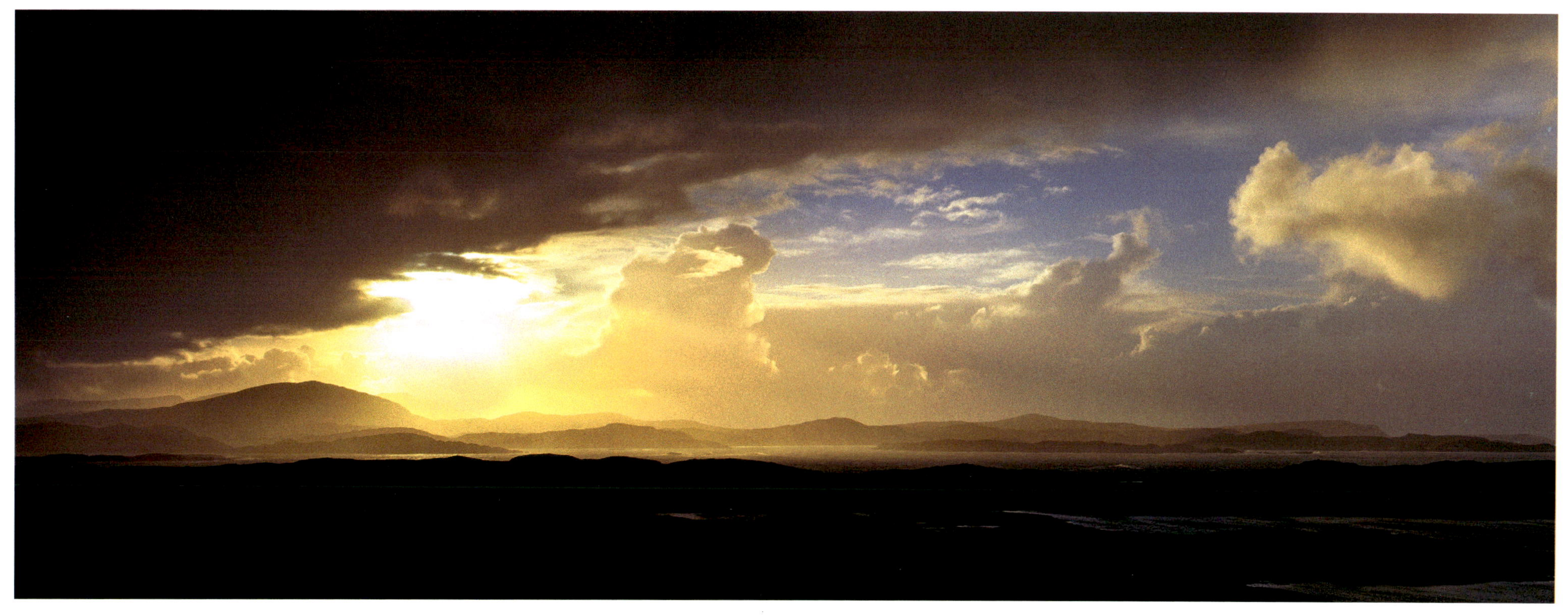

Wild Light, Isle of Lewis

becomes an individual project that might require months of planning, many hours of travel and perhaps an overnight camp, all in the hope of arriving at that magical moment when land and light combine to perfection.

Having said that, some of my favourite images have been more spontaneous in nature. Mountain environments can be extremely dynamic places; they tend to generate their own localised weather and this element of unpredictability means that anything can happen, regardless of the forecast. A large part of being a photographer in the wild is always being aware of what is happening around you so you can respond to the ever-changing surroundings. Given how remarkably changeable the Scottish weather can be, a rule of thumb is to expect the unexpected and capitalise on unforeseen opportunities if they arise. In this theatre of erratic conditions, all the meticulous planning in the world does not guarantee the

desired result. Luck will always play a significant part.

Whether a planned image requires a night-time ascent, an overnight camp or just a long walk over difficult terrain, the challenges involved can be considerable. However, I find that the feeling of reward and satisfaction derived from capturing a pre-planned image increases with the level of difficulty involved. To capture the first light of dawn on the flanks of Ladhar Bheinn, for example, requires a deep knowledge of the landscape and a significant level of planning and commitment. The many hours – or even days – spent on a project like that allows the photographer to become immersed in the landscape and really familiar with their surroundings. It is an awe-inspiring feeling and one that I attempt to express through my images, shining a light on a landscape that would otherwise remain unknown to the vast majority of people.

Another challenge that I find with landscape photography is one that is self-imposed: my choice of camera, or more specifically, the use of a film camera as opposed to digital equipment. Although my earliest images were taken using a digital SLR, the digital workflow is one I have never wholly connected with. I moved to using a Hasselblad panoramic film camera in 2006, and I feel that film helps to maintain the level of authenticity that I am looking for. The reaction between the film and the light retains some of the actual character of the moment, and the use of film means that the light captured is as close as possible to what I actually experienced. I feel that film allows me to retain something of the essence of being there in the wild, and that, to me, is just as important as the image itself. I also enjoy the practical challenge of working with film. I have a very limited number of shots available, meaning that a much more

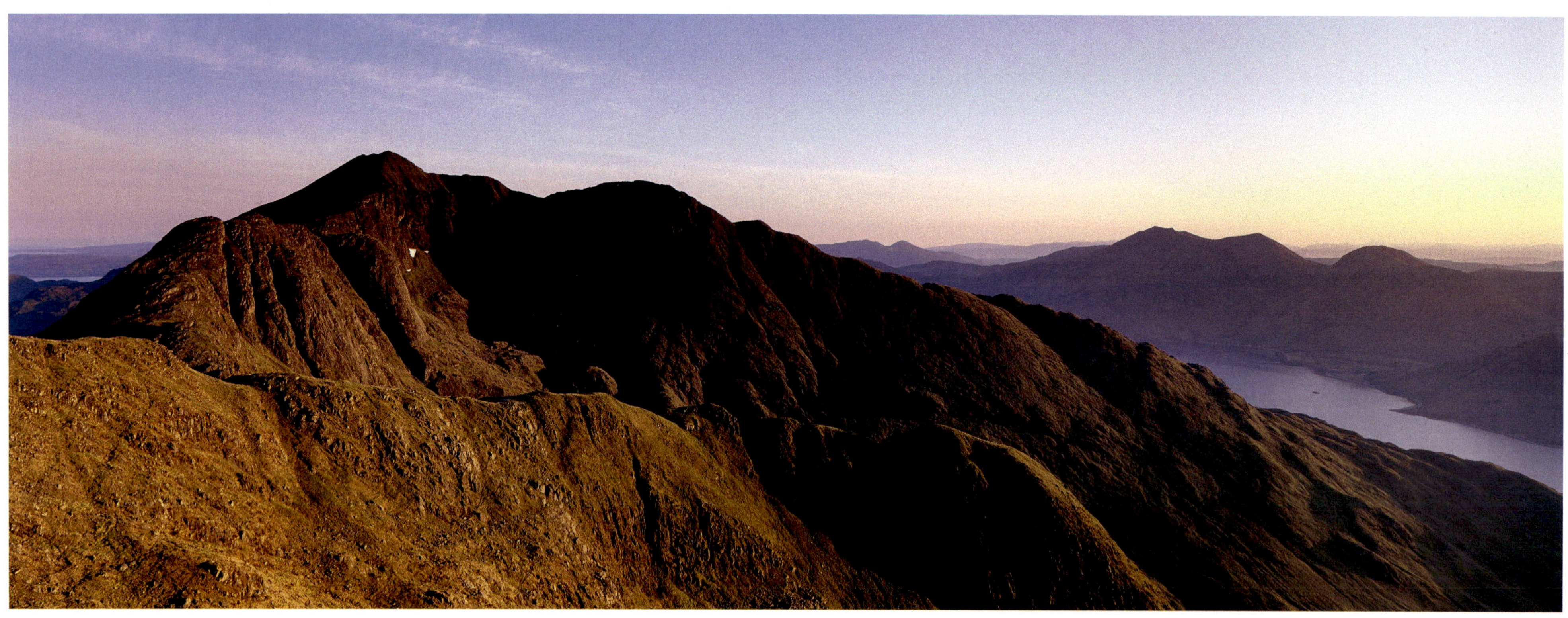

Ladhar Bheinn, Knoydart

disciplined approach is required, with images being carefully planned and executed. Working with prime lenses also imposes further restrictions in terms of composition and focal length, but delivers superb quality. The somewhat convoluted workflow associated with the use of film also allows a sense of space and time to develop between capturing the image and getting the final results. It might be a couple of weeks between releasing the shutter and seeing the final image. During this time a greater sense of perspective becomes possible and helps prevent me from being too close to the image. I find this helps to see the image in a wider context and with a more critical eye.

As my confidence and workflow developed I realised that with the right amount of pre-paration, photographs I had initially thought out of reach were now potentially possible. An image that I had long had in my sights

was that of An Teallach. Lying on the fringe of Fisherfield amongst hugely dramatic scenery, its fabled saw-toothed skyline of tiered slabs and terraced spires are straight from the pages of a Tolkien novel. For a long time I had wanted to stand on Bidein a' Ghlas Thuill, the mountain's most prominent summit, to capture the first light of dawn striking this jewel in the crown of the North West Highlands. It is an obvious place for an image and one I was fixated upon.

Having made two ascents of the mountain months before, I had become familiar with its landscape and terrain. More importantly, from these surveys I had determined the best time and place that would deliver the definitive image I sought. At any time of the year the outlook from Bidein a' Ghlas Thuill is outstanding, but for a photograph to do it appropriate justice I wanted the added drama and aesthetics that come with winter. I therefore planned my attempt for late

February when the conditions would be ideal.

As the time neared, I kept an increasingly anxious eye on the mountain weather forecast, hoping for an opportunity to arise. On the last weekend of February a promising window of high pressure developed following a particularly severe bout of storms that had left deep snow lying to low levels across much of the North West. The stage was set. I left Glasgow the day before to ensure I was in prime position for an early start the following morning. Waking at 3 a.m. I prepared myself for the climb and set off from Dundonnell with only the light of my head torch guiding the way. A night-time ascent of any Scottish mountain, particularly in full winter conditions, is not something to be taken lightly, but I felt sufficiently confident in my preparation and mountain craft as I began my climb through the darkness. The well-established path which meanders its way up the north-eastern flank

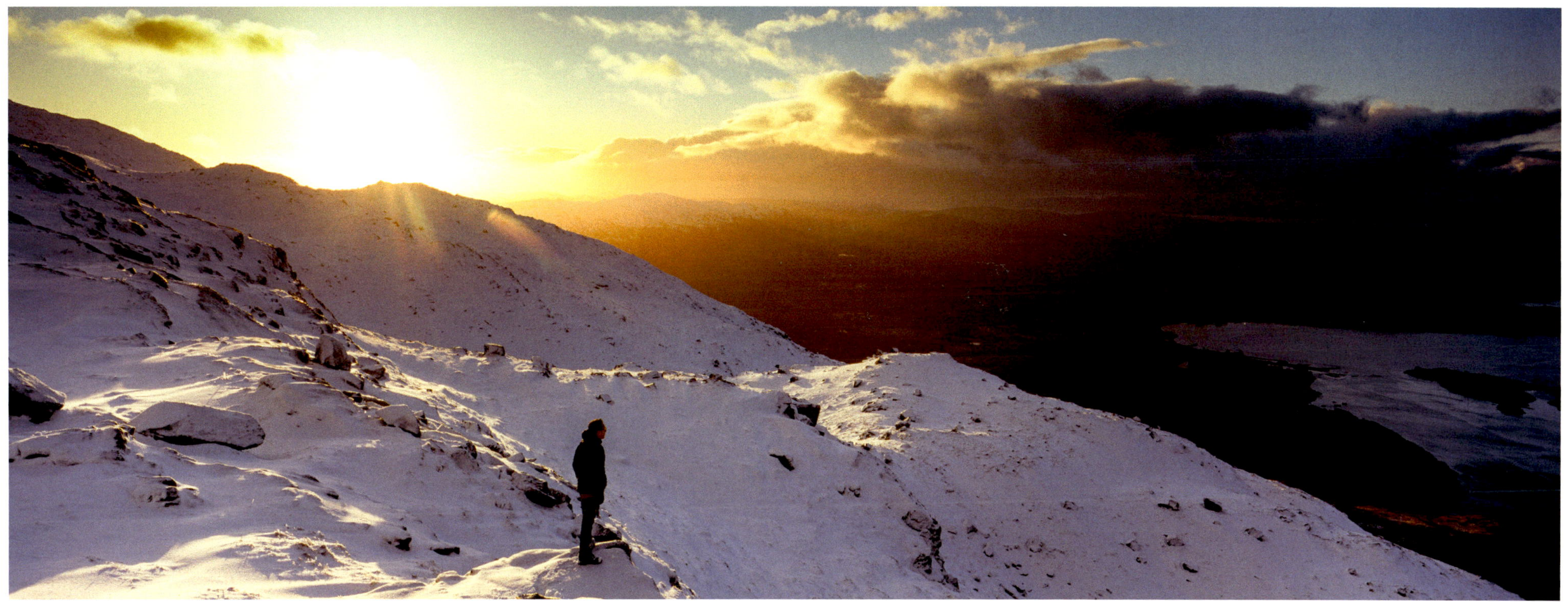

of the mountain was completely hidden by the pristine blanket of snow, making navigation quite difficult. My progress was also much slower than anticipated due to the relentless chore of wallowing through the ever-deepening snow. Breaking trail is always hard work and I pushed on hoping that the reward at the top would make the effort worthwhile. I soon reached a point where conditions became so challenging that I began to have second thoughts. As I slowly gained height I hoped the snow conditions higher up would improve, having consolidated enough overnight to support my weight and thereby alleviating my struggle. But it was still fresh from the previous day and the final, steep ascent became a brutal trial of endurance.

Finally I arrived at the summit with some time to spare, allowing a chance to recover and space to enjoy the moment. I was aware of the stark contrast between how different everything looked compared to my previous trips only months before. Alone on the mountain in the moments before dawn, I felt a familiar sense of comfortable isolation. The full moon was now beginning to set and as the light grew, the moment arrived. I set up and composed my camera as the first rays of dawn struck the face of Sgùrr Fiona. The morning light crept slowly down the mountain filling the vast corrie before me, vanquishing the shadows as its spectrum moved from pink to orange and then to yellow – the transformation nothing short of sensational. All around me the snow glowed with such intensity its appearance seemed to echo that of 'the forge' – the Gaelic description from which the name An Teallach is thought to derive. I loaded some film and metered the scene, dialled in the exposure settings and shot through two rolls as the sun rose, bracketing my exposures as I went. Months of planning and effort reduced to one brief fraction of a second that I hoped would capture the essence of the moment. Eventually, the warm light hardened to daylight, signifying the end of the golden hour. I packed up feeling relieved and elated in equal measure. As I turned to start the long journey home, my own footprints in the snow caught my eye as they wound their way up the mountain; I reflected on how quickly they would disappear, a reminder that we are but fleeting visitors in the vast and beautiful landscape of the Highlands.

Craig Aitchison
April 2018

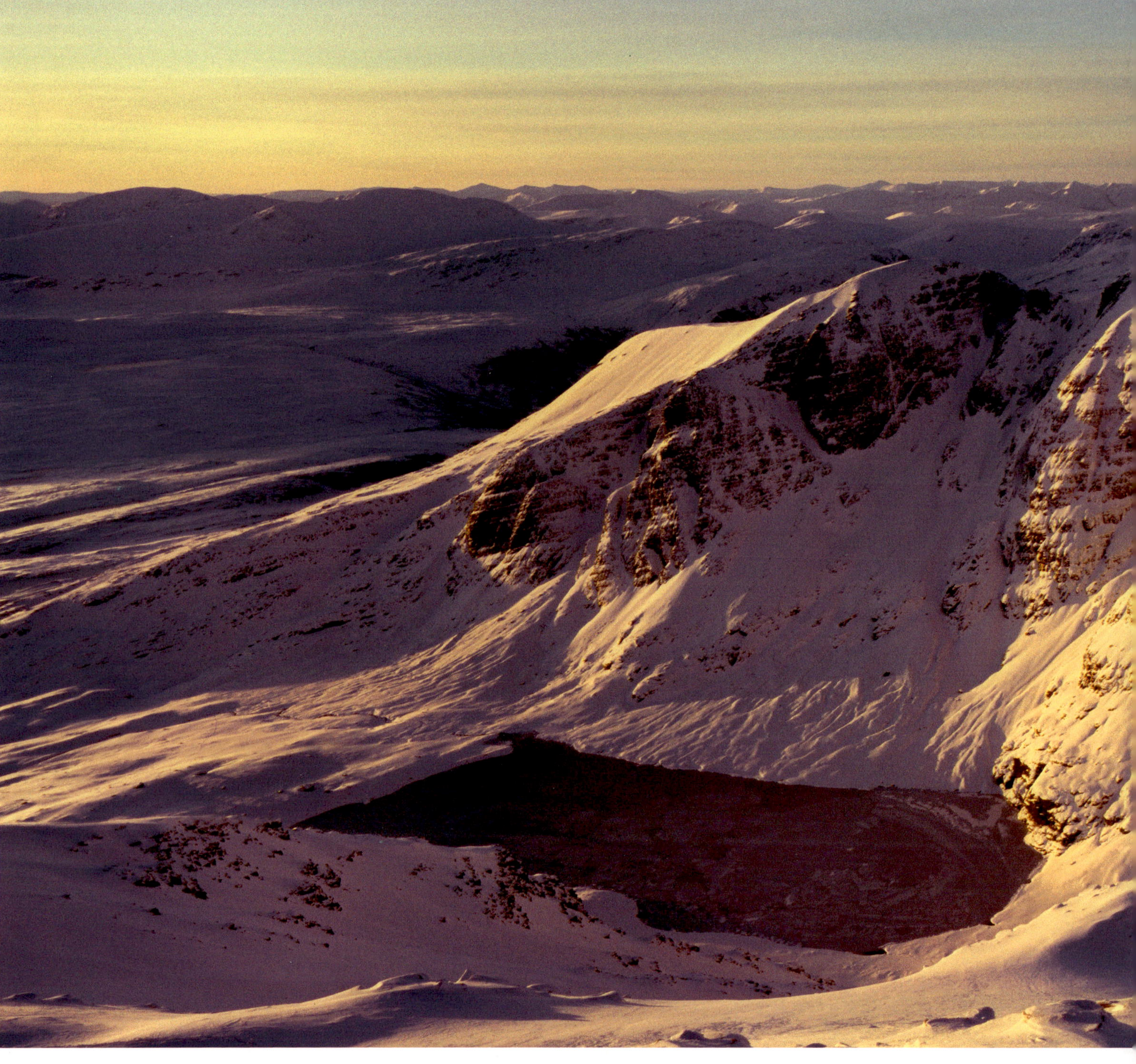

An Teallach, Dundonnell
February 2016

The first light of dawn ignites the chiselled slopes of
An Teallach on a perfect winter's morning. After years
of waiting for the right conditions, I finally achieved the
image I had hoped for and realised a long-standing
photographic ambition.

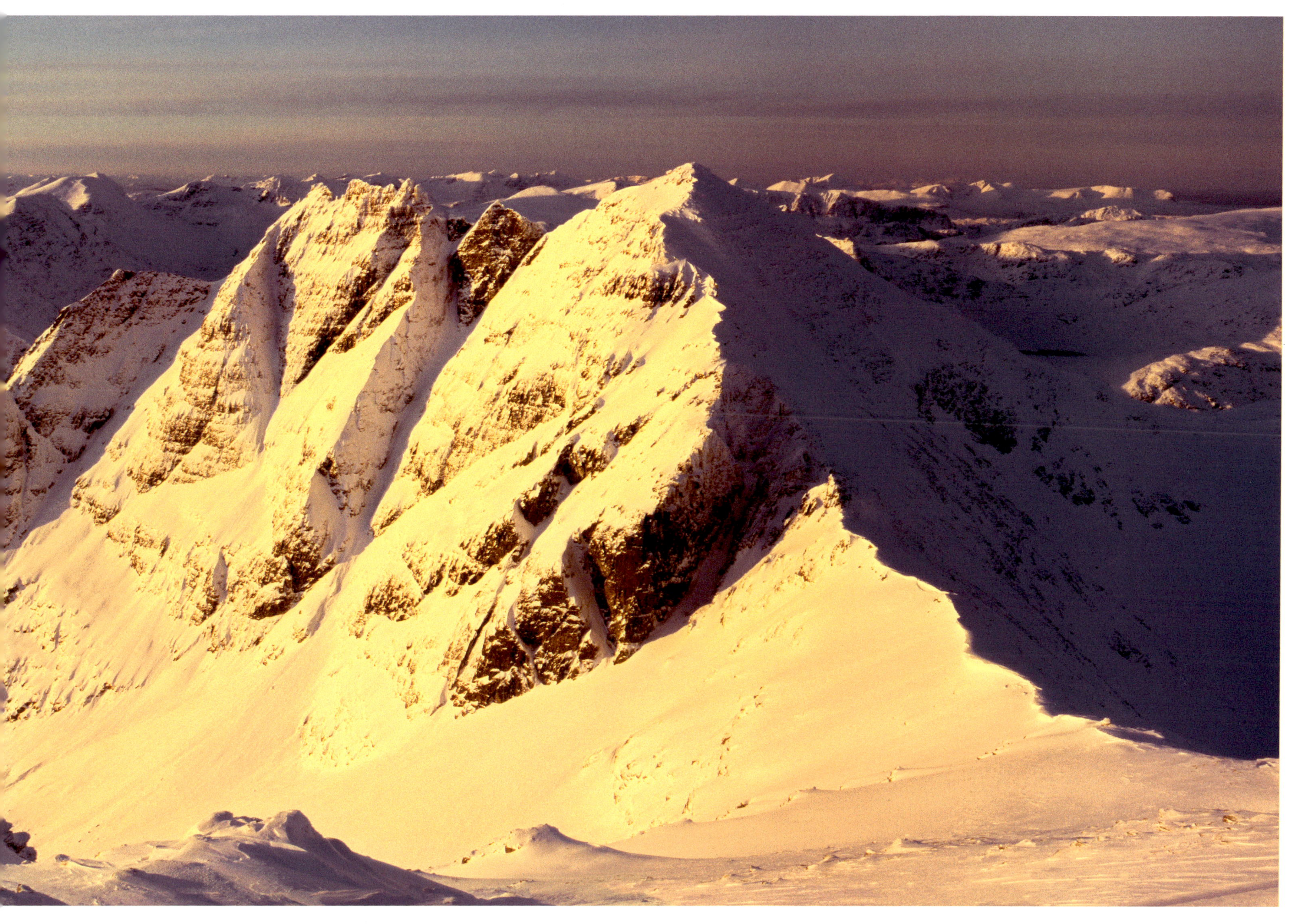

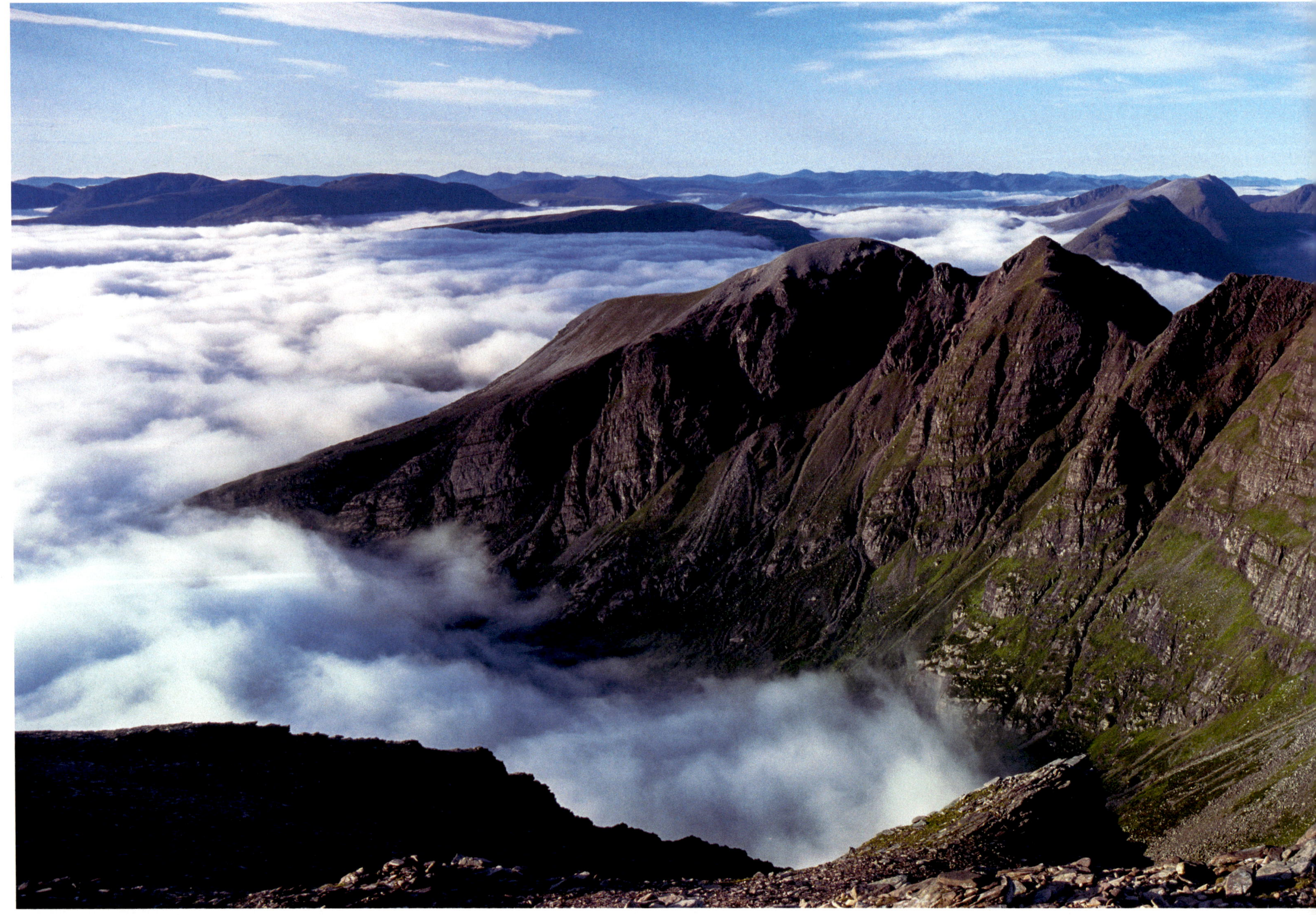

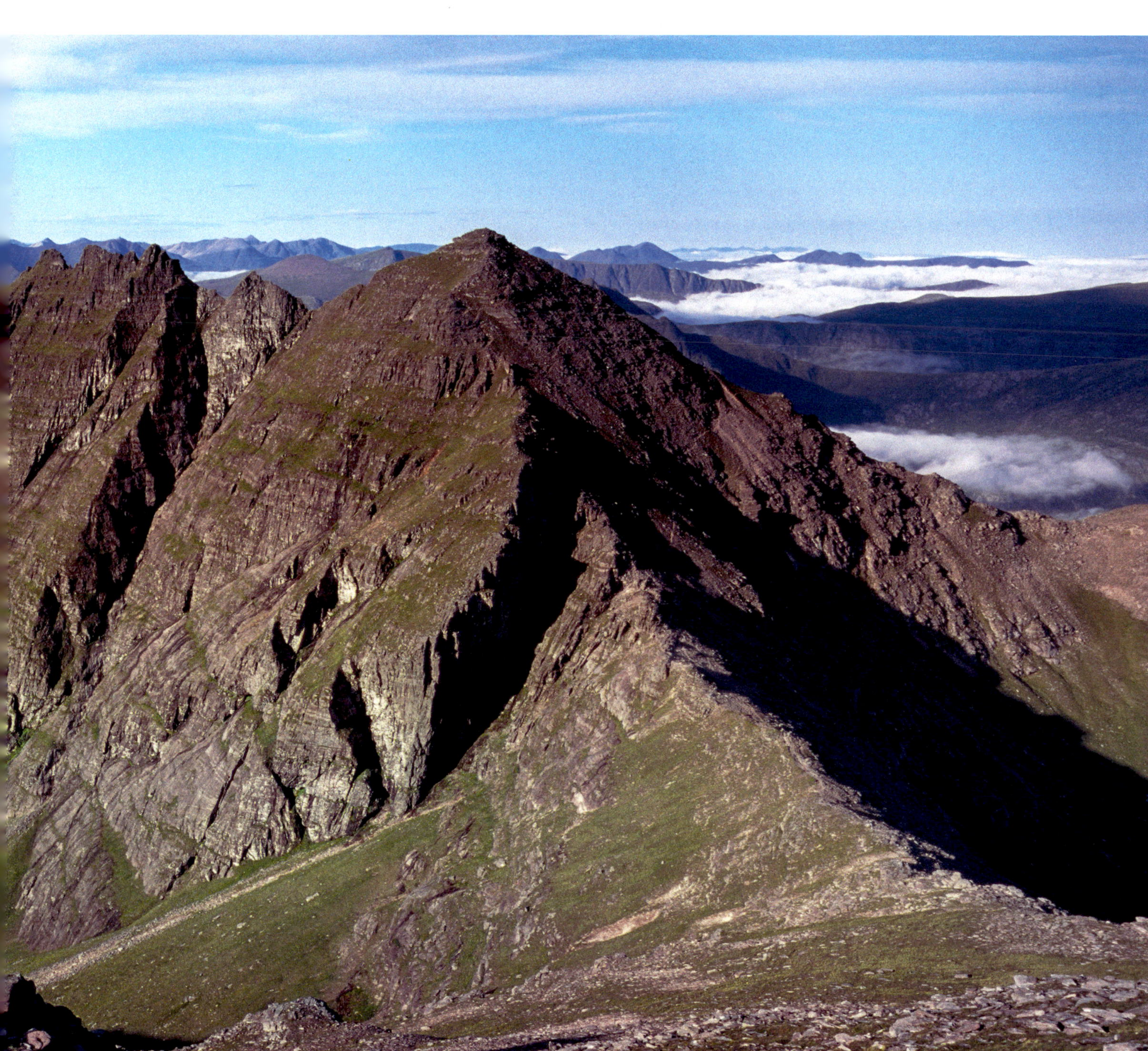

An Teallach, Dundonnell
July 2017

Standing at the foot of An Teallach in the predawn light I knew from experience that the low-lying cloud above me was indicative of a potential cloud inversion surrounding the mountain. With the thought of what might lie above I pushed on hard, hoping to capture this rare phenomenon before it burnt off. In a little over ninety minutes I had reached the summit. I was in luck: above the cloud it was warm and windless, the silence – absolute. I immediately set up my camera to capture the stunning conditions; I made my exposure and only after that could I finally relax. I sat down to recover, taking it all in. Two hours later I was still there: it was almost impossible to leave, but as the sun gained height the sea of cloud gradually dissipated and I returned home sunburnt and happy.

Following Page
The Lairig Ghru, Cairngorms
December 2012

The Lairig Ghru is a high mountain pass that carves its way through the heart of the central Cairngorm plateau, one of the wildest areas in the country. This great gorge features some of Scotland's most revered winter mountains and this image shows its western aspect. From left to right are the summits of The Devil's Point, Cairn Toul and Braeriach.

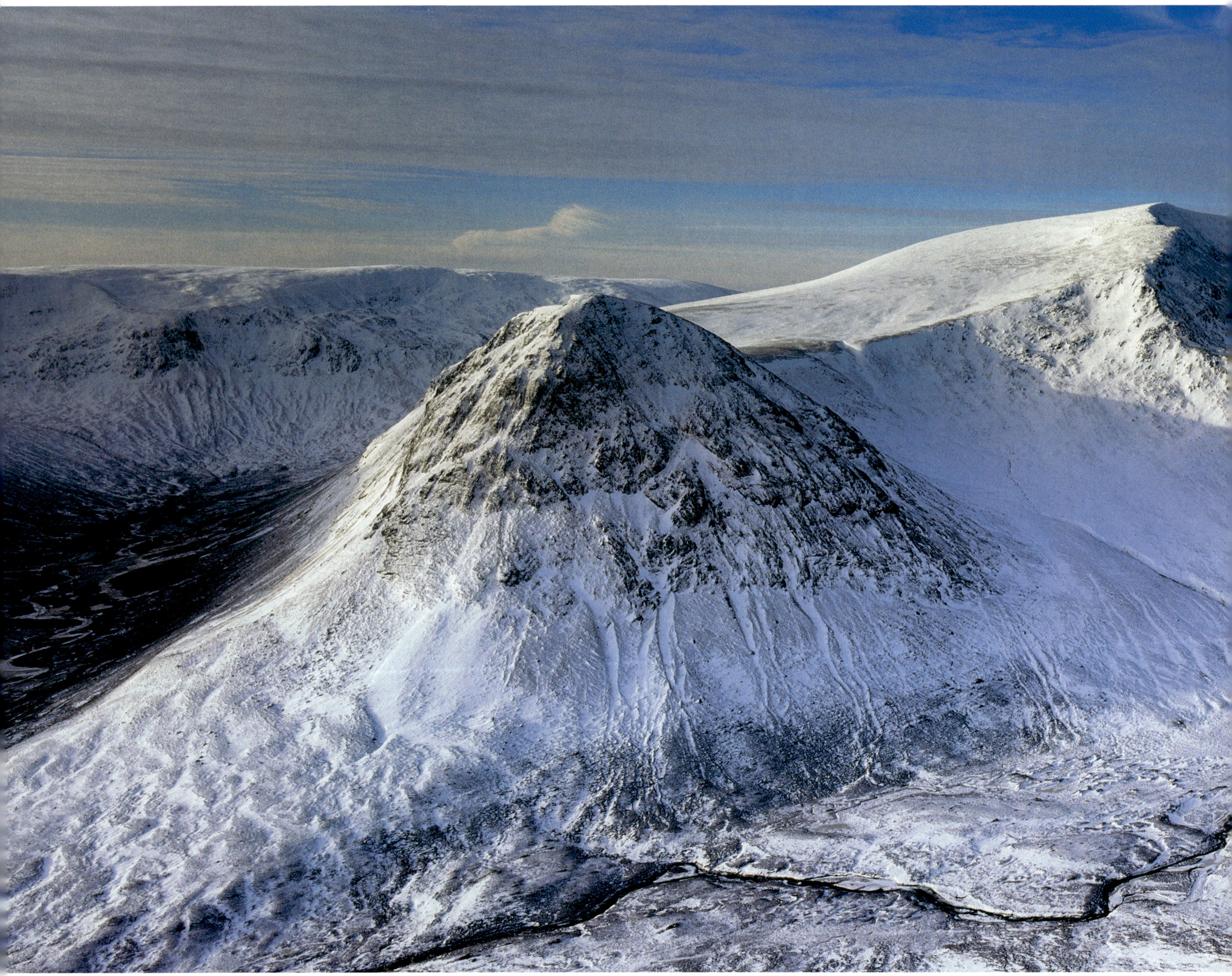

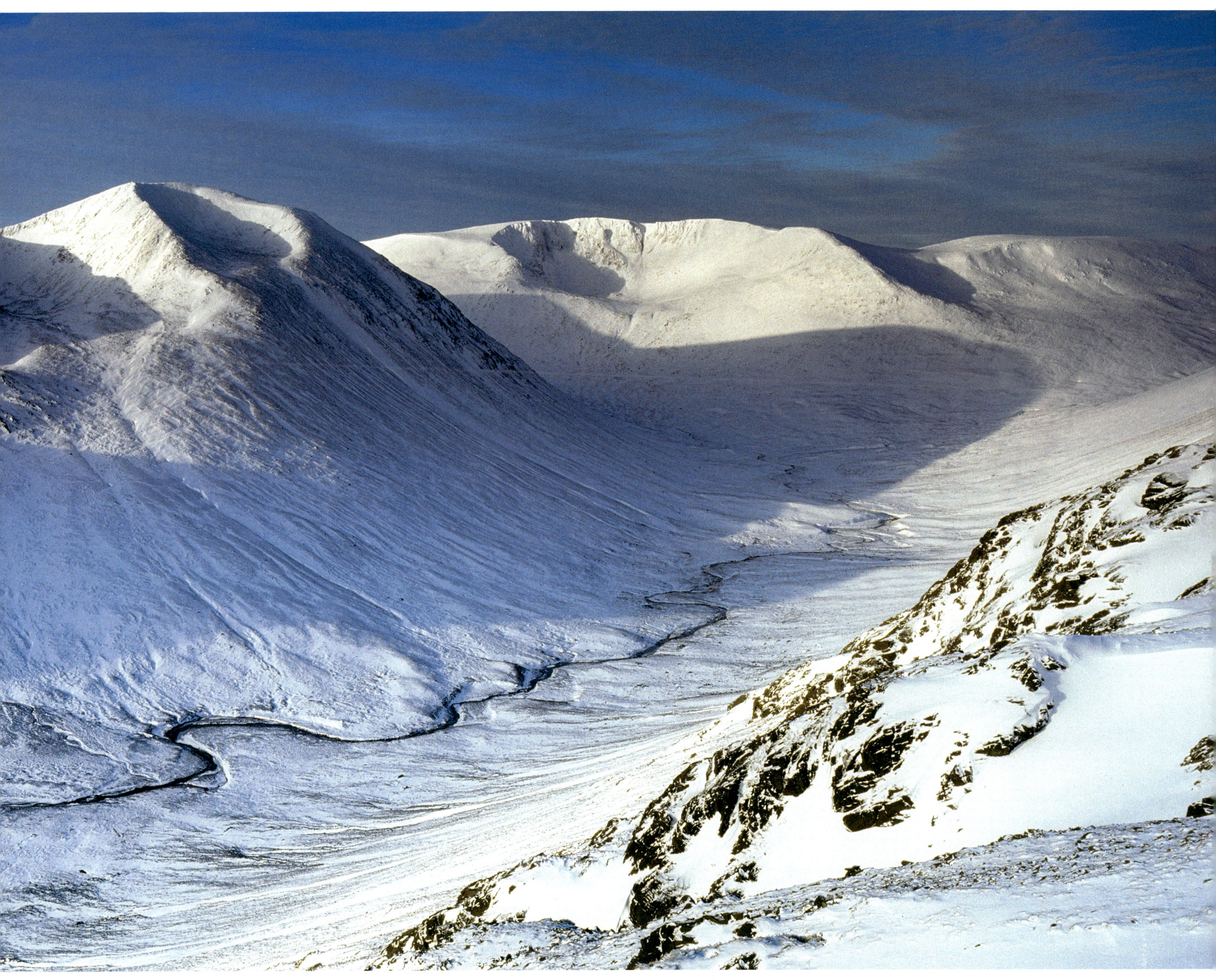

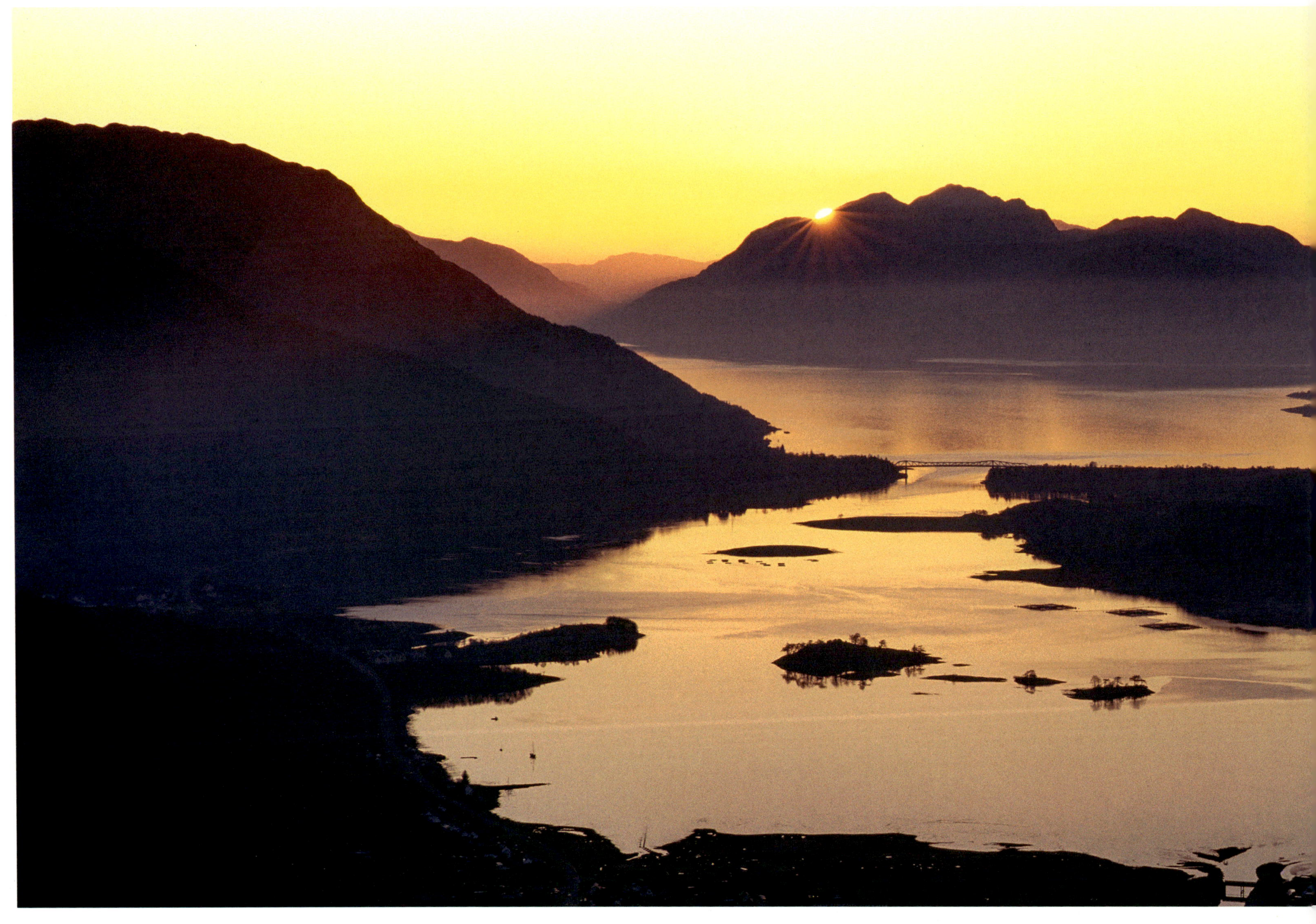

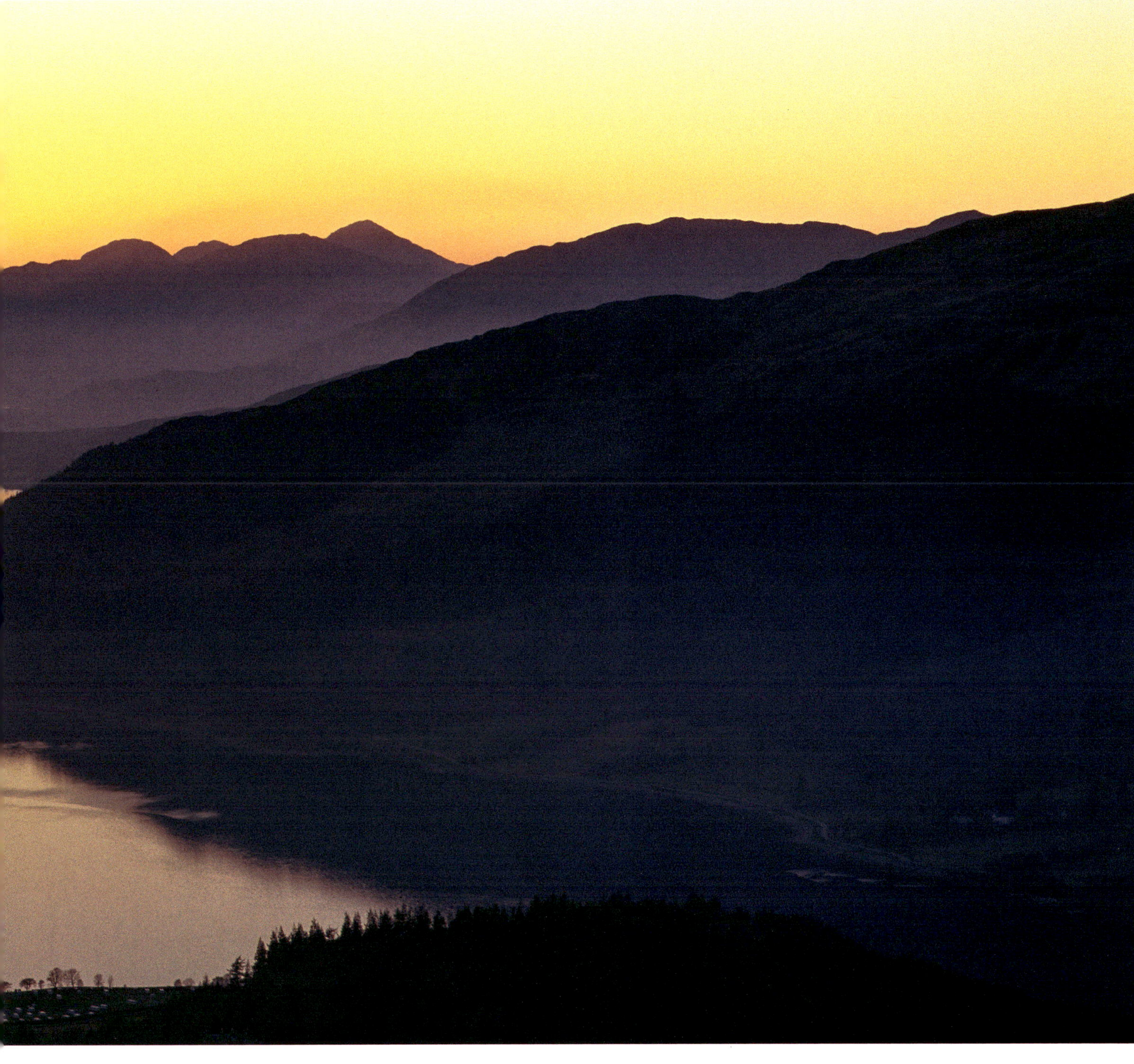

Garbh Bheinn, Loch Leven
March 2012

During an unseasonably warm spell in March I climbed to an elevated position high above Loch Leven. At this time of the year the sun sets due west over the loch and the mountains of Ardgour. Keen to avoid unwanted lens flare I waited until the sun had almost completely disappeared behind Garbh Bheinn before making this exposure.

Canisp and Suilven, Loch Druim Suardalain, Assynt
May 2014

The mountains of Assynt are fashioned from the oldest
strata found in Britain, some 3,000 million years old.
Although not eminent in height, the separated, individual
peaks of Canisp and Suilven contain more character than
most. They are viewed here from the shores of Loch Druim
Suardalain, as the sun dropped below the cloud canopy,
flooding this ancient landscape in fine evening light.

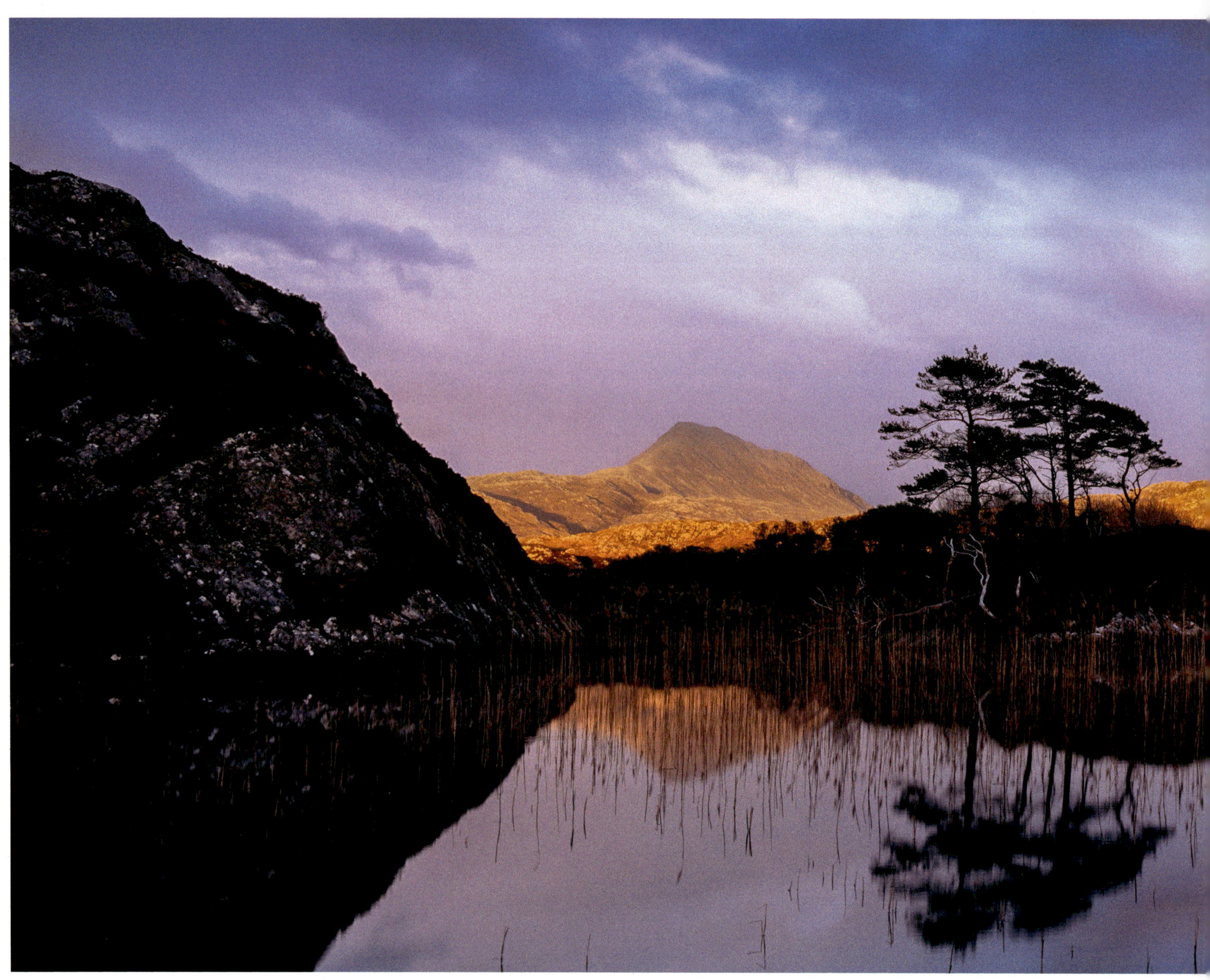

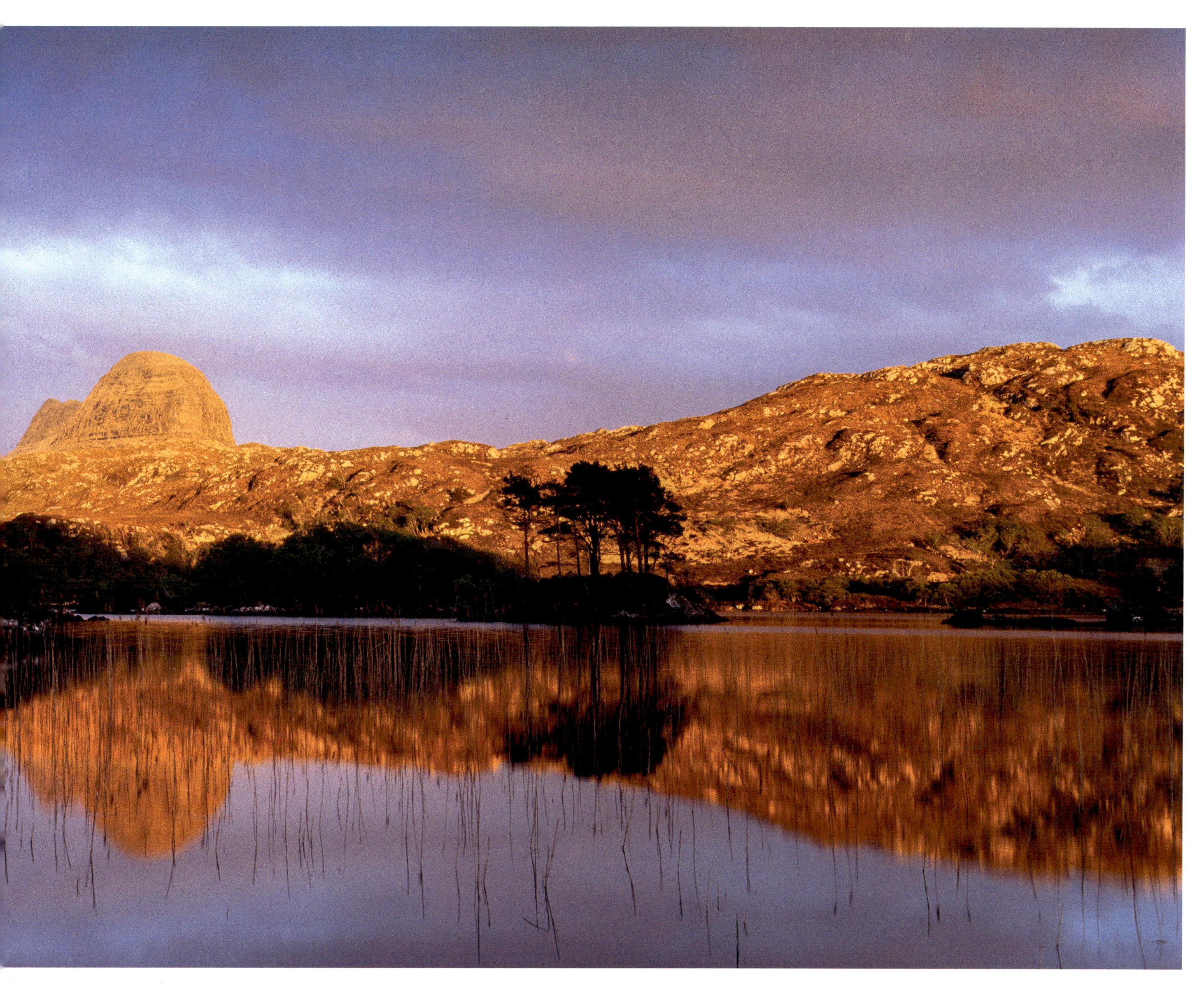

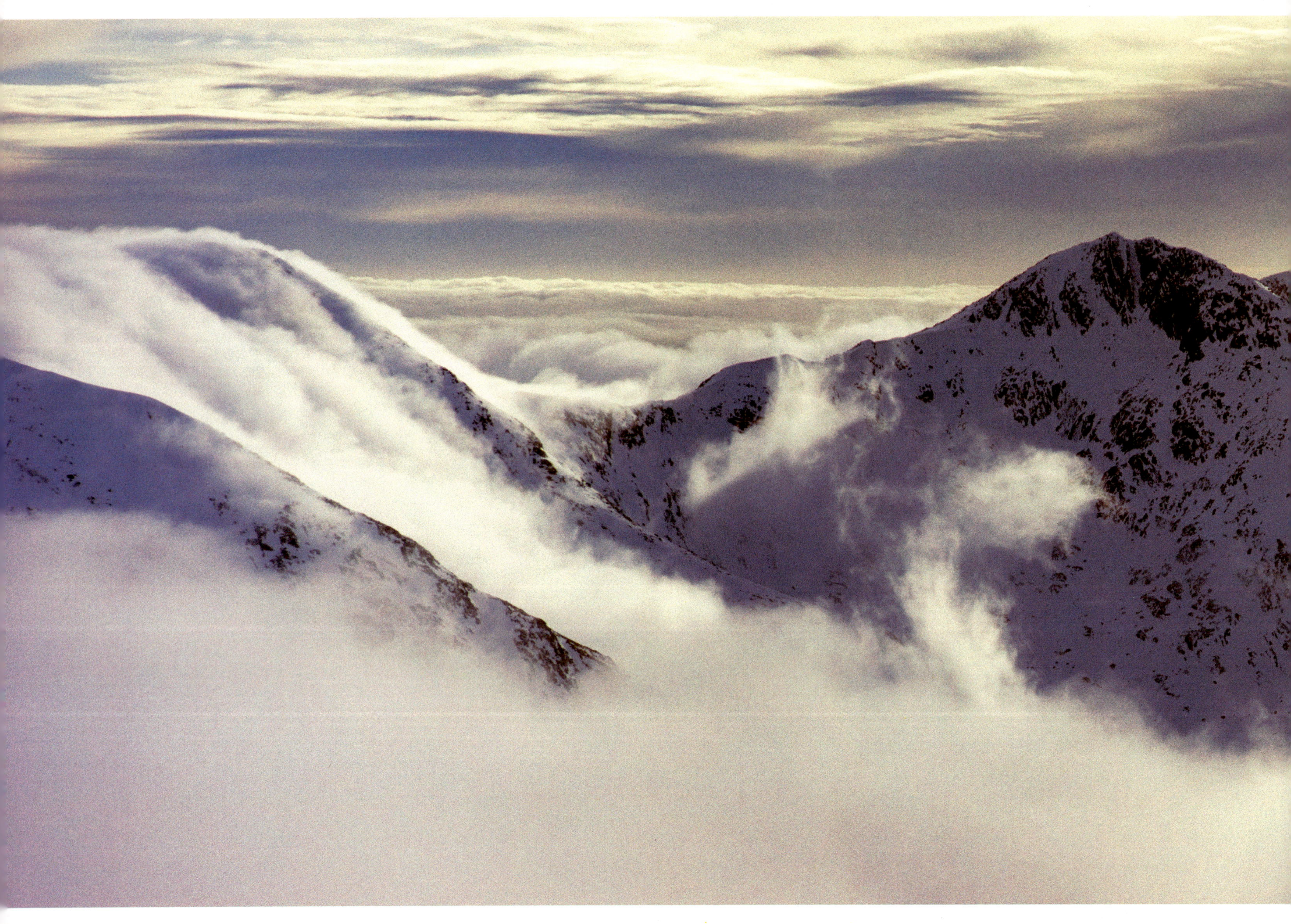

    WILD LIGHT

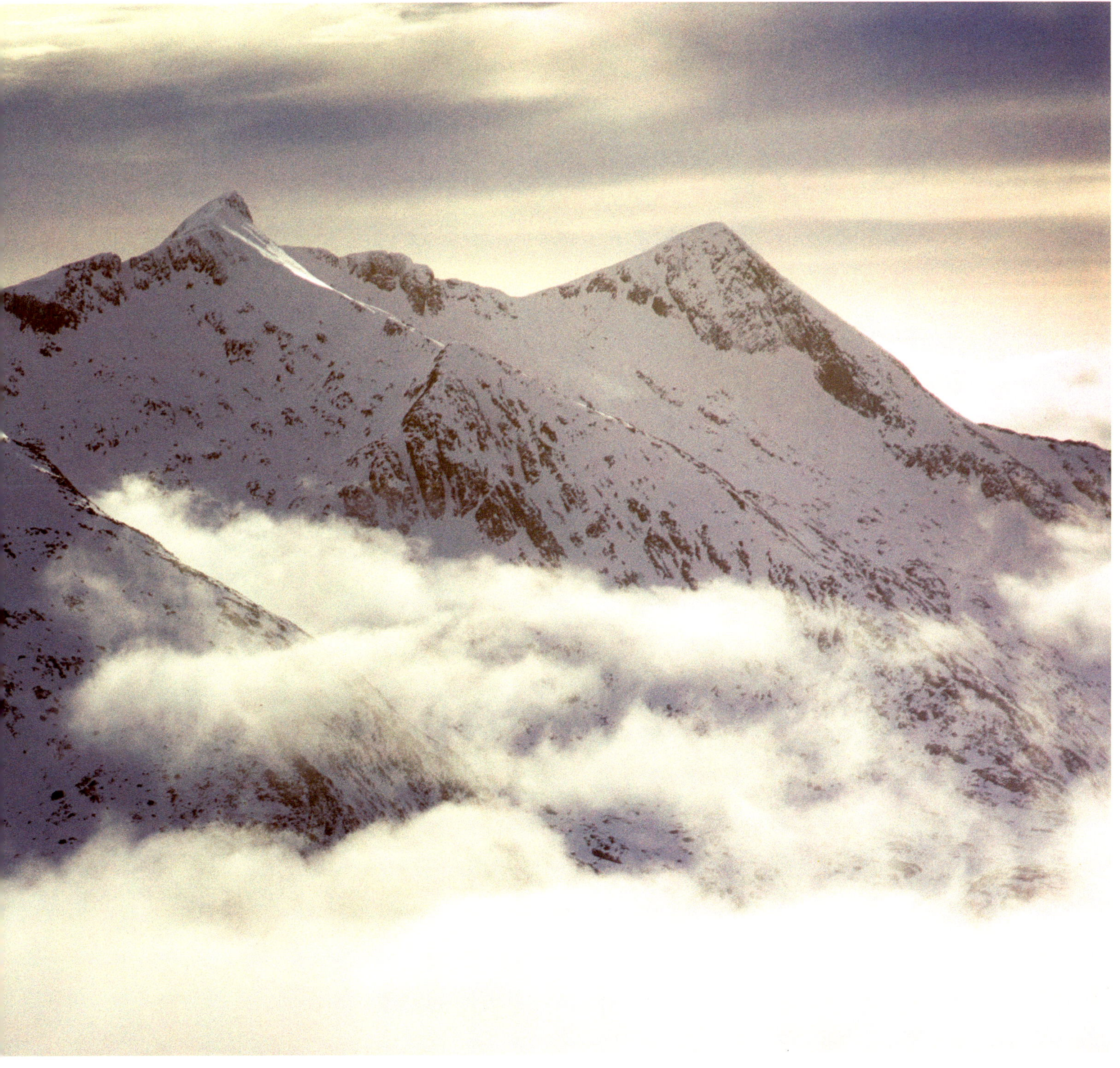

Ben Cruachan, Argyll and Bute
March 2018

Being high on a mountain above the clouds is always a joyous experience. I spent many hours here on the windless summit of Beinn a' Chochuill watching and photographing this dynamic inversion ebb and flow around the contours of the Cruachan massif. I had decided to wait for the evening light, but by late afternoon the wind had increased significantly and brought with it a dramatic change in weather. The temperature had dropped and an advancing front was approaching fast, engulfing even the higher peaks around me. It was time to leave, but just before I set off down, the sun momentarily appeared, lighting the scene before me. I had time to set up and fire one single frame before the weather, conspicuous on the left of the frame, moved in permanently, reducing the visibility to nil.

Following Page
Loch Clair, Glen Torridon
October 2017

To the photographer, the autumn colours of the silver birch are always a welcome sight, boldly announcing an end to the monotonous palette of green that plagues the summer landscape. Although strong in colour, their small triangular leaves are particularly delicate and vulnerable when exposed to the winds. So, after a week of typical autumnal weather that saw two major storm systems consecutively hit the North West, I was a little apprehensive on returning to this position above Loch Clair and was pleasantly surprised to see enough foliage had survived.

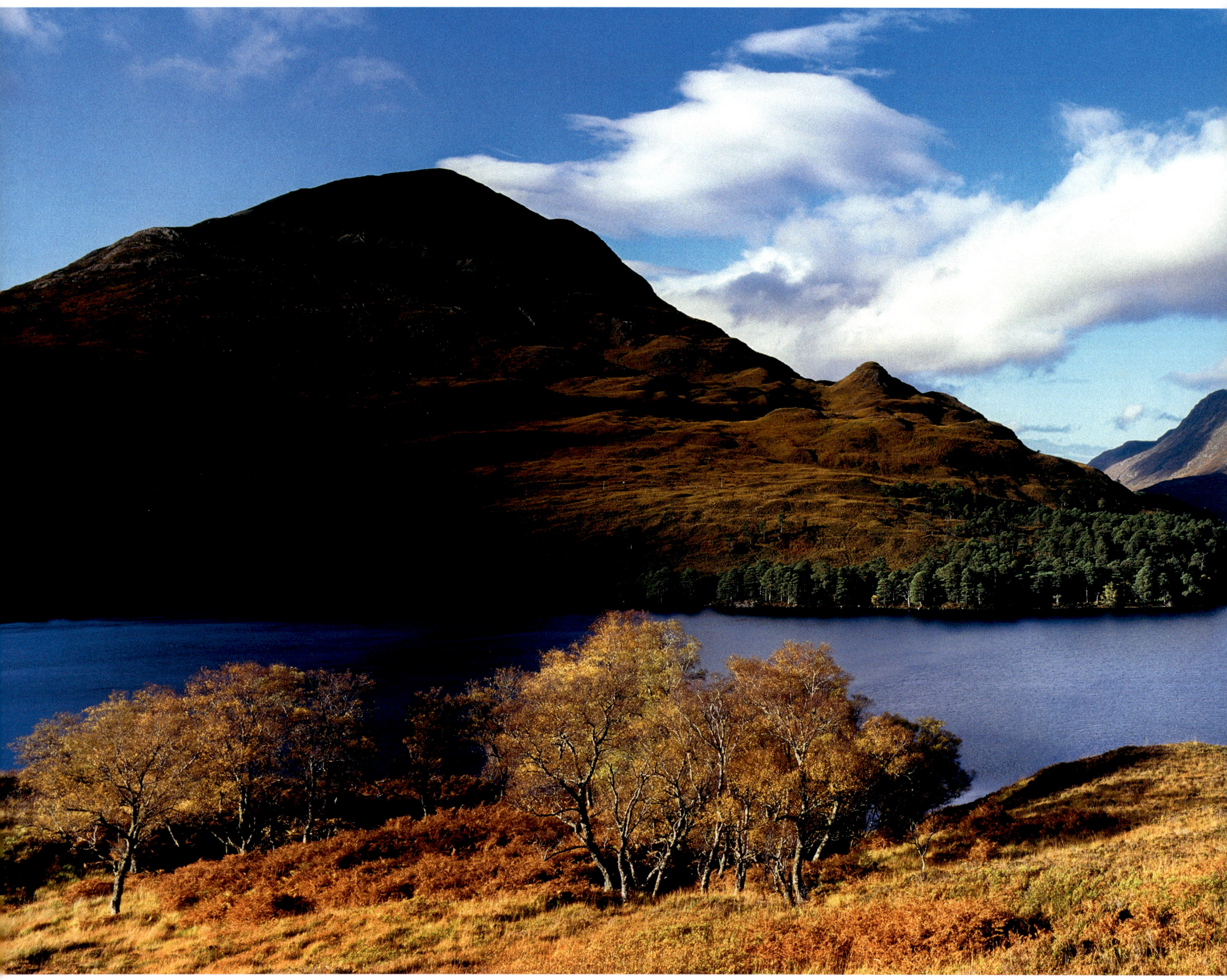

    WILD LIGHT

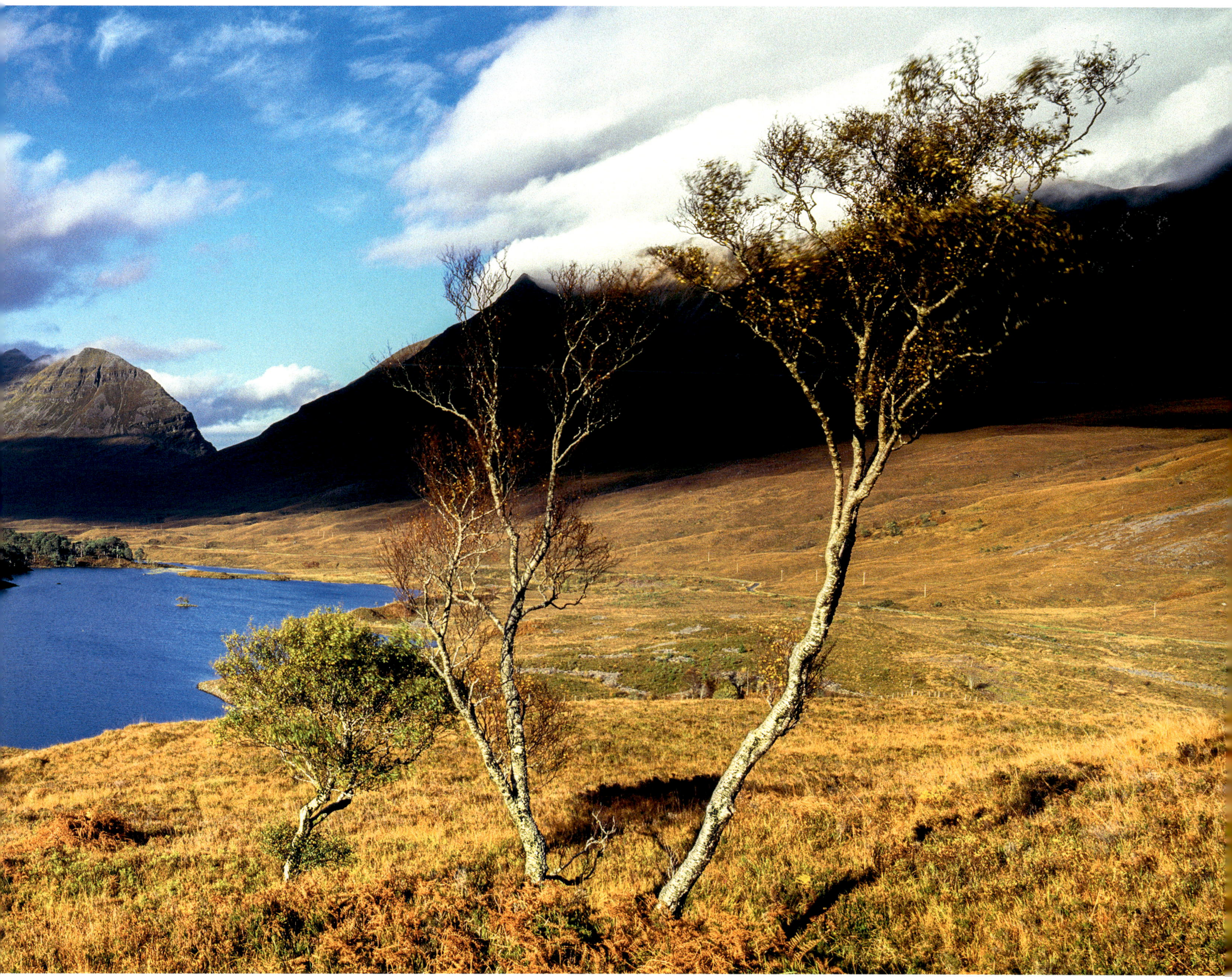

Loch Affric, Glen Affric
March 2017

The wonderful natural environment surrounding Loch
Affric has the perfect combination of ancient woodland,
moorland and dramatic mountain scenery that makes
this a classic Scottish landscape. The native trees are
a mix of birch, oak, Scots pine and Douglas fir that
represents one of the largest remaining belts of habitat
that once covered much of this land.

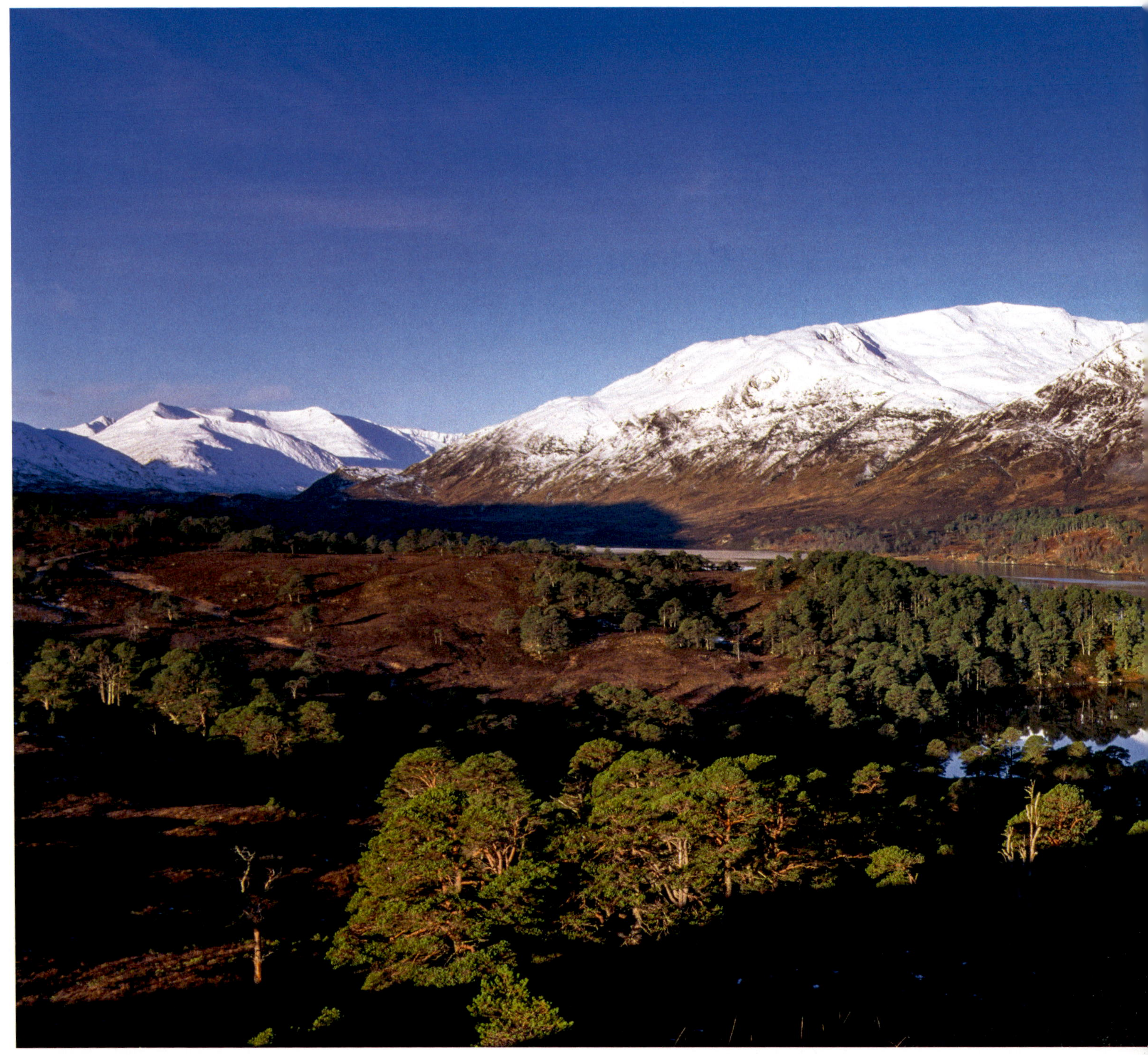

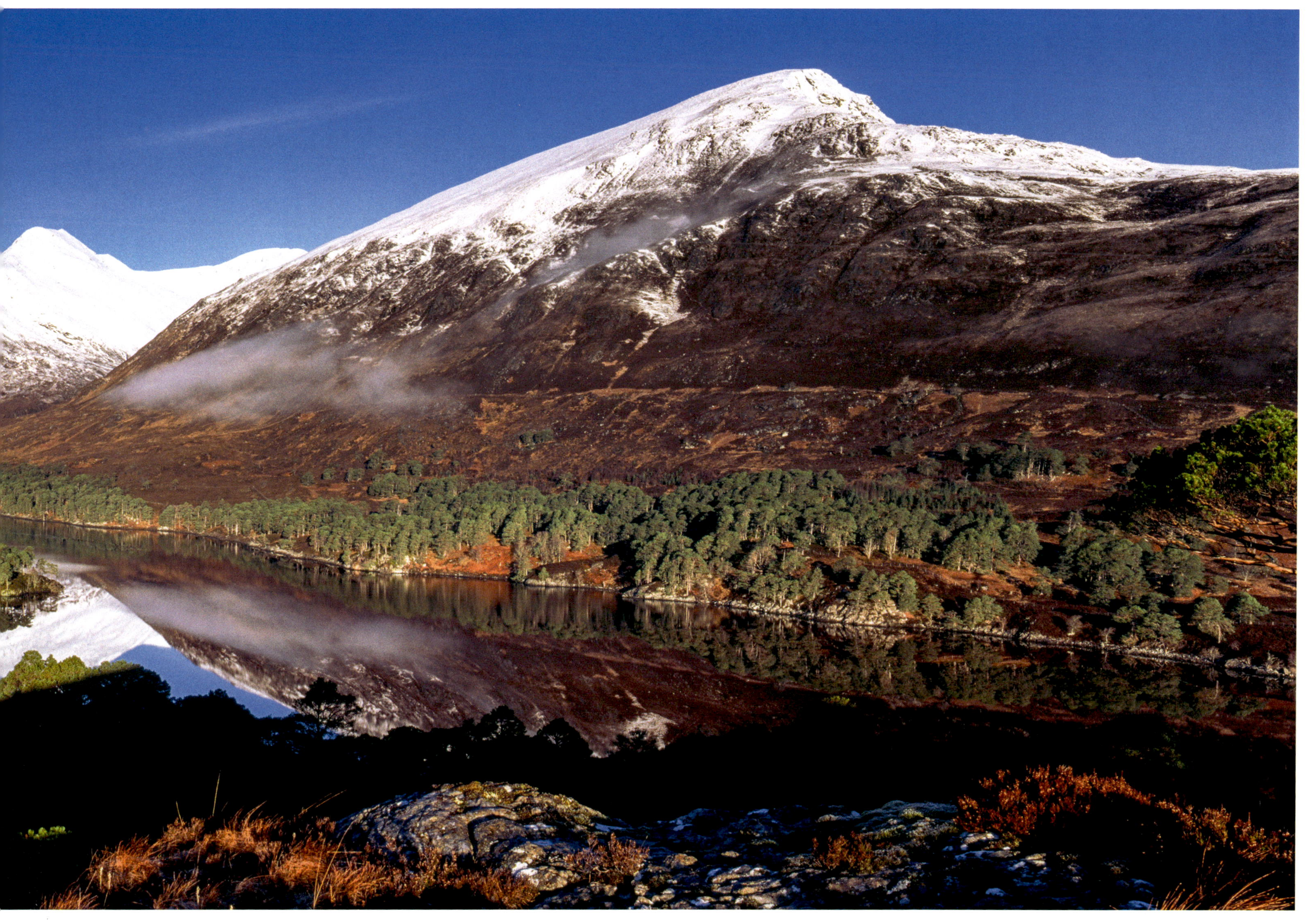

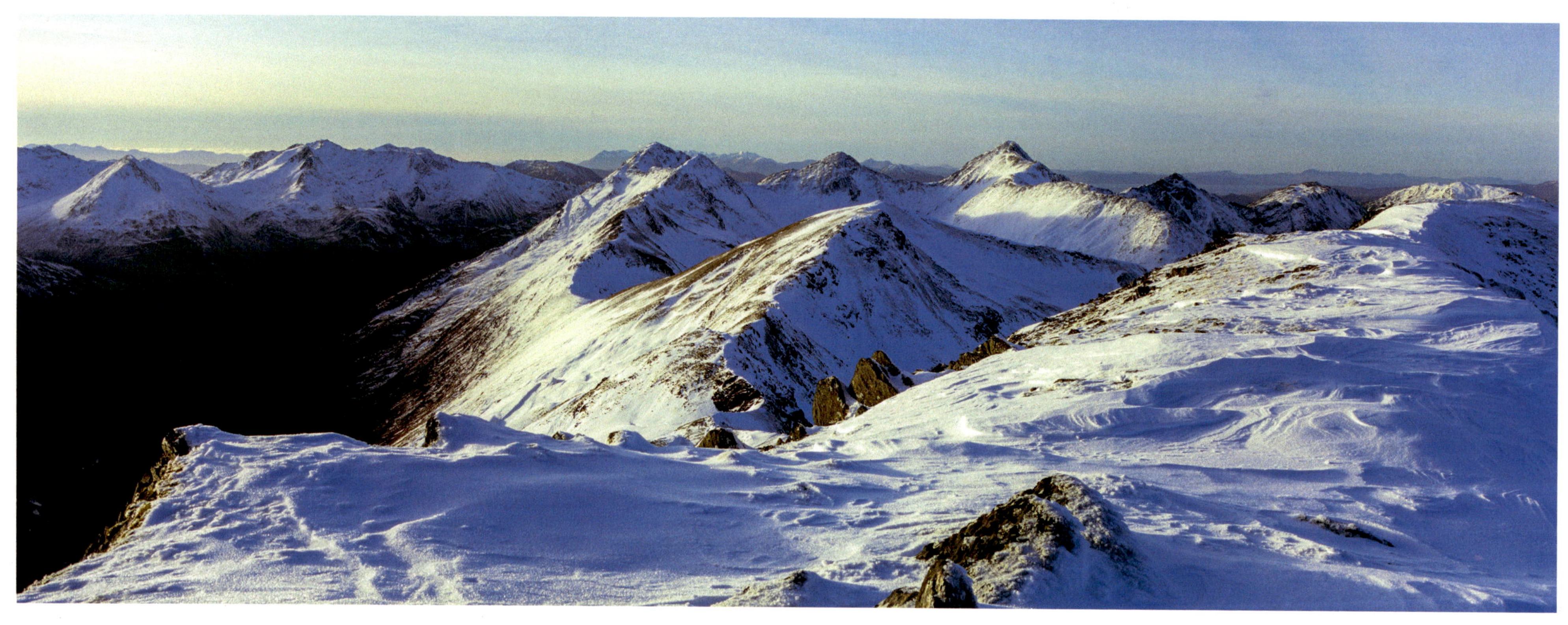

Kintail, West Highlands
January 2017

For high-level ridge walking, Kintail is hard to beat.
The northern aspect of Glen Shiel is formed from
a concentrated number of steep-sided mountains
creating a weaving chain of 3,000-foot (900-metre)
summits stretching for over six miles.

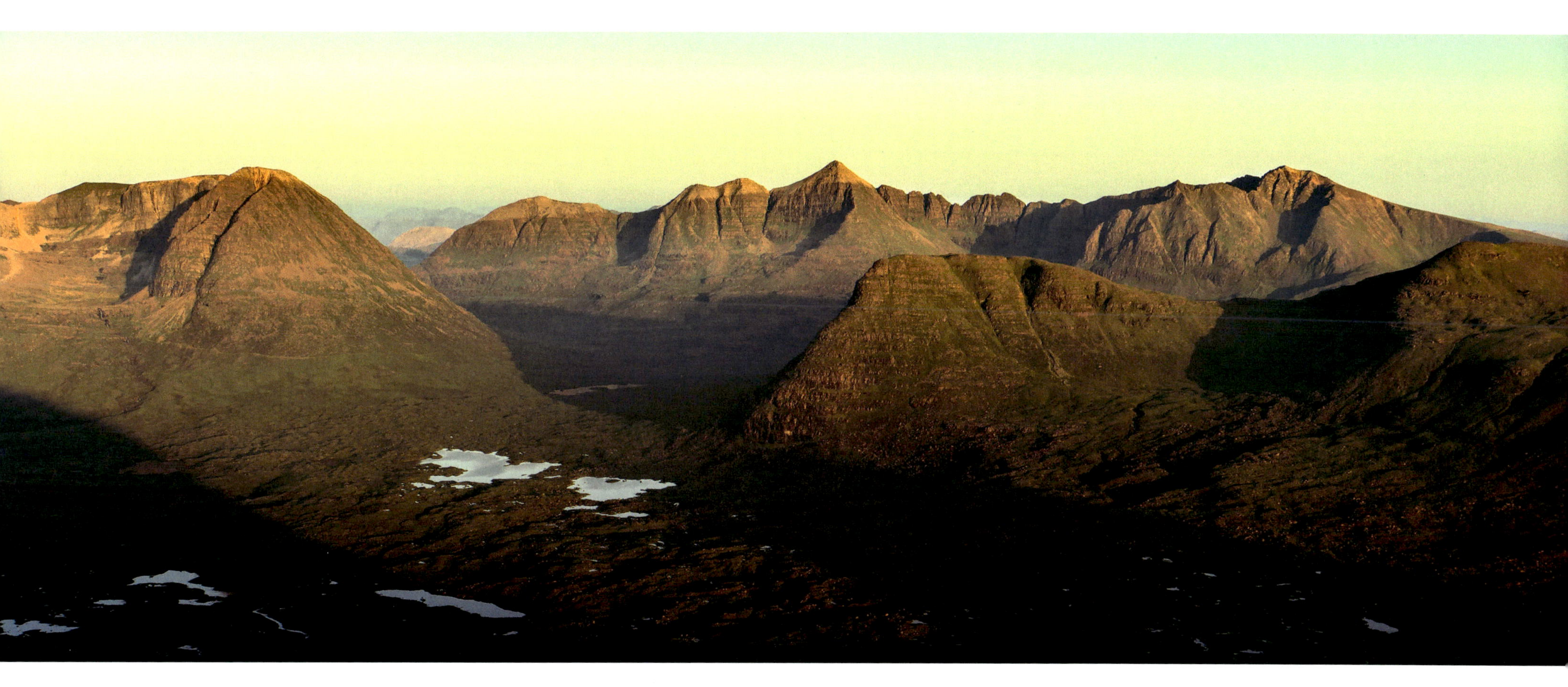

Torridon, Wester Ross
July 2013

On a blisteringly hot summer's day I set off for the remote mountain summit of Beinn an Eòin. Located deep within the Flowerdale Forest this lesser-known Torridon peak offers one of the best alternative views into this renowned area. From my rocky promontory there were many recognisable mountains, but it was Liathach that took centre stage.

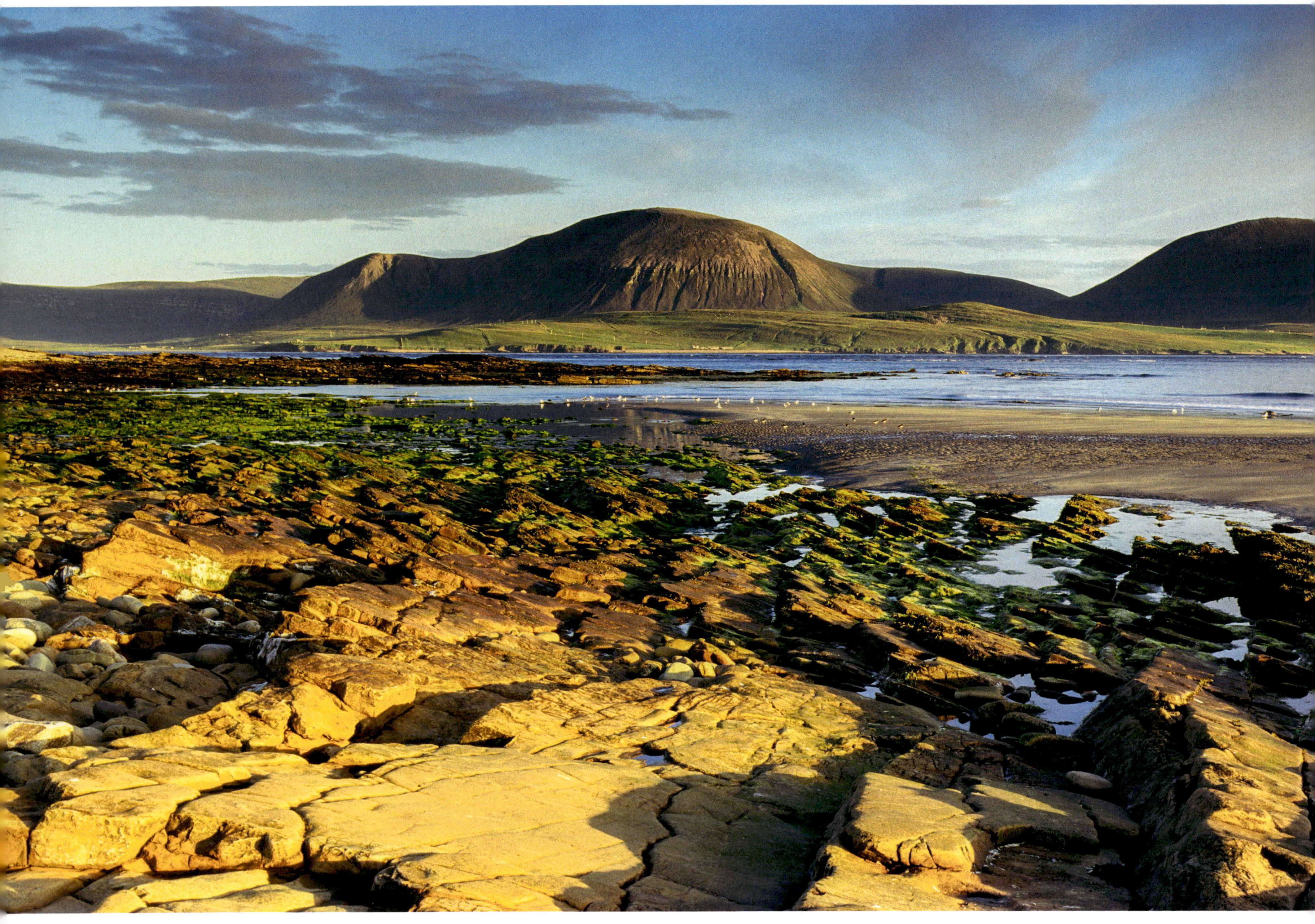

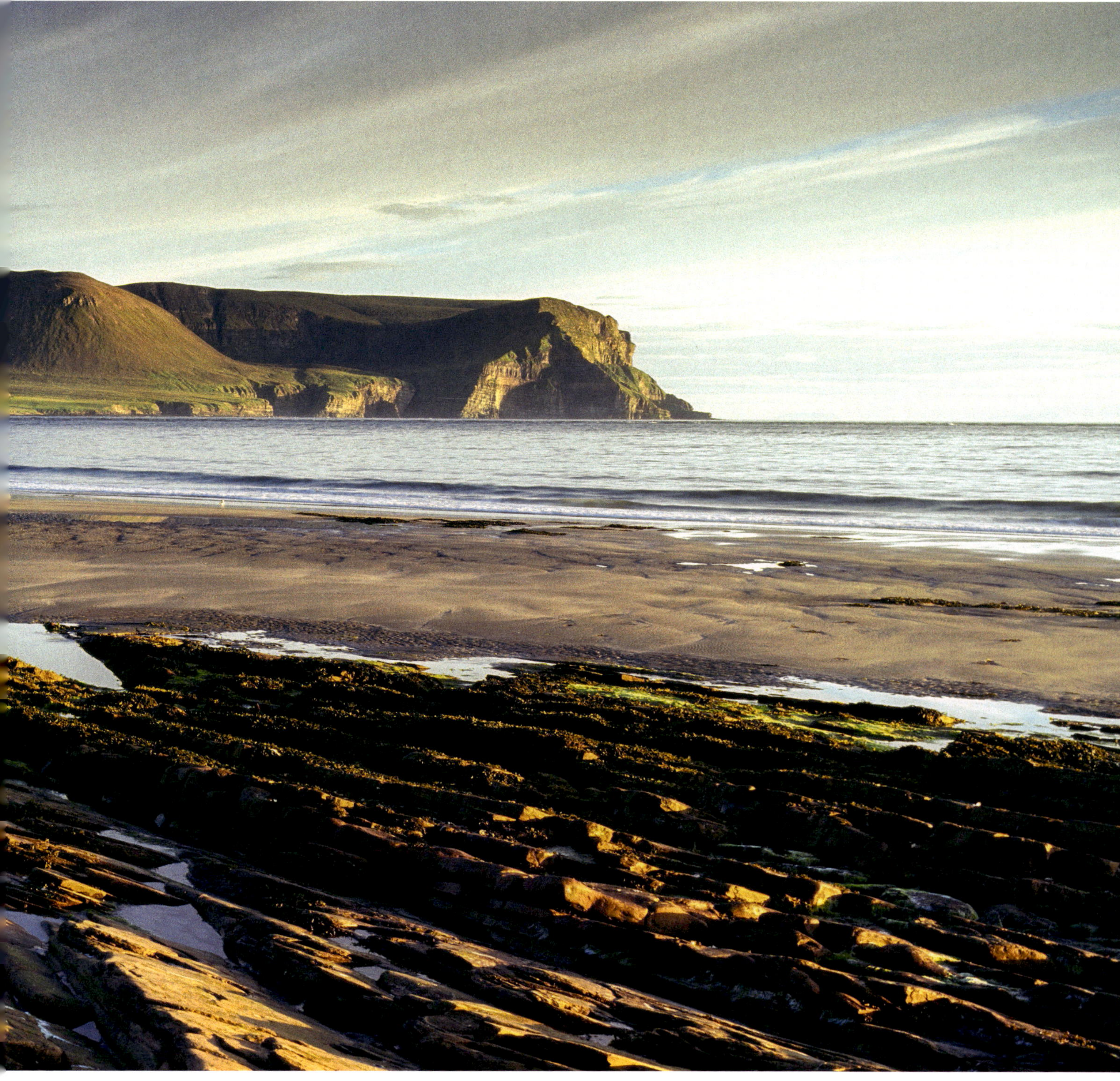

Hoy Sound, Orkney
July 2014

The Orkney archipelago is a collection of seventy or so
diverse isles and skerries located just off the northern
coast of Scotland. Separated from the mainland by
the Pentland Firth, the majority of these lands are
mainly low-lying save for Hoy. Famous for its sharply
rising sandstone cliffs and high, rounded summits,
its distinctive profile is best seen from Stenigar,
Stromness, as the sun sets low in the summer sky.

Glen Etive
February 2016

Deep in Glen Etive, the outlook from Beinn Maol Chaluim
looked bleak. A strong, cold easterly wind was bearing
some threatening skies that looked likely to snuff out the
only window of clear sky that remained out west. I waited
close to the summit in the hope that an opportunity
might arise and was about to give up when the sun
suddenly broke through and put on a spectacular
last-minute light show.

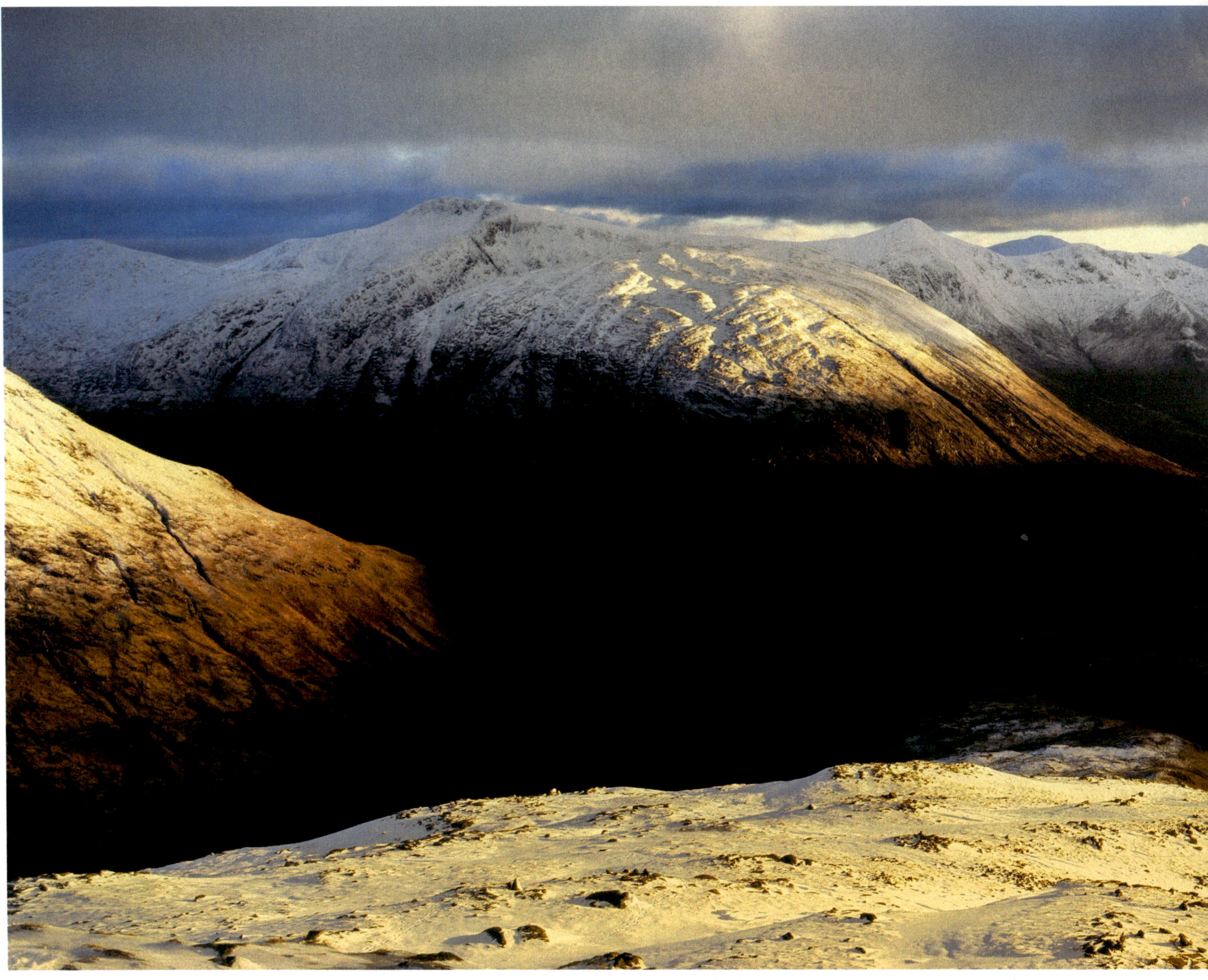

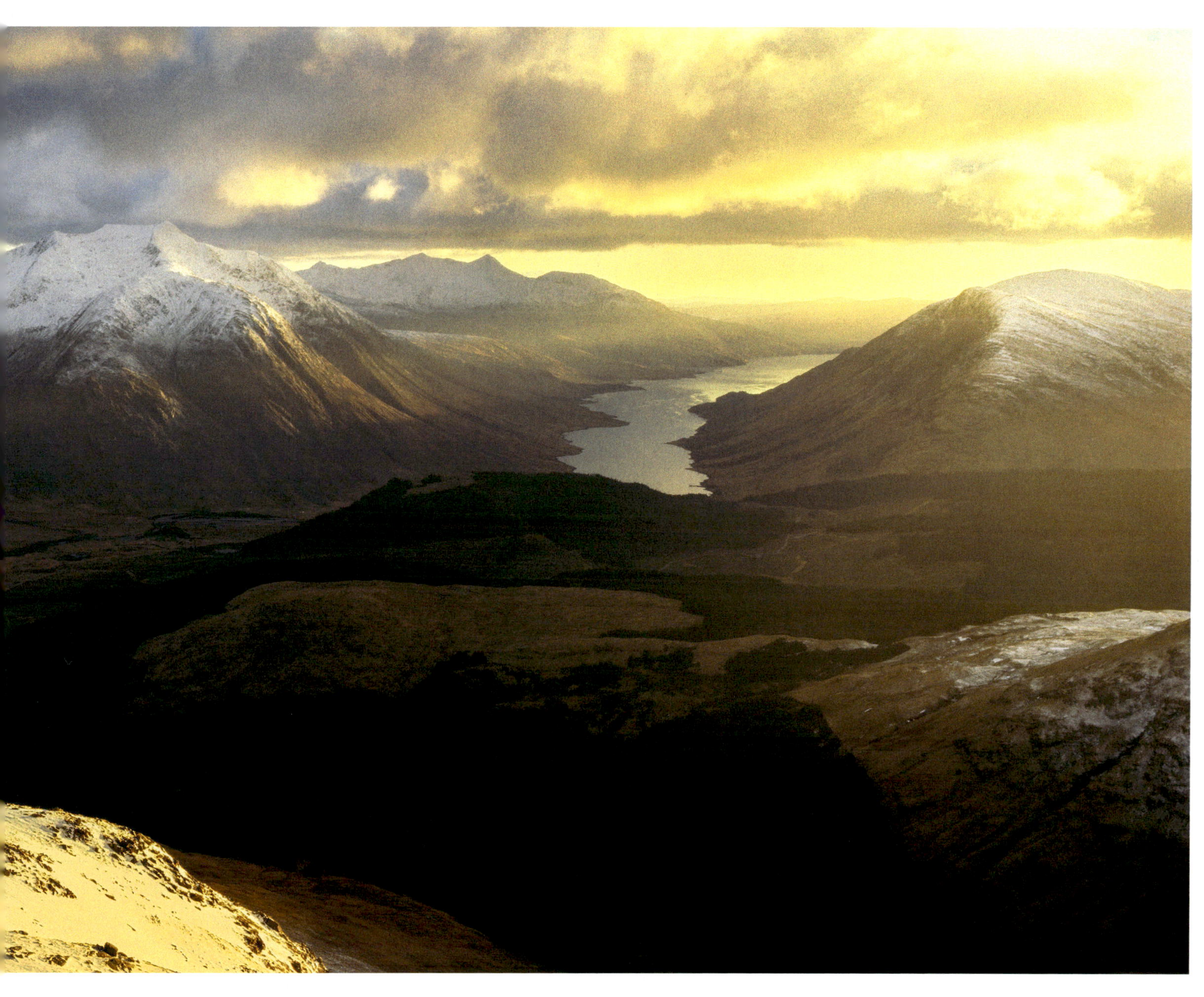

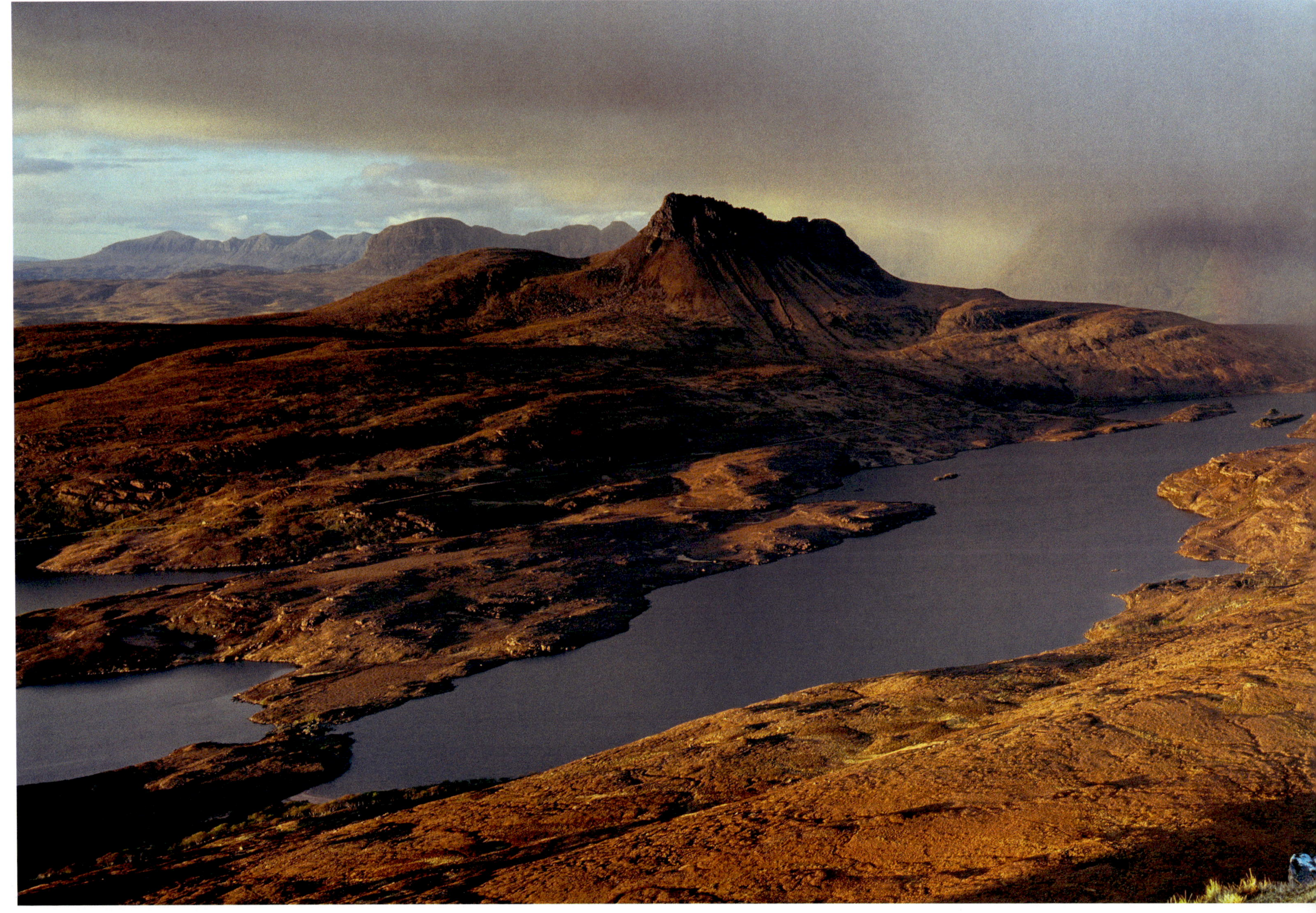

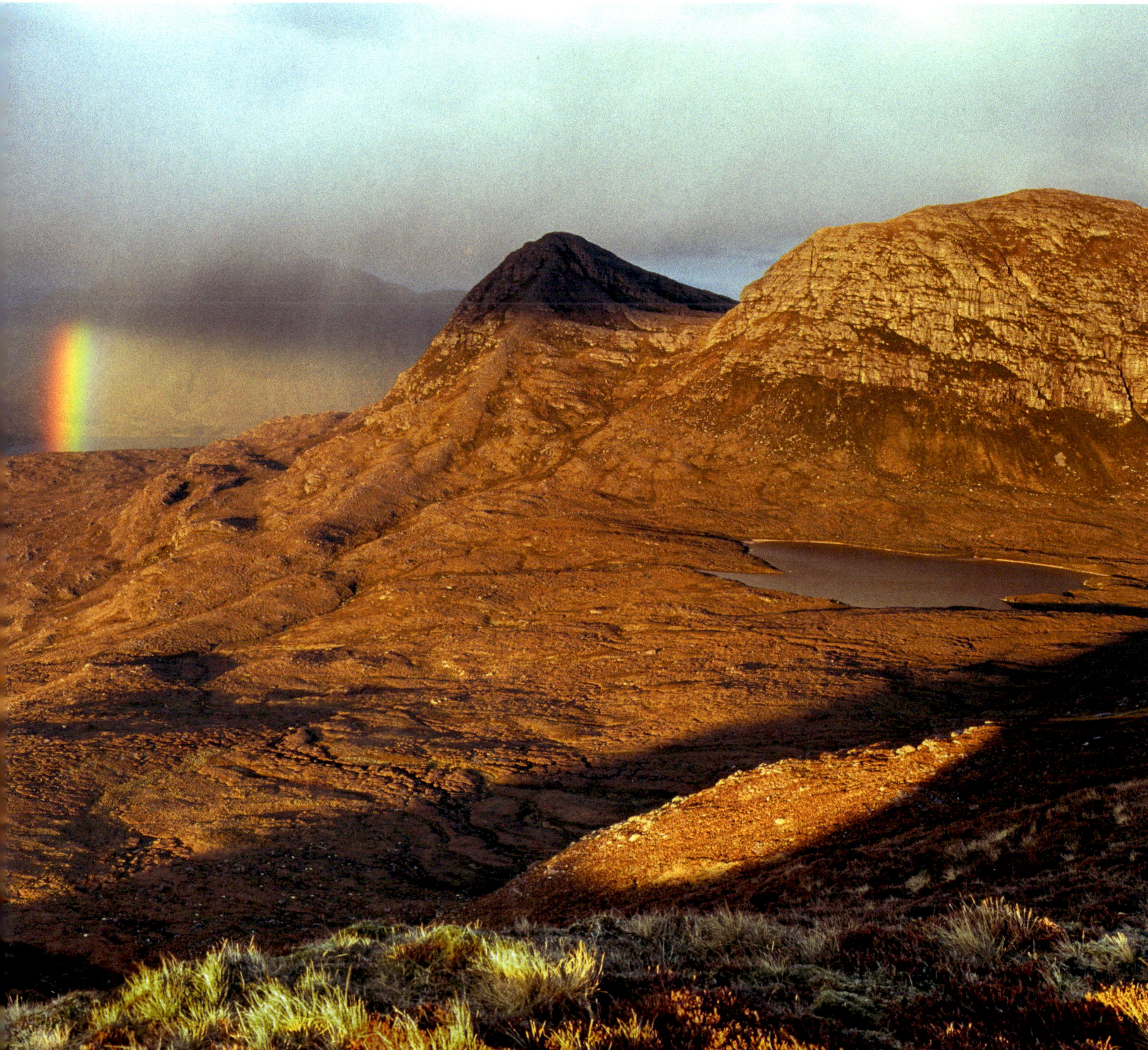

Loch Lurgainn, Inverpolly
April 2012

The unpredictable weather conditions surrounding me
were producing intense downpours across the landscape.
When I reached the edge of the summit plateau I
watched the next maelstrom make its way towards me,
perfectly timed to collide with the late evening light.

River North Esk, Angus
October 2011

The ancient woods and narrow confines at the Rocks
of Solitude on the River North Esk dictate that it can
be extremely difficult for light to penetrate sufficiently
to fill a panoramic frame. From previous experience
I knew of a gap in the trees that would allow a very short
window of morning light to reach the shadowy gorge;
this window corresponded with my visit in autumn,
adding a vital canopy of colour to the scene.

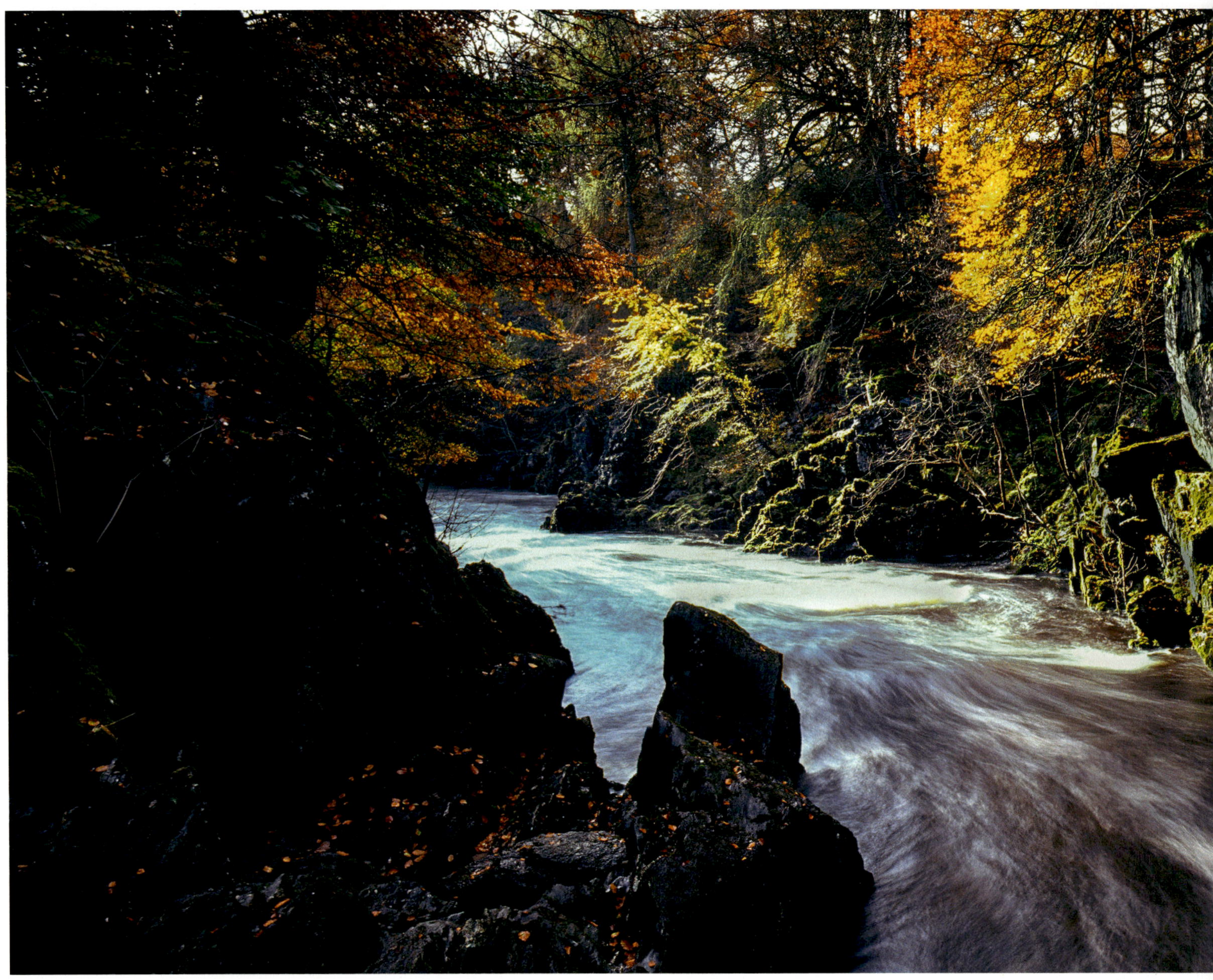

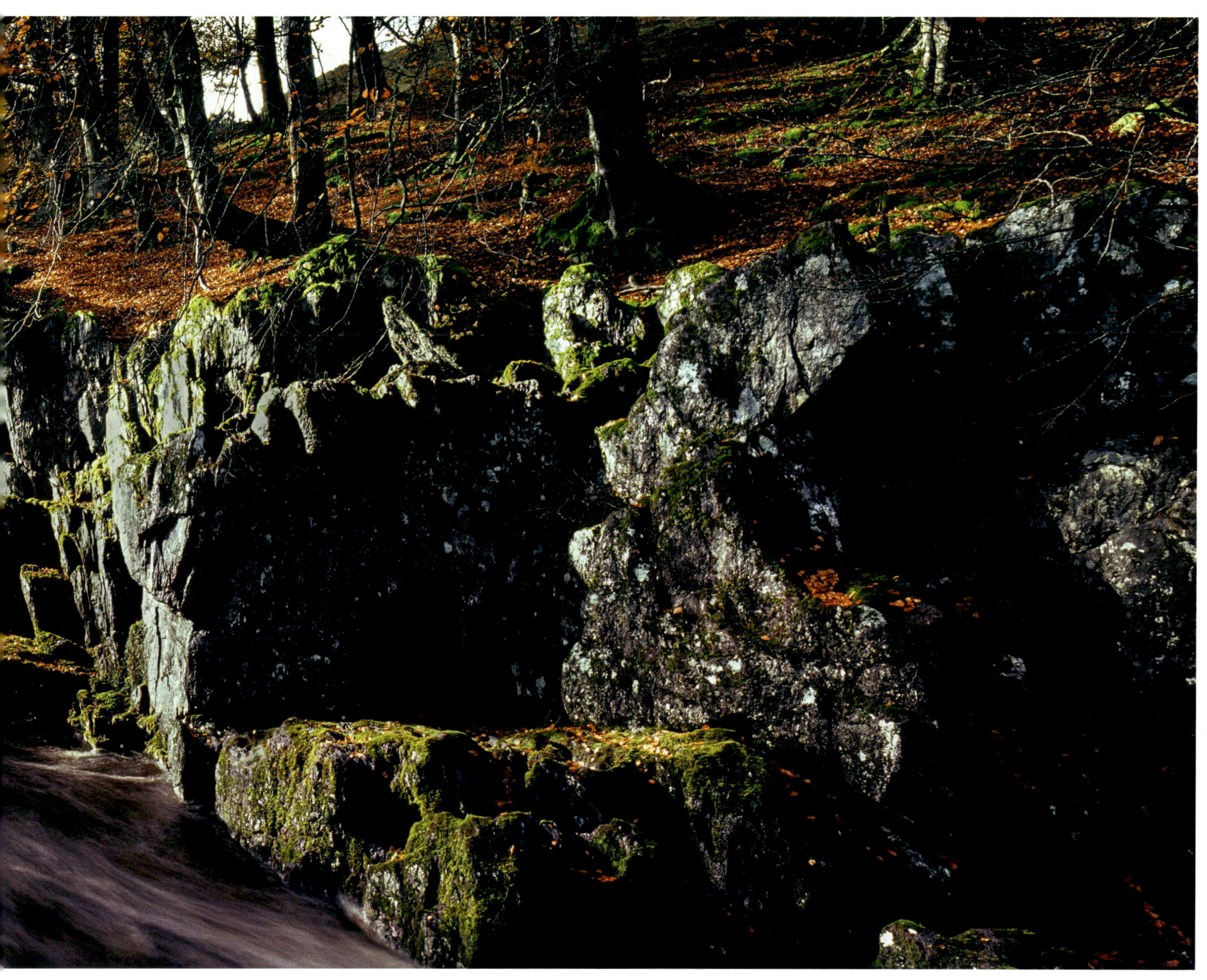

Following Page
Suilven, Assynt
May 2017

The unique structure of Suilven means it can appear
to shape-shift depending on where in the landscape
you view it from. Seen here from the south-west,
its distinctive profile rises from the lochan-scattered
wilderness of Assynt.

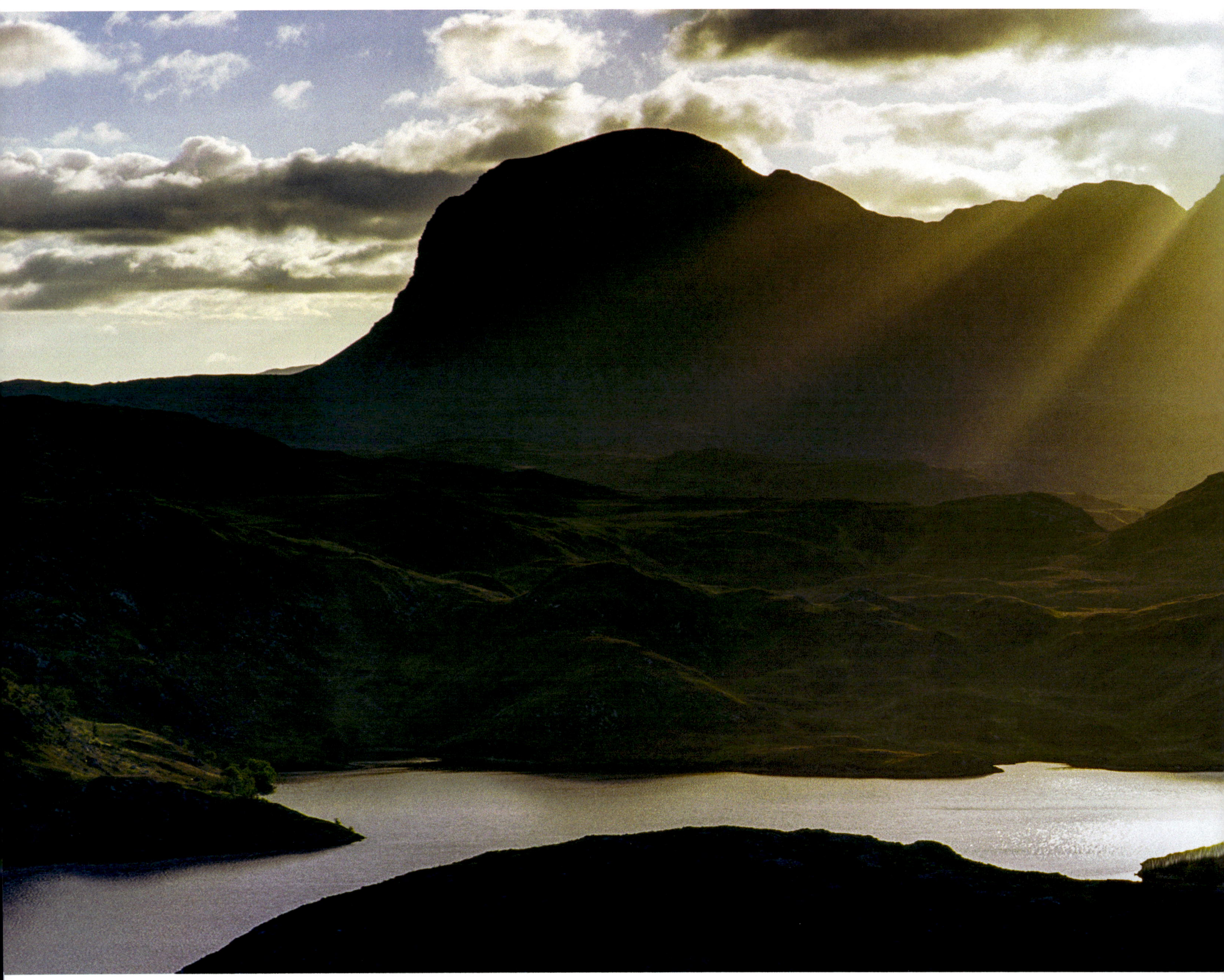

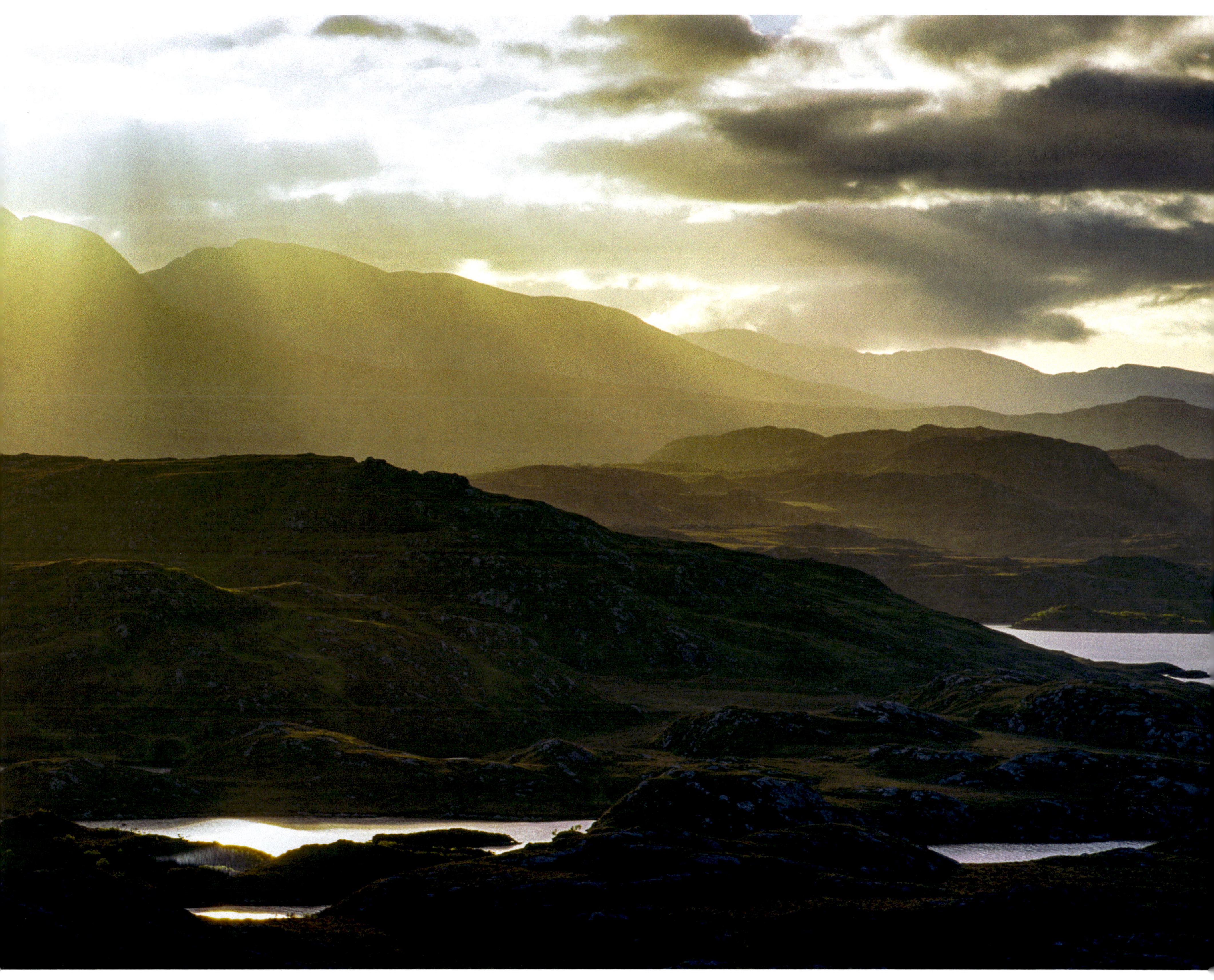

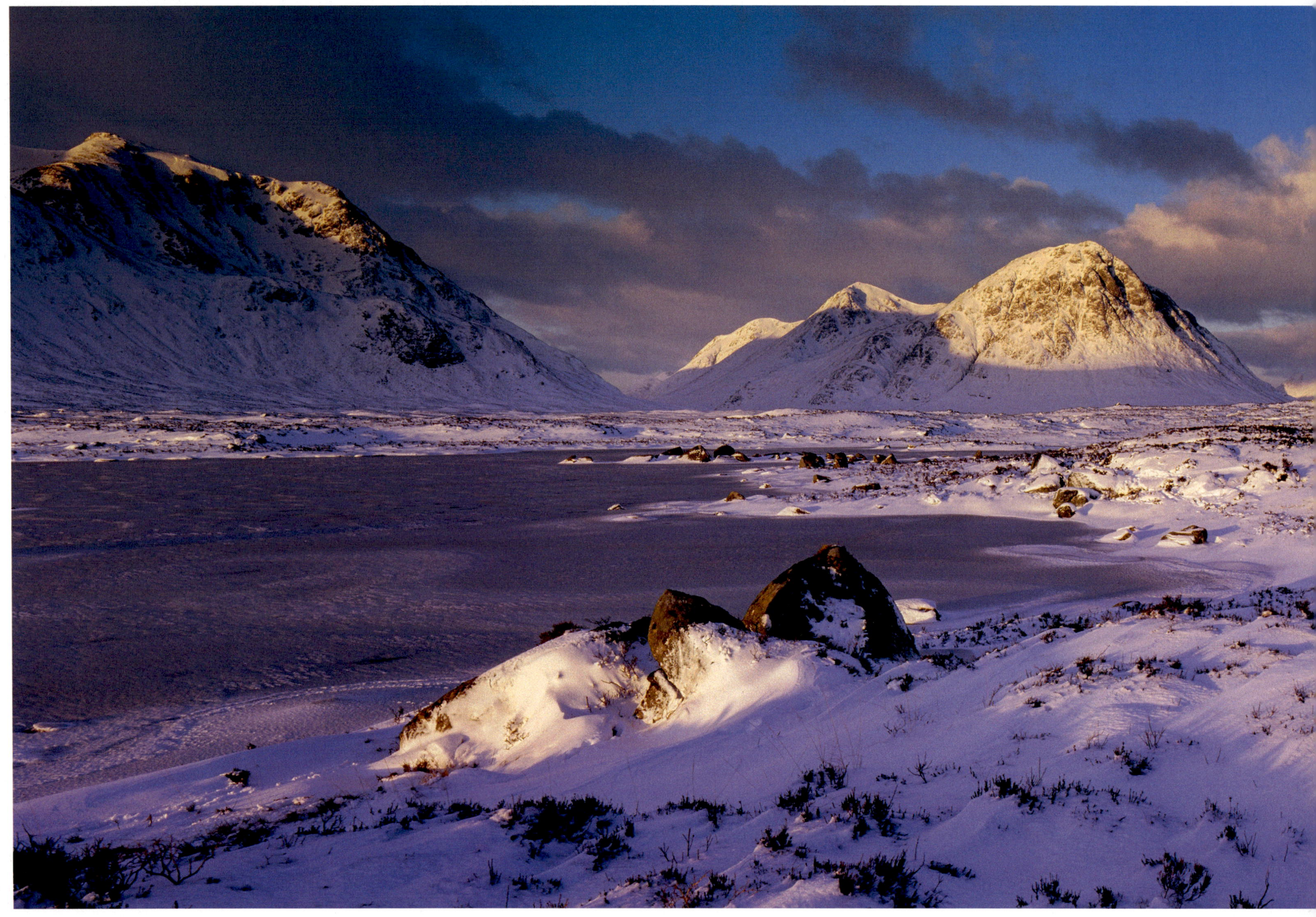

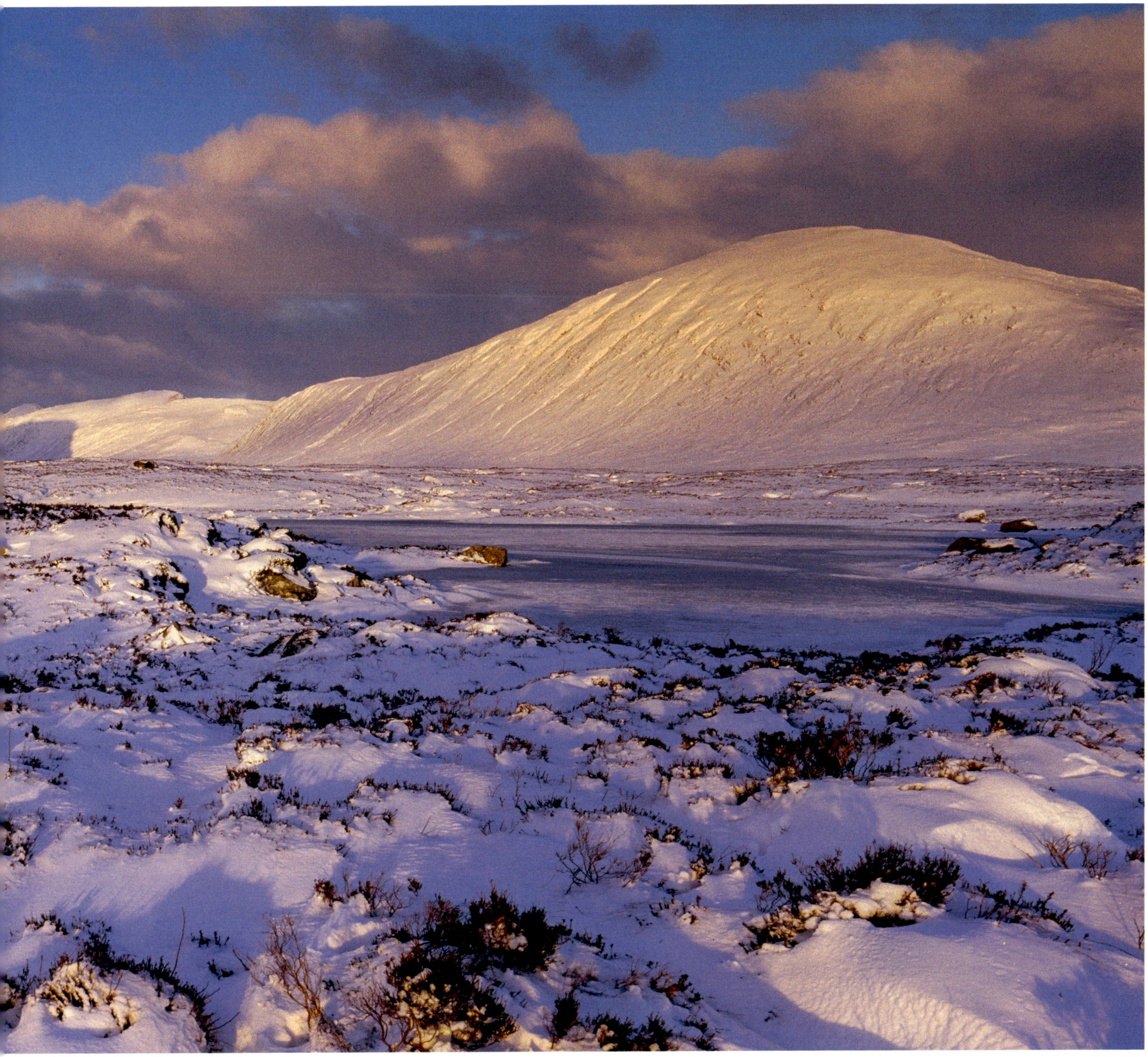

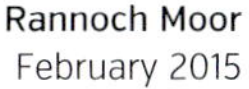

Rannoch Moor
February 2015

Rannoch Moor is a vast plateau of blanket bog,
lochans and streams that sits close to an altitude of
300 metres. This idyllic expanse covers approximately
fifty square miles and is surrounded by mountains on all
sides, including Buachaille Etive Mòr, left of centre here.
While Scottish novelist Robert Louis Stevenson famously
wrote of Rannoch Moor, 'A wearier-looking desert
man never saw', you could more appropriately
regard Rannoch Moor as a place of wonder and
one of the few remaining wild places in Scotland.

Shieldaig Forest, Wester Ross
June 2017

From the summit of Sgùrr Mòr on Beinn Alligin,
I witnessed this sunset unexpectedly develop into
something of a light show. Perched high above the
waters of Loch Toll nam Biast I quickly set up
my camera to capture the spectacular colours
with the sinister silhouette of Baosbheinn looming
on the horizon.

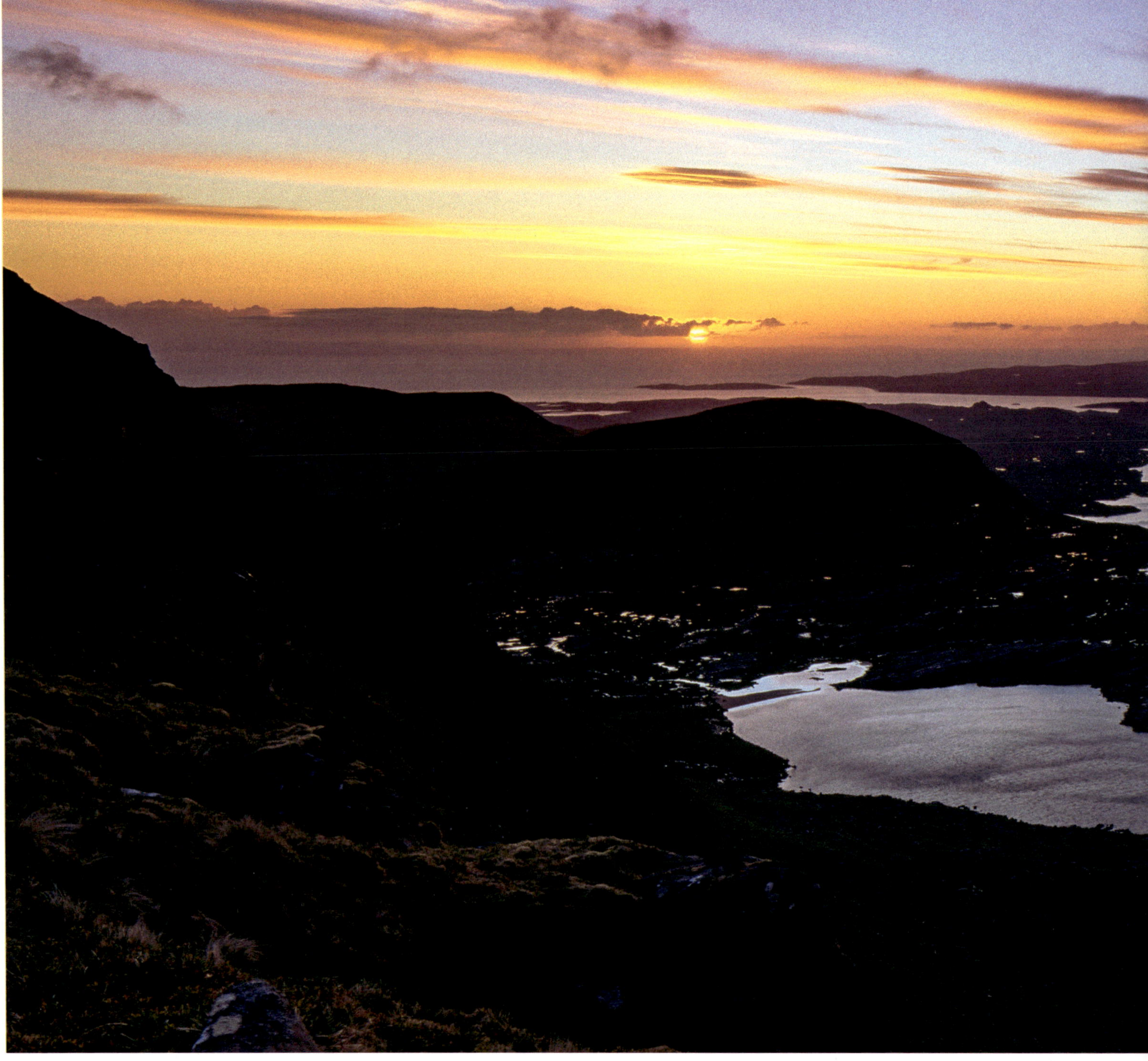

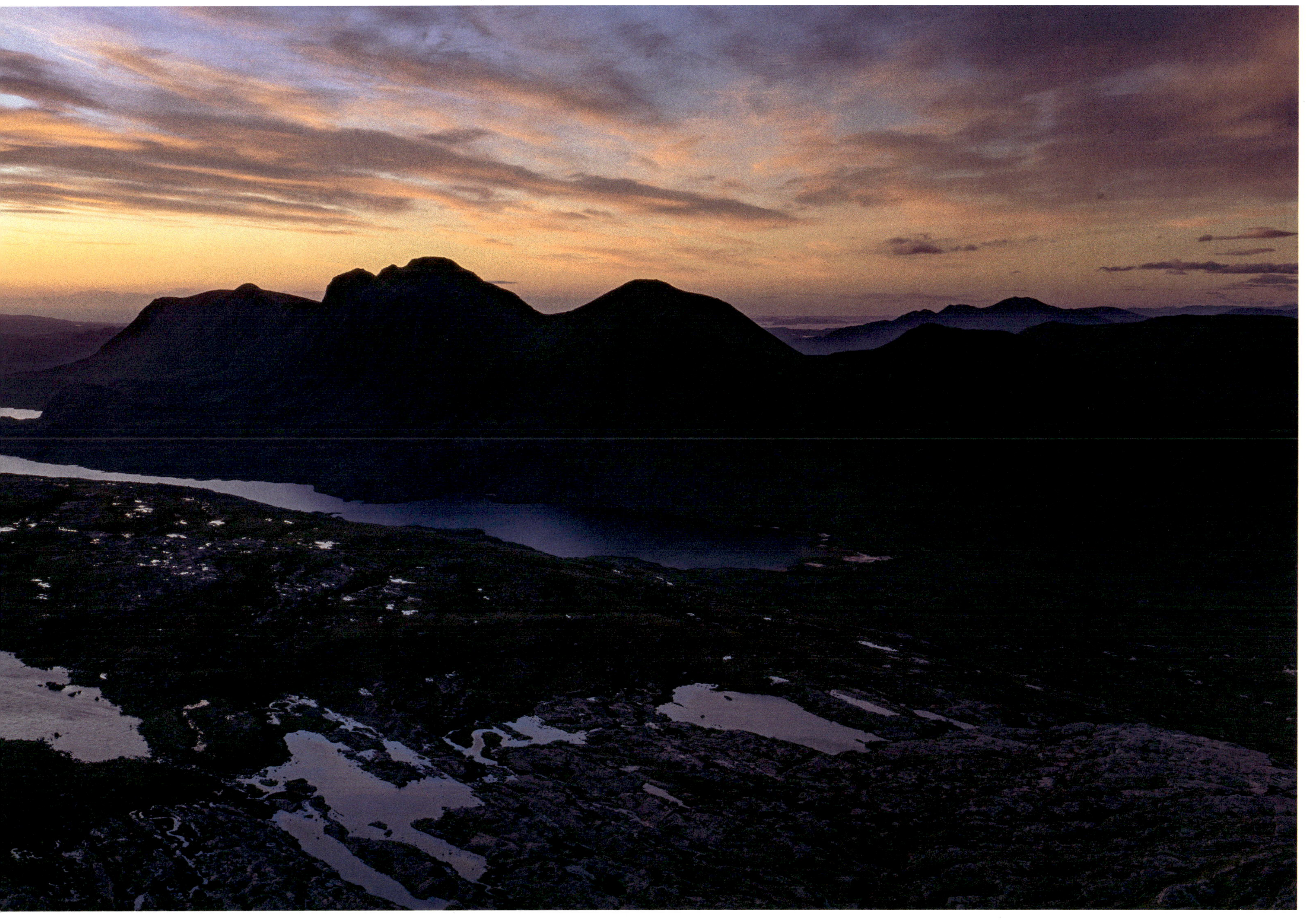

Following Page
Oldshoremore, Sutherland
September 2012

Nestled within the rugged coastline of the North West
Highlands, the fine white sands of Oldshoremore are
naturally protected from the worst of the elements by
the surrounding sea cliffs and mature dune system.

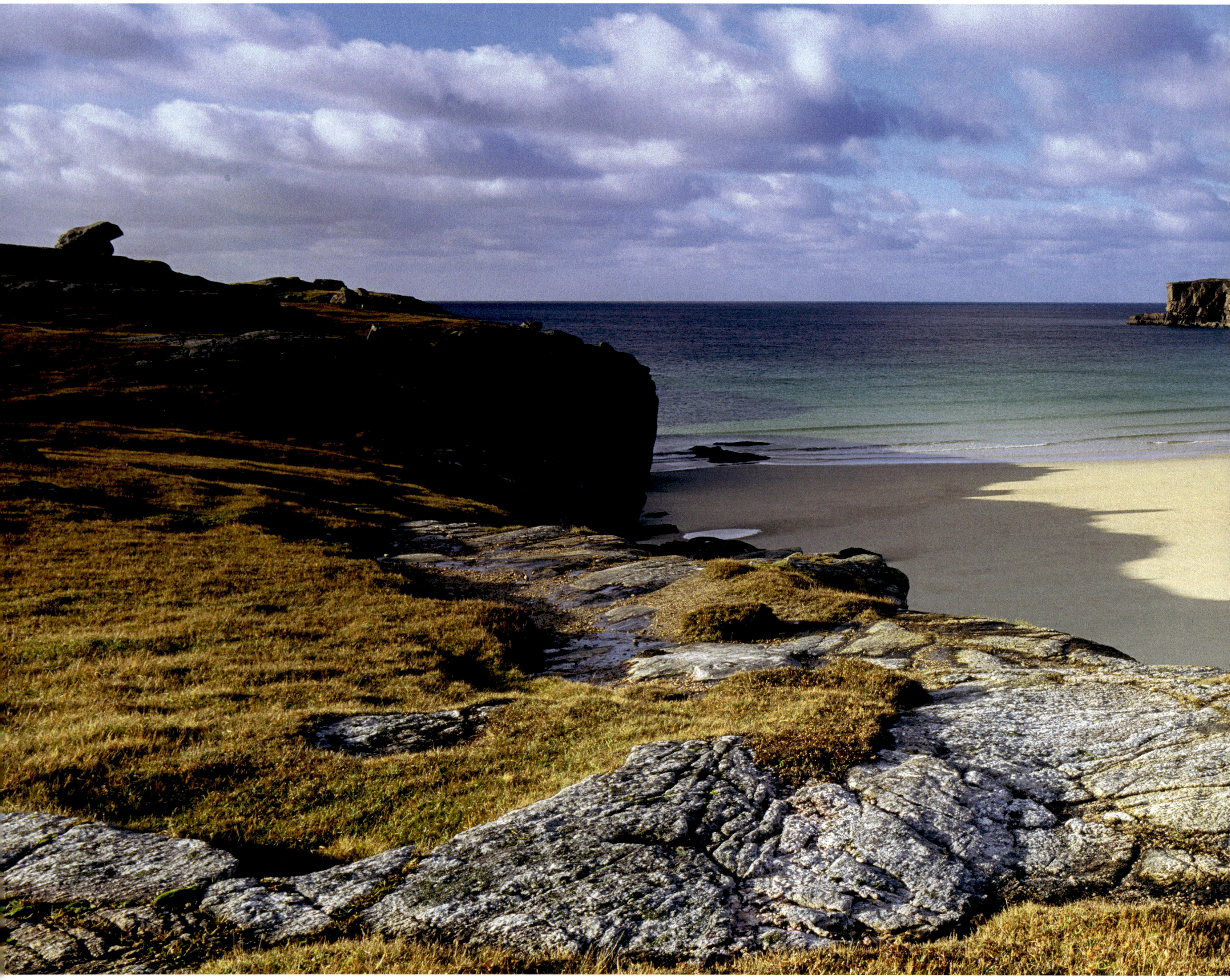

 WILD LIGHT

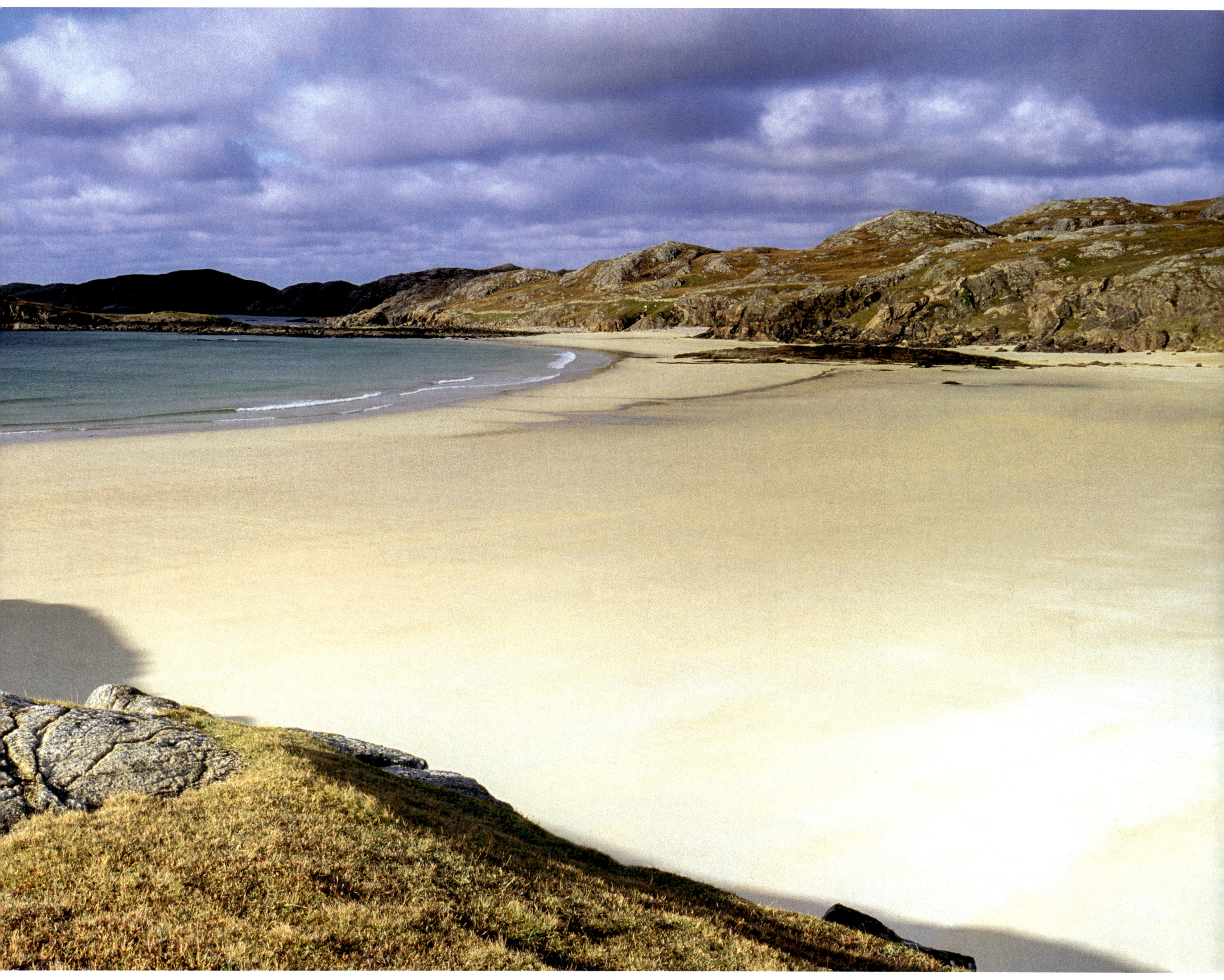

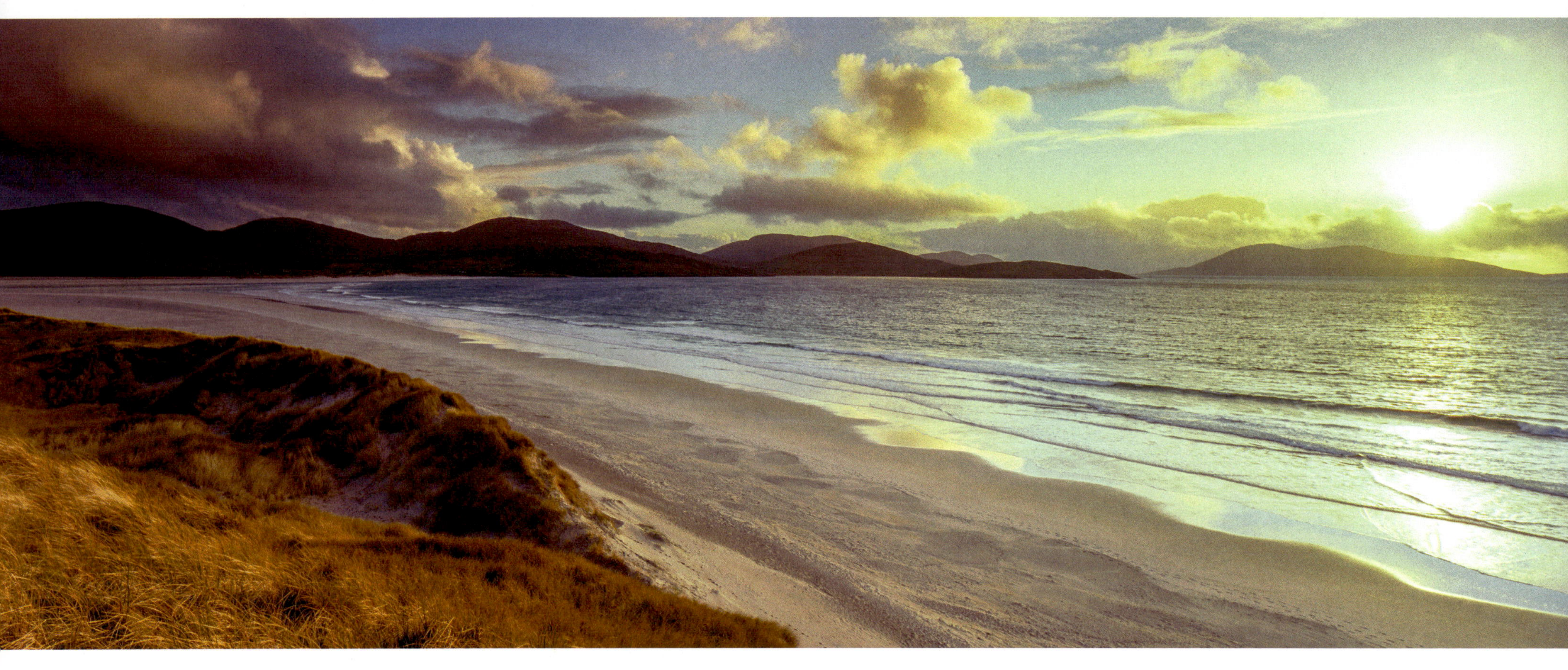

Luskentyre, Harris
November 2011

Often regarded as one of Scotland's finest beaches,
Luskentyre is an exquisite stretch of brilliant white sand
on the west coast of Harris. Backed by immense dunes
and surrounded by mountains, it is an environment of
huge contrasts that epitomises all that the Outer
Hebrides are renowned for.

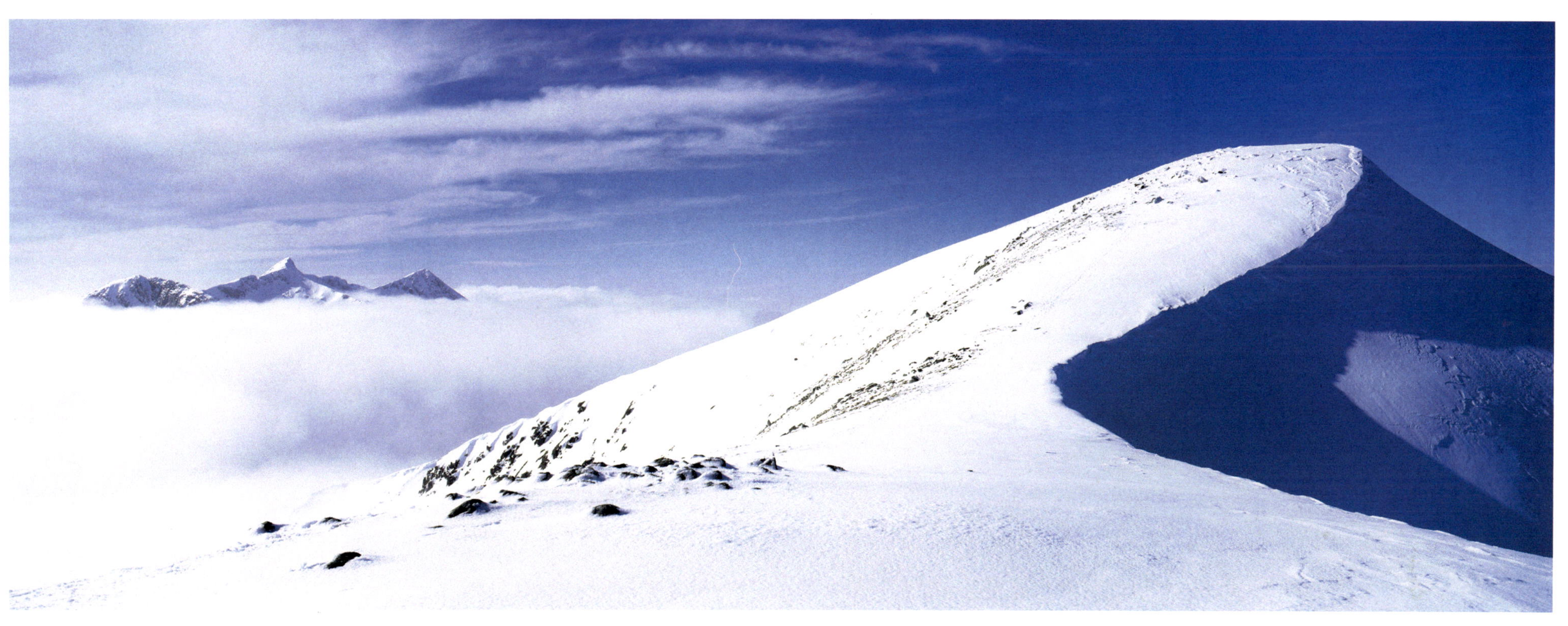

Beinn a' Chochuill, Argyll and Bute
March 2018

Beinn a' Chochuill in Argyll is a favourite mountain of mine and one I have climbed many times and in all seasons. The broad, rolling ridge that links its neighbouring Munro peak of Beinn Eunaich is the perfect place for a walk above the clouds and gives the definitive views towards another favourite, Ben Cruachan.

Liathach, Glen Torridon
February 2013

Loch Clair in Glen Torridon is perfectly placed for framing
the apparently impregnable mass of Liathach. This aspect
actually hides its true size as it stretches for a further
four miles down the glen, presenting a challenging
traverse to those wishing to claim its two principal
peaks, Spidean a' Choire Lèith and Mullach an Rathain,
both of which are Munros.

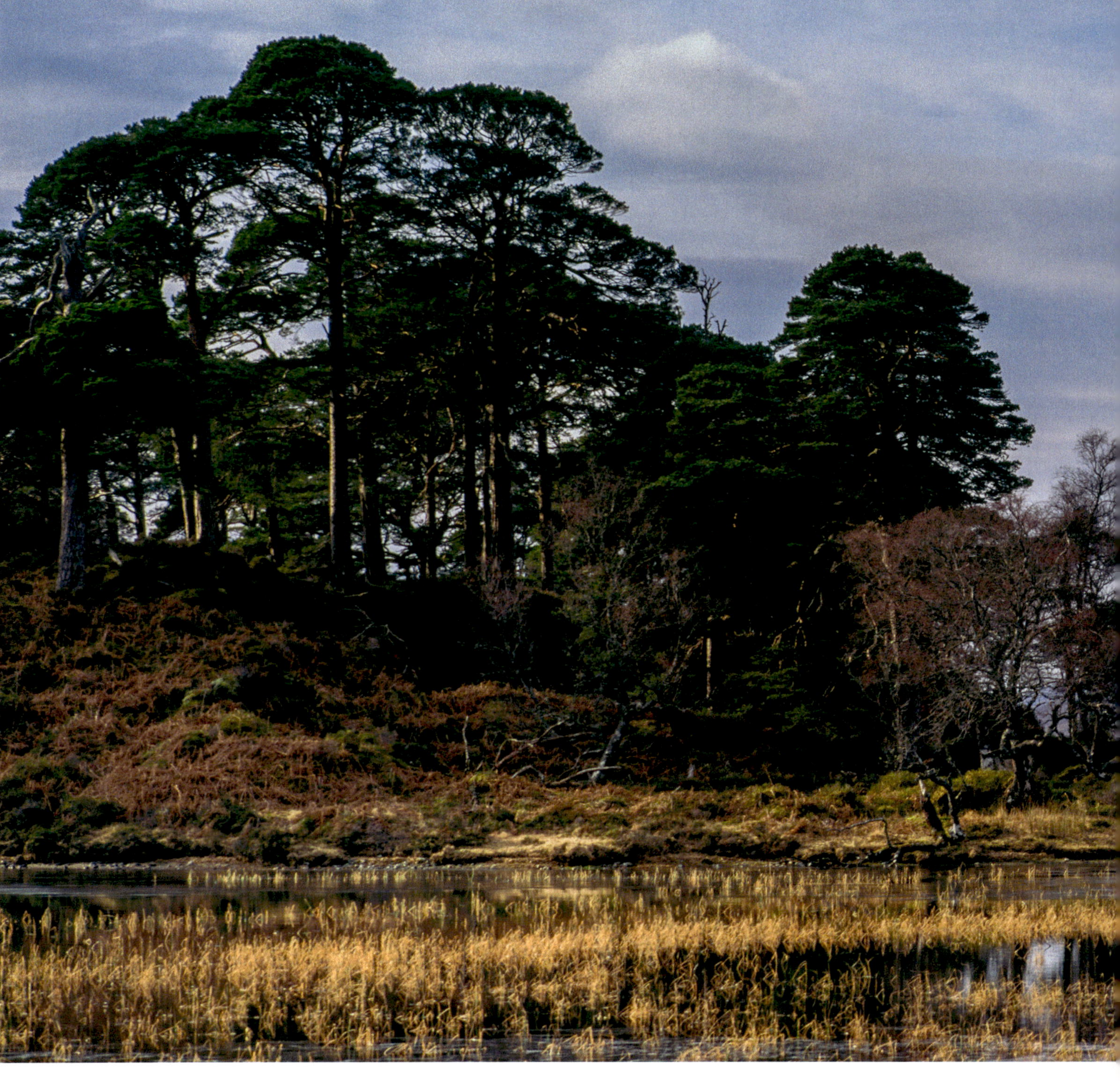

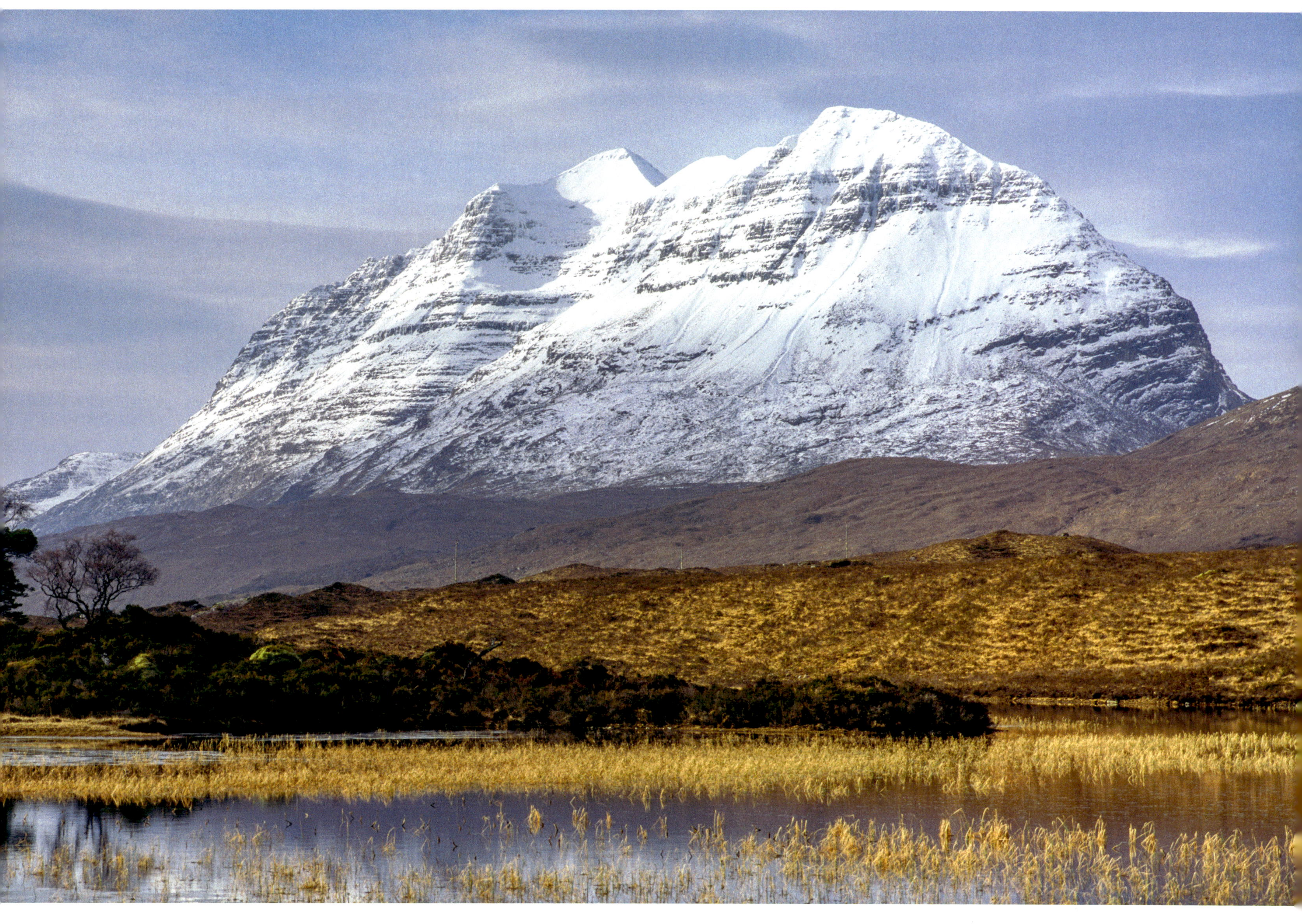

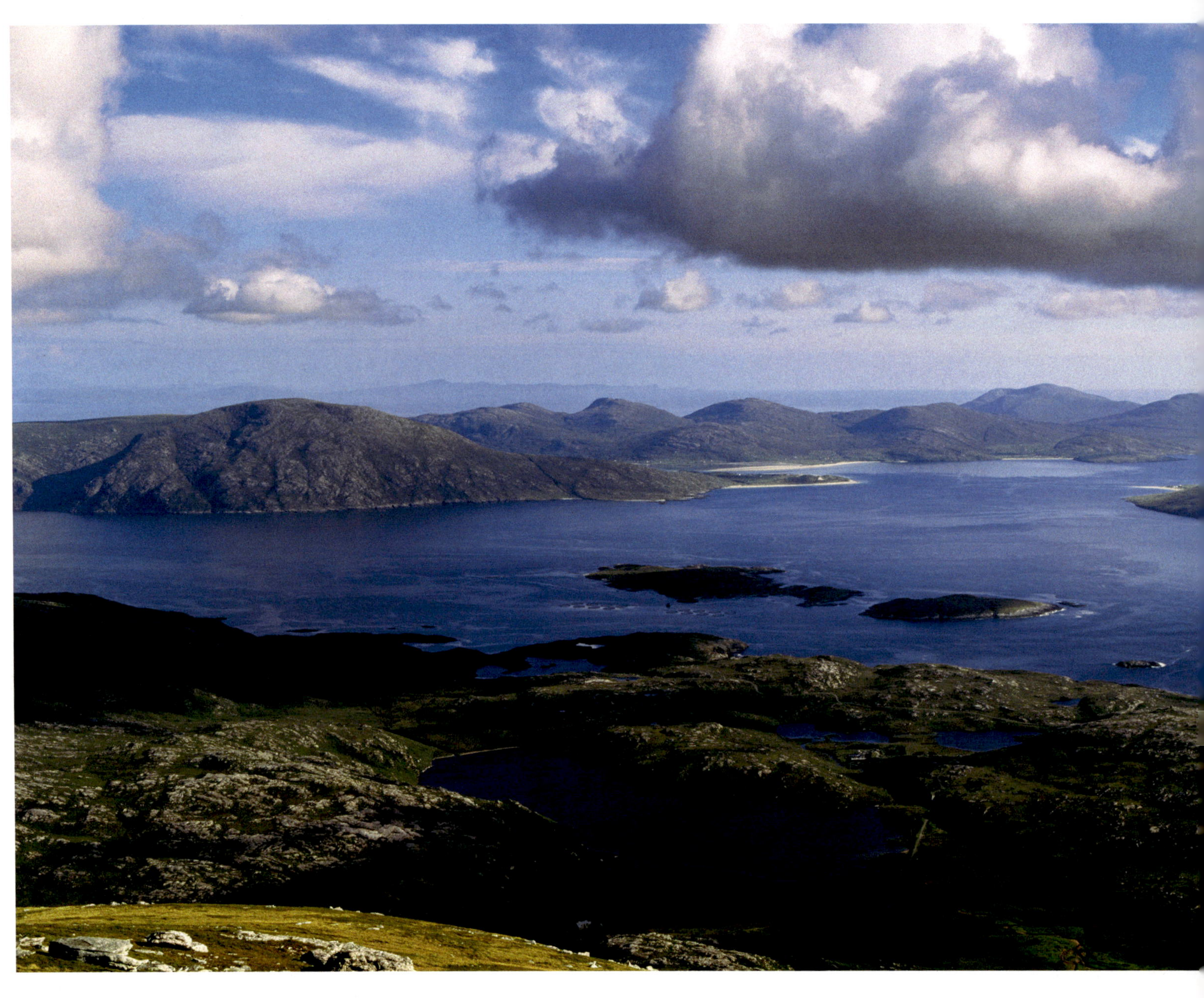

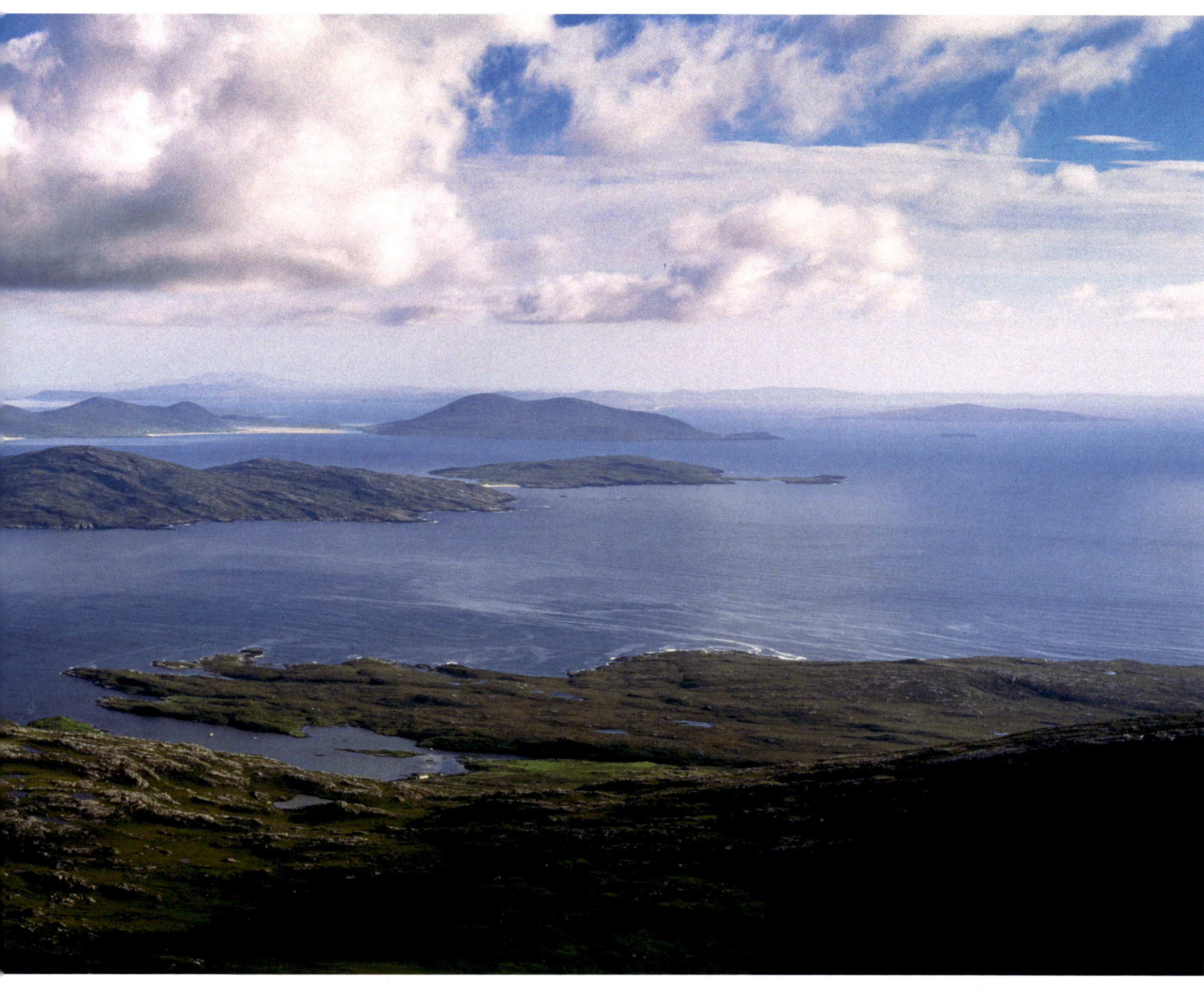

The Sound of Taransay, Harris
August 2012

Tiorga Mòr in North Harris has one of the most
spectacular summit panoramas in Scotland. From high
above the Sound of Taransay it is possible to identify
each of the pristine beaches that the coast here is
renowned for. Not only that, thanks to the superb
visibility I was also able to clearly see the isolated
archipelago of St Kilda, Boreray and the Stacs
over sixty miles away, far out to the west.

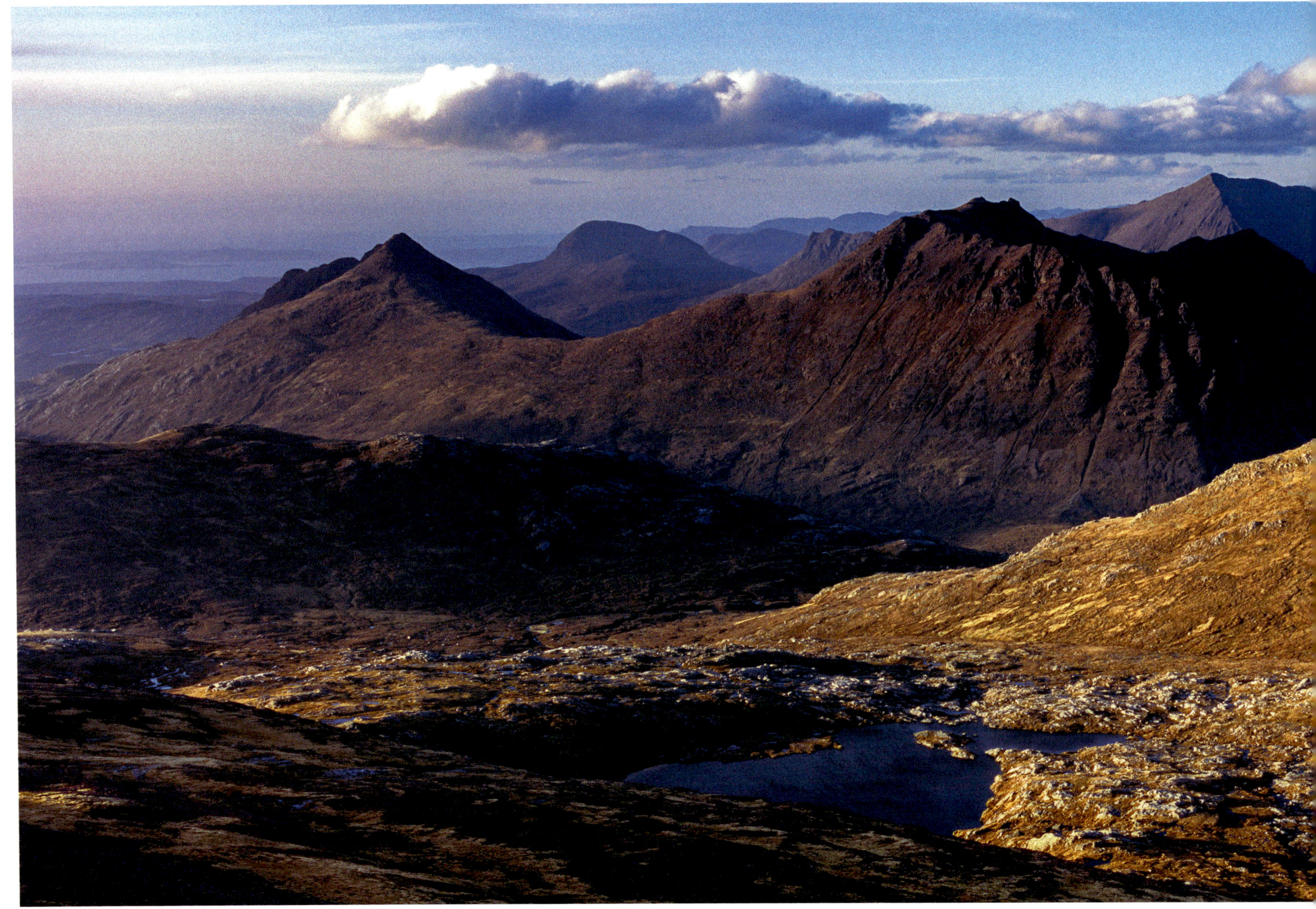

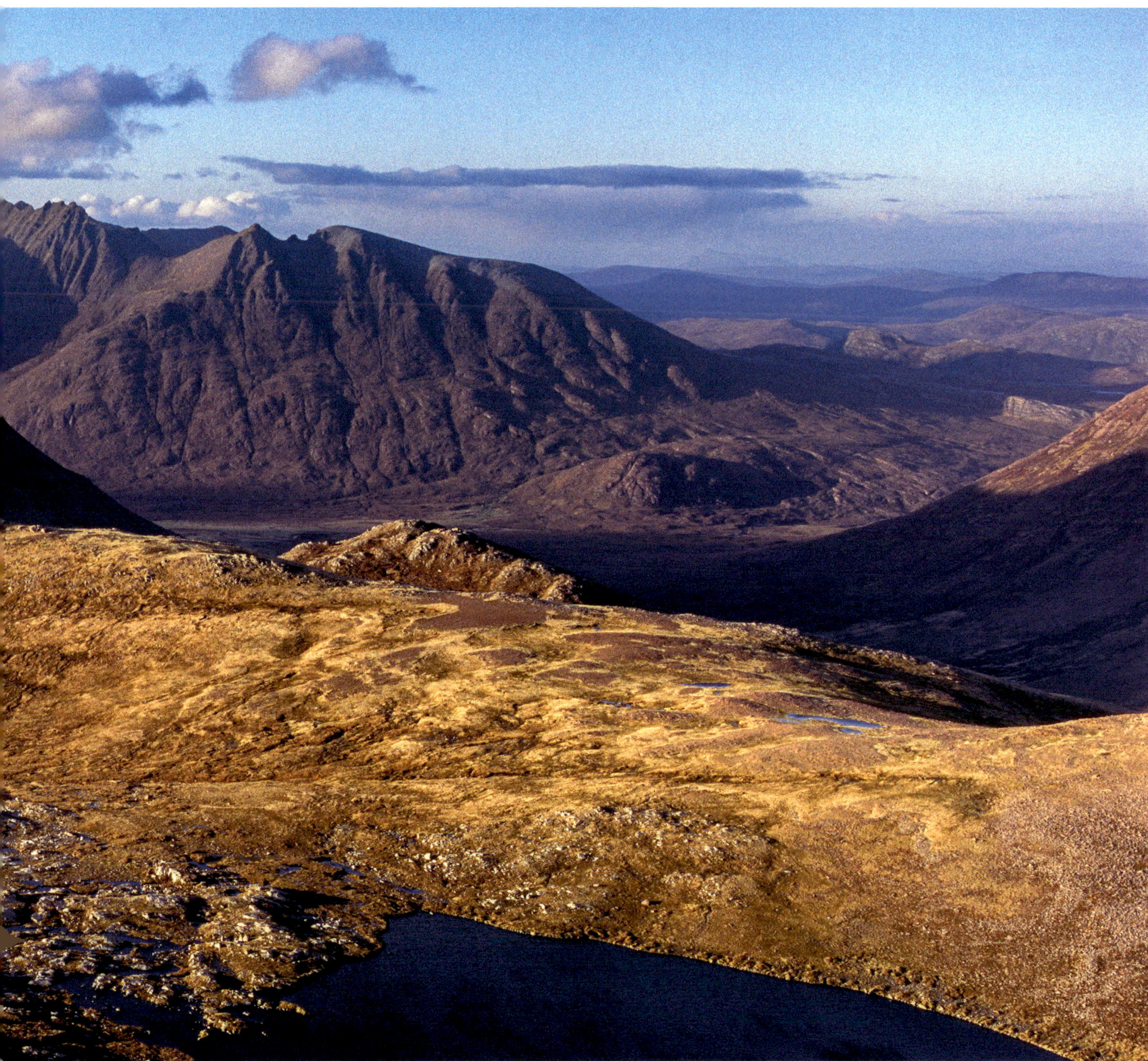

Ruadh Stac Mòr stands high and proud in the middle of the famed Fisherfield Forest. Alongside its close neighbour A' Mhaighdean, these two mountains are often regarded as the most remote of all 282 Munros. They can be reached by a number of different approaches; I made mine from Incheril, making good use of my mountain bike on the excellent Land Rover tracks and stalkers' paths that infiltrate this area. After seven miles the trails abruptly stop near to Lochan Fada from where it is a pathless slog of another five miles across open hillside to achieve the 918-metre summit. After three previous failed attempts I finally managed to capture the shot I had planned, the superlative view north-east across this great wilderness towards Beinn Dearg Mòr and An Teallach.

Following Page
Stob Dubh, Stob Coire Sgreamhach and Bidean nam Bian, Glen Coe
January 2018

Of all the mountains in Glen Coe, Buachaille Etive Beag is by far the easiest to climb. Its two peaks, Stob Dubh and Stob Coire Raineach are linked by an undulating high-level ridge that provides outstanding views in all directions. Stob Coire Sgreamhach and the Bidean massif are foremost in this image.

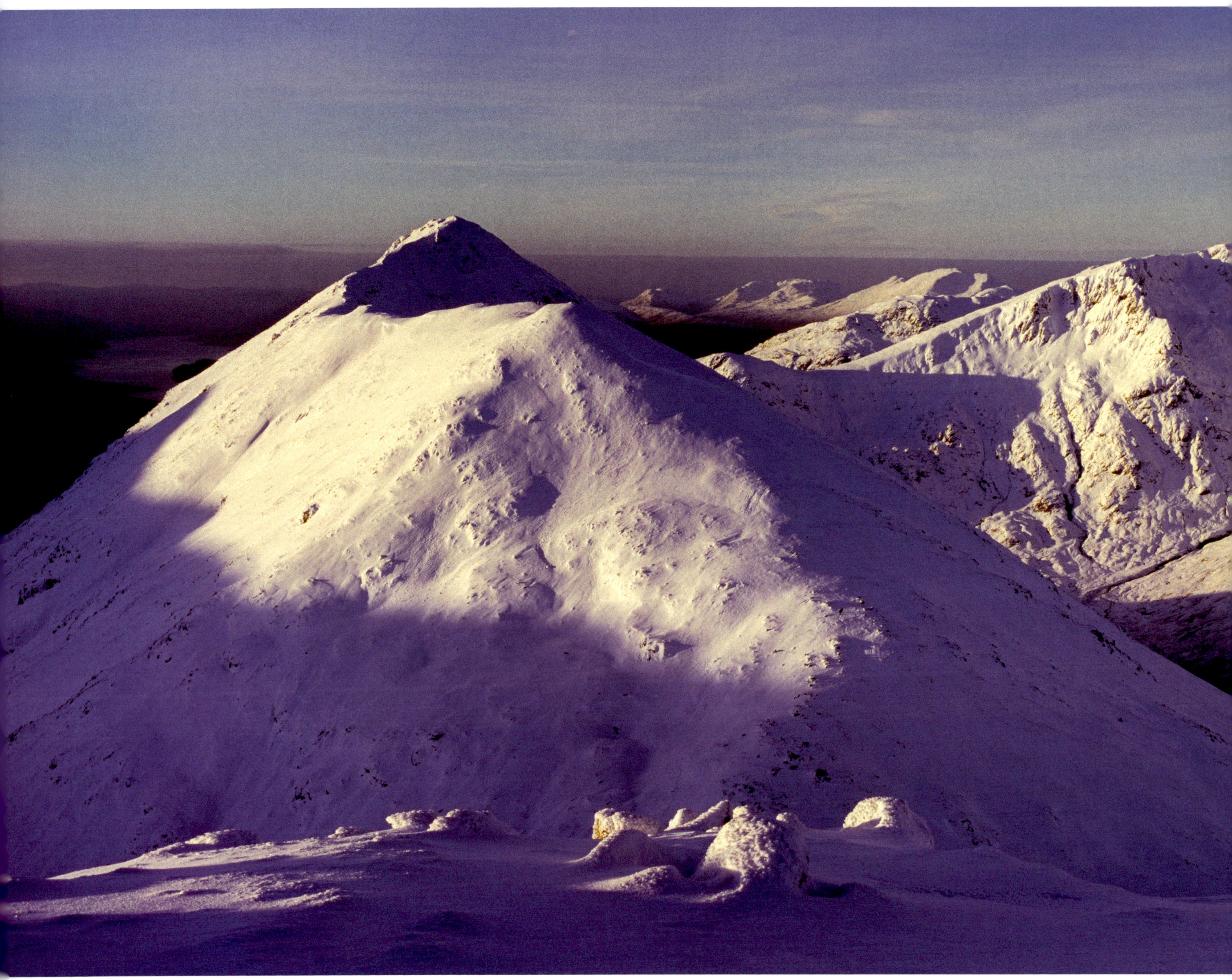

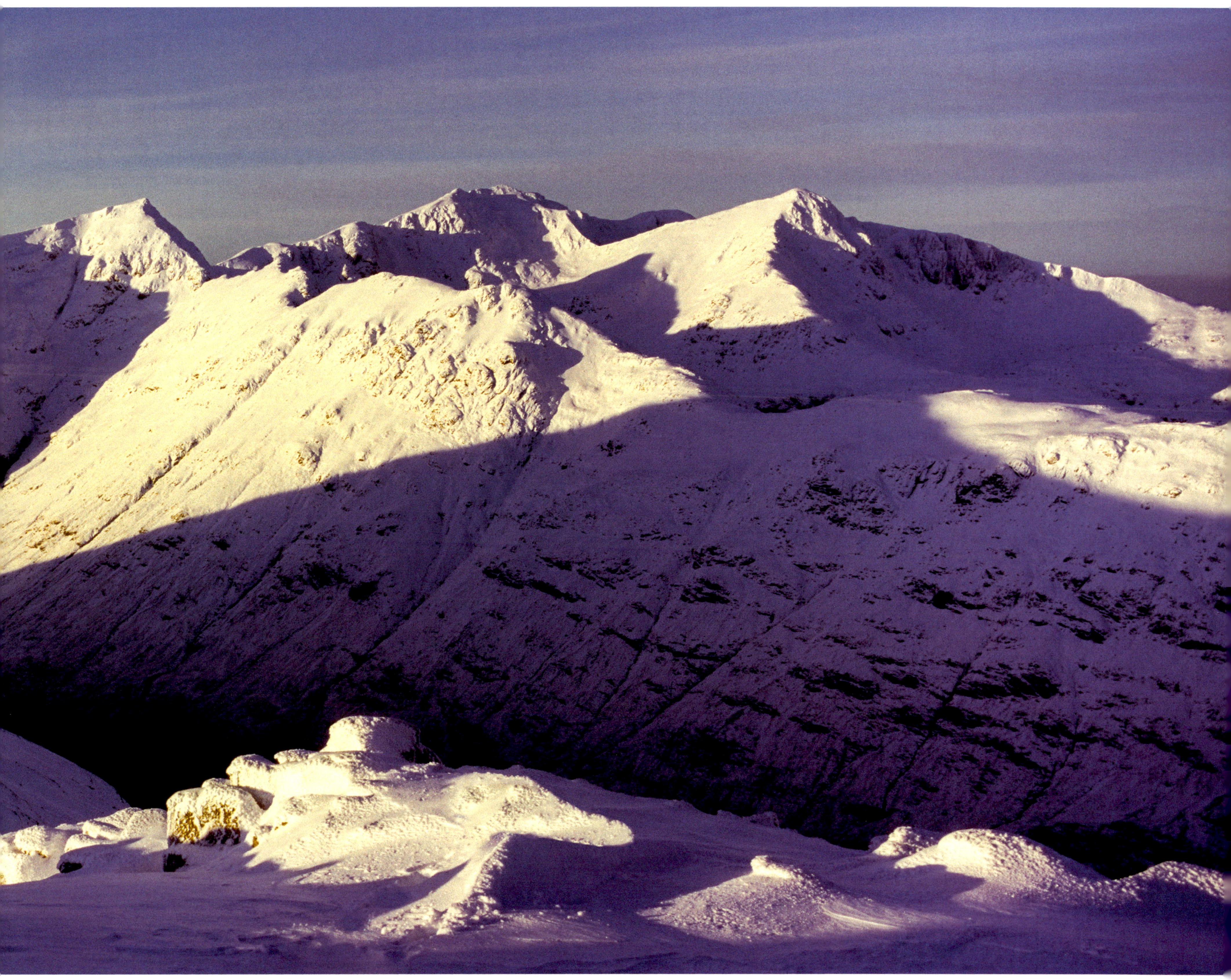

Loch Bad a' Ghaill, Inverpolly
May 2017

The typical dreich weather that had stubbornly persisted
all day was slowly retreating eastwards, and as the
evening approached so too did a change in weather.
With clear skies developing far out to the west, the sun
eventually sank low enough to illuminate the cloud-laden
skies above.

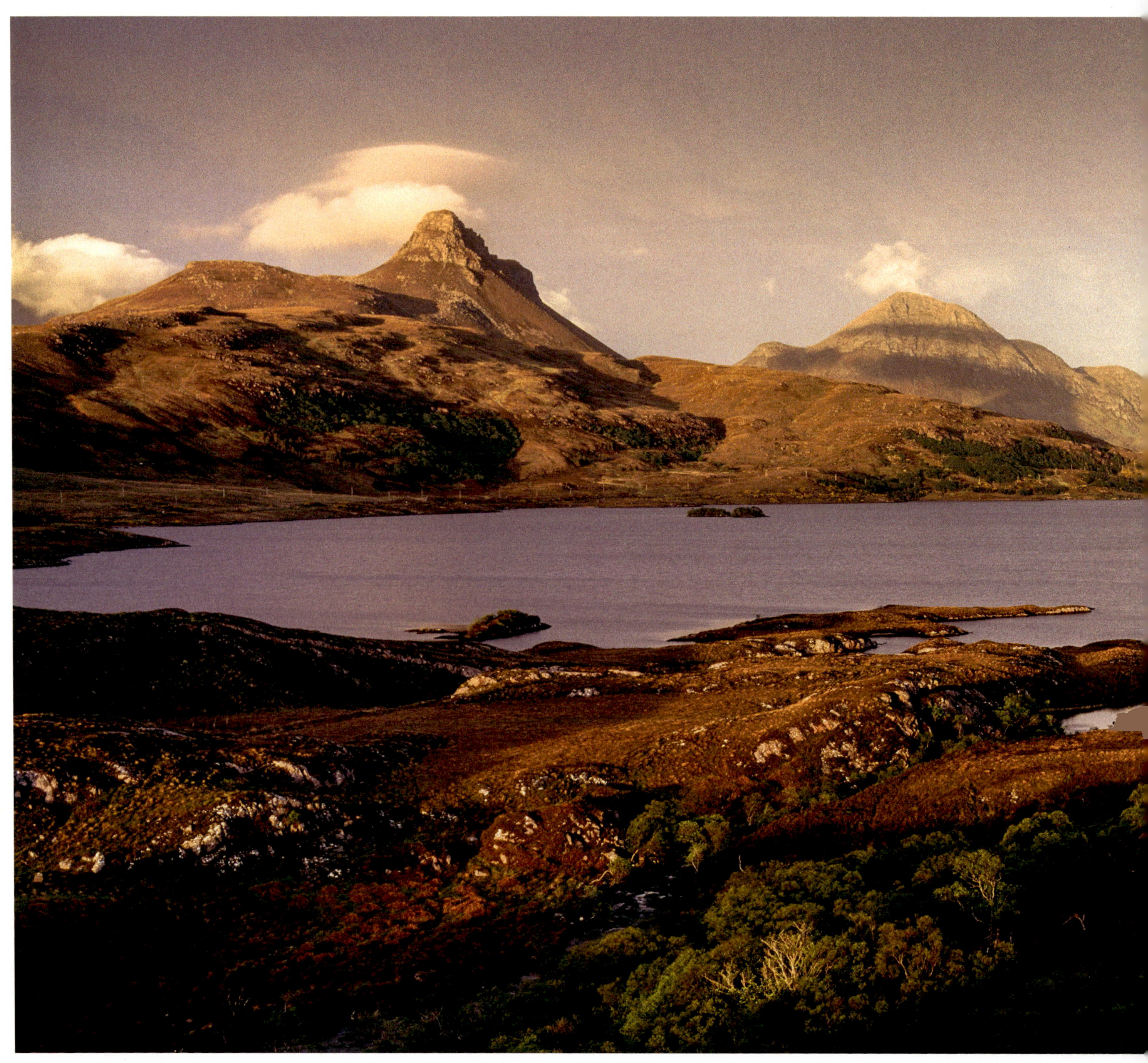

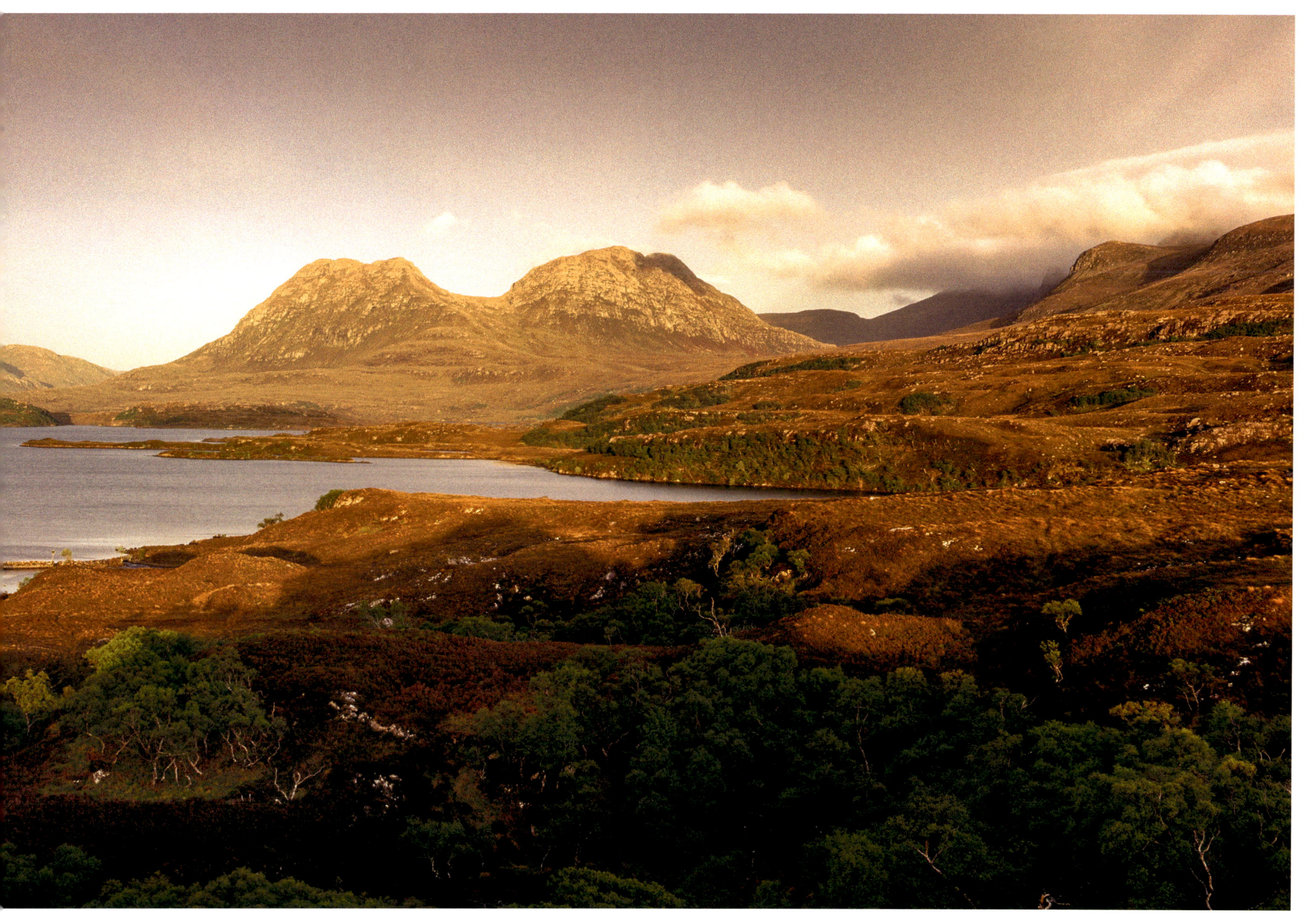

Loch Leven
August 2016

The narrow fjord-like trench of Loch Leven is a typical
example of the many sea lochs found along the west
coast of Scotland. From its bay at Kinlochleven the deep
waters extend for over eight miles to the narrows of
Ballachulish and eventually out to sea via Loch Linnhe.

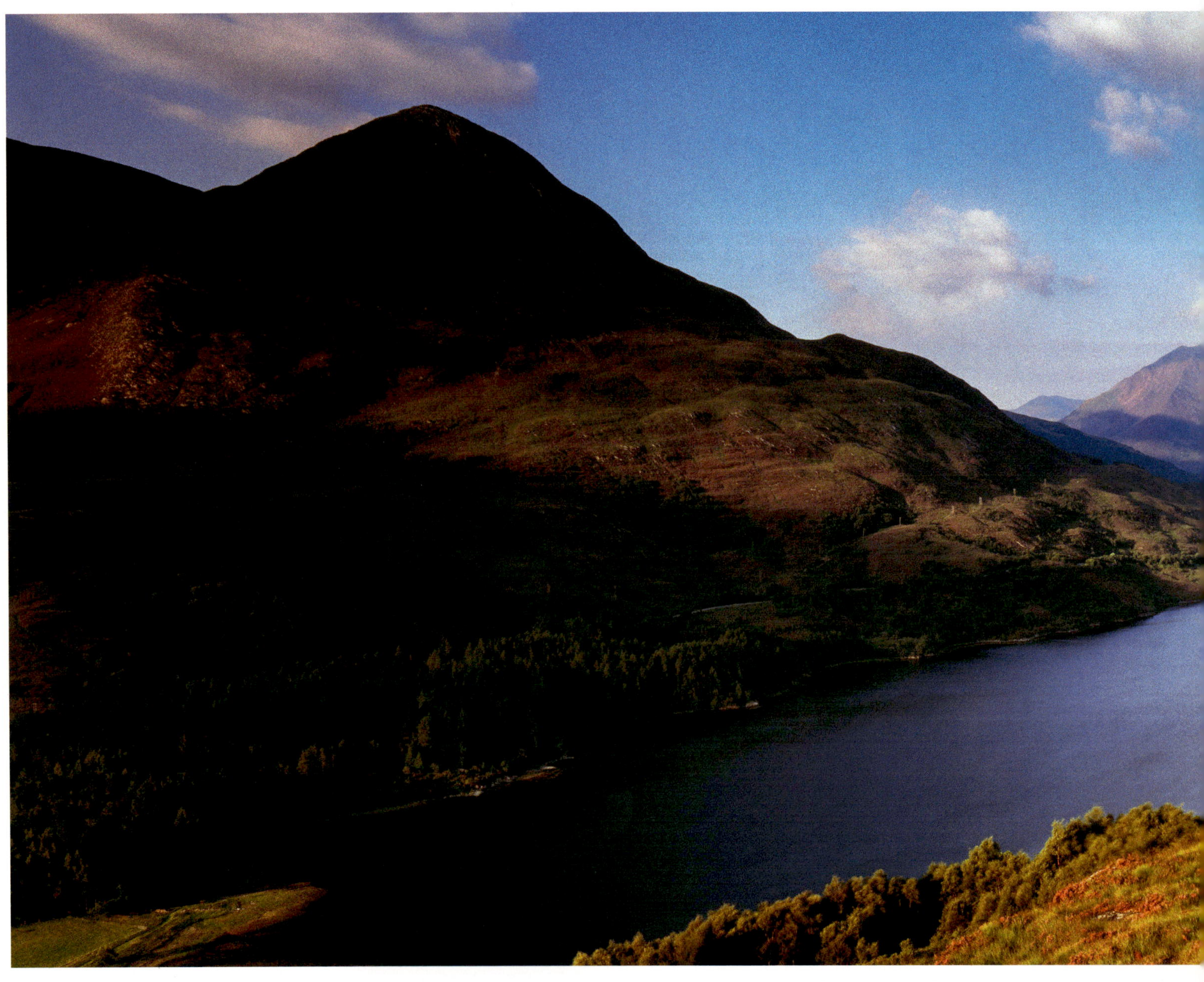

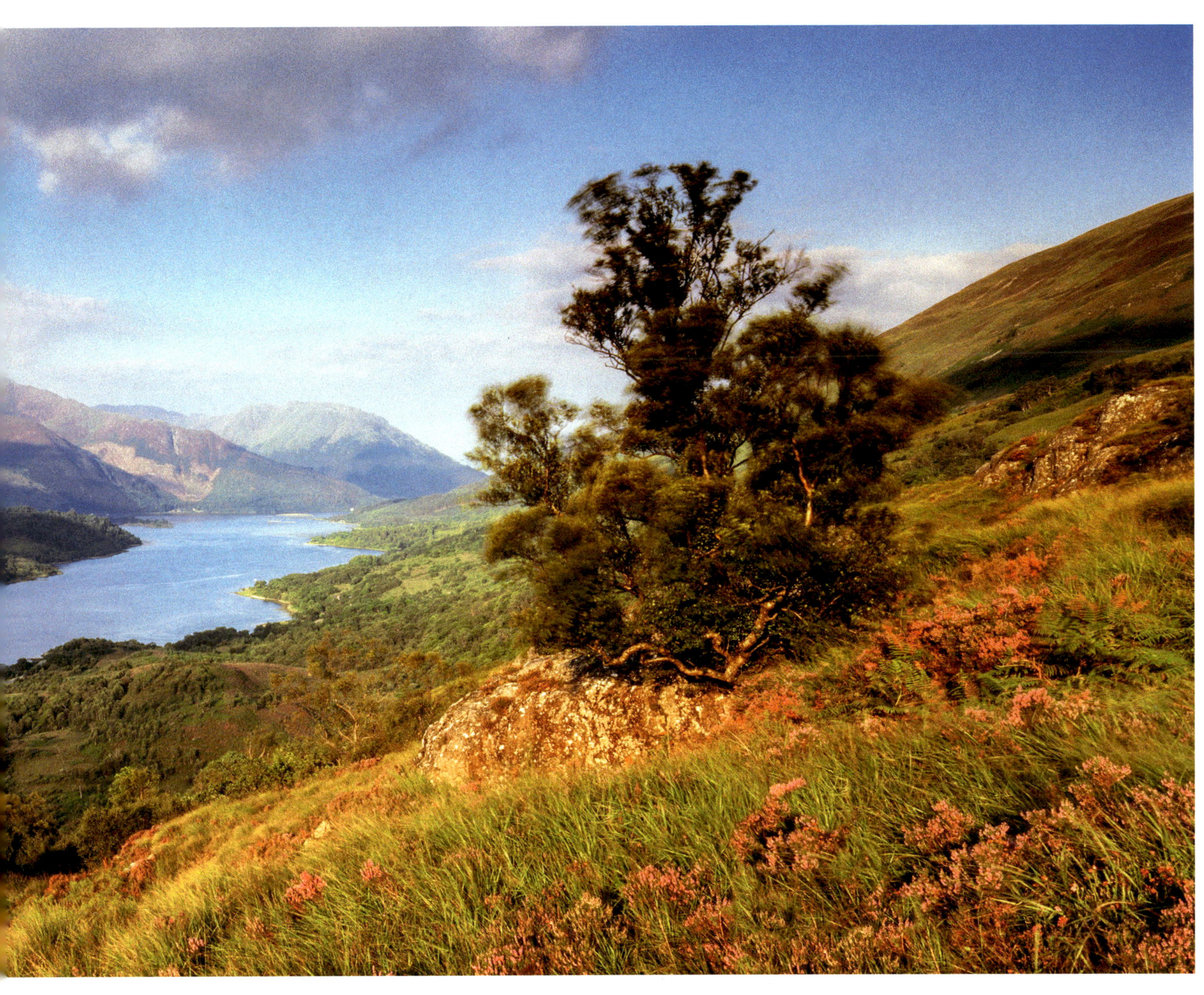

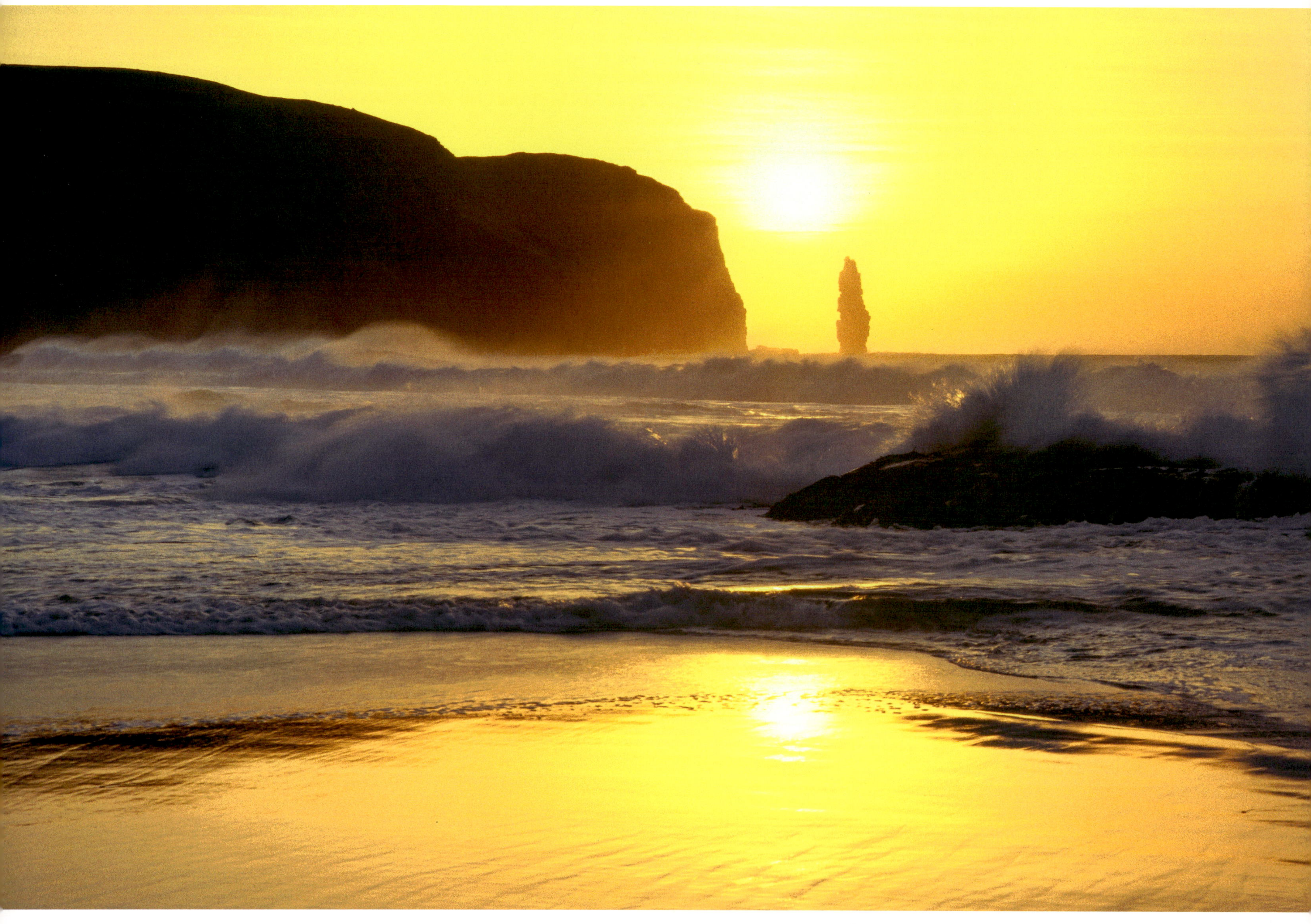

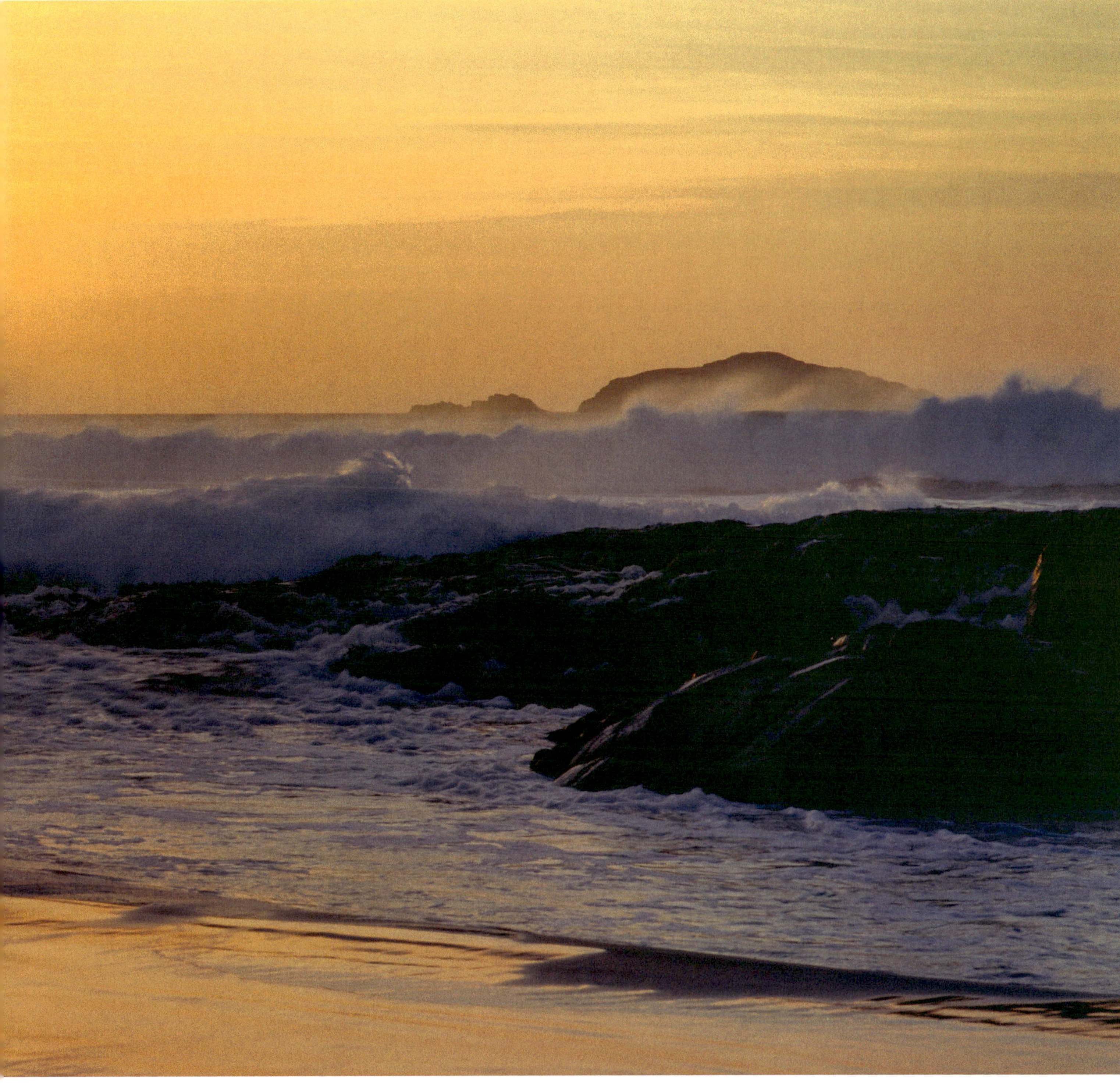

Am Buachaille, Sandwood Bay
March 2015

Lying at the end of a four-mile track, this magnificent
stretch of coastline faces north-west, straight into the
teeth of the North Atlantic. As a result, the pounding surf
is mesmerising to watch and was something I wanted to
capture on film.

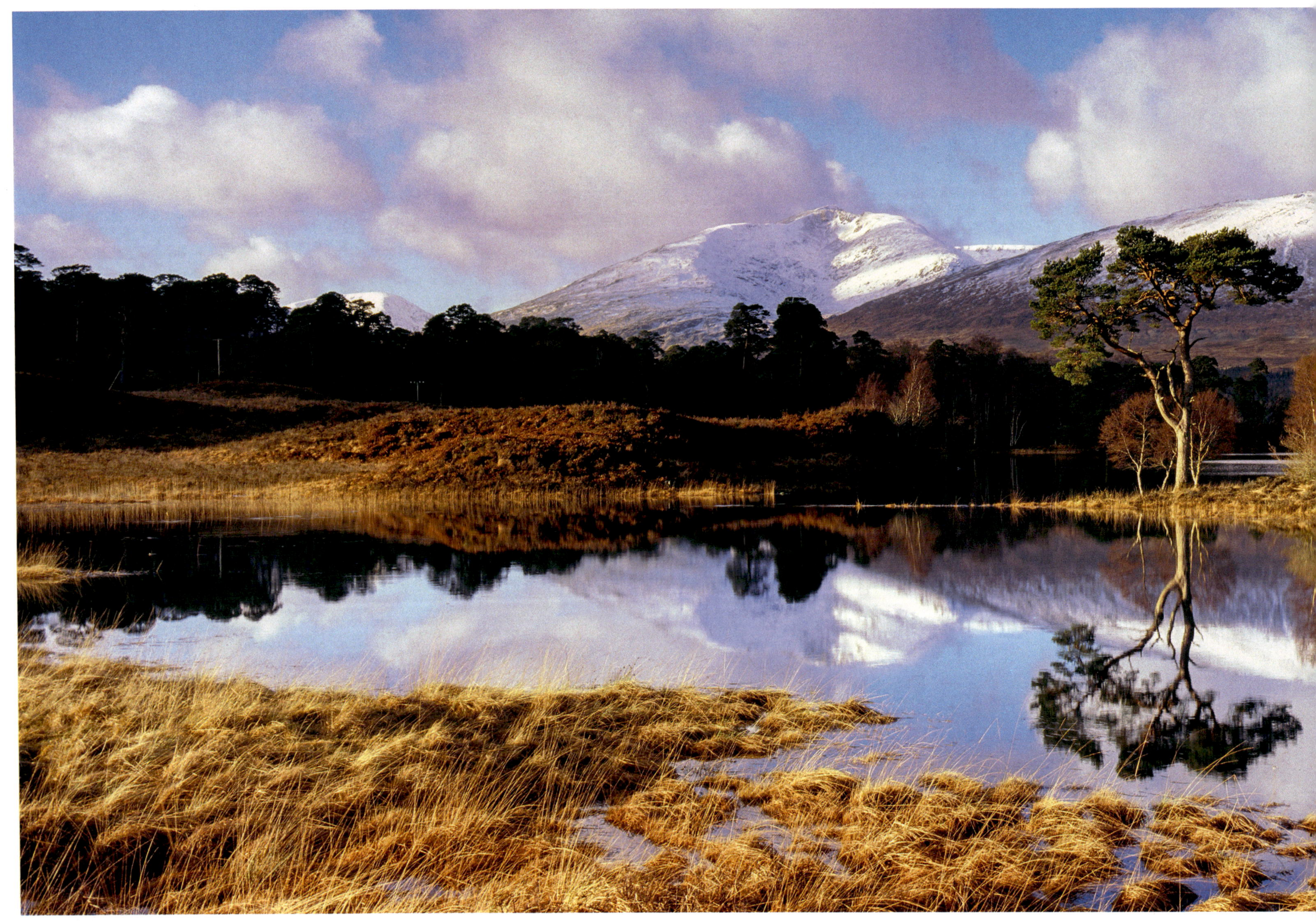

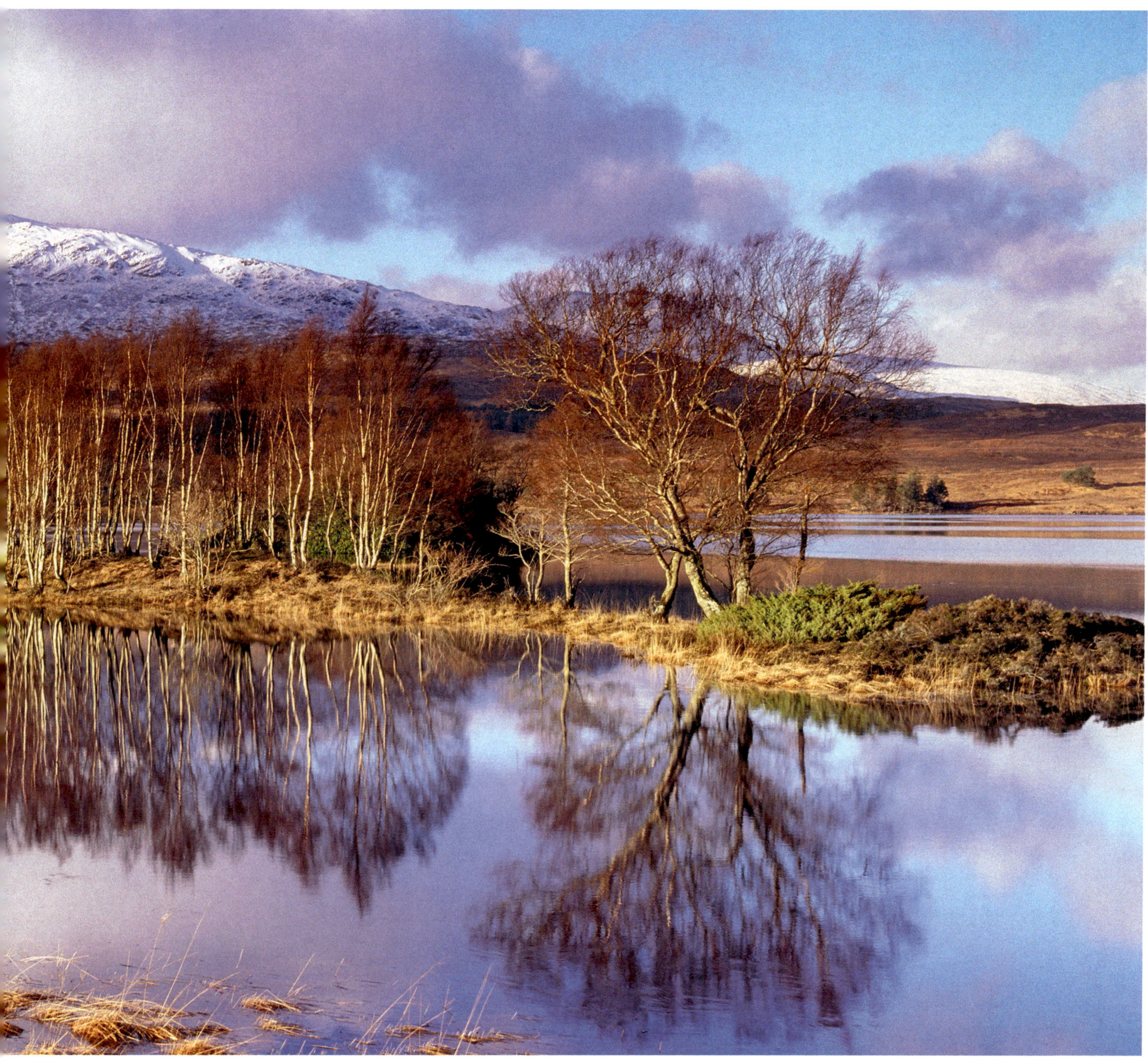

Loch Tulla and Stob Ghabhar
January 2015

The area around Loch Tulla is a favourite place. I found
it an excellent location for learning and exploring and
one I frequented often when I first began photographing
the western Highlands. The waters here are dominated
by Stob Ghabhar and surrounded with surviving
remnants of the ancient Caledonian pine forest
– to me the perfect combination that makes
this landscape quintessentially Scottish.

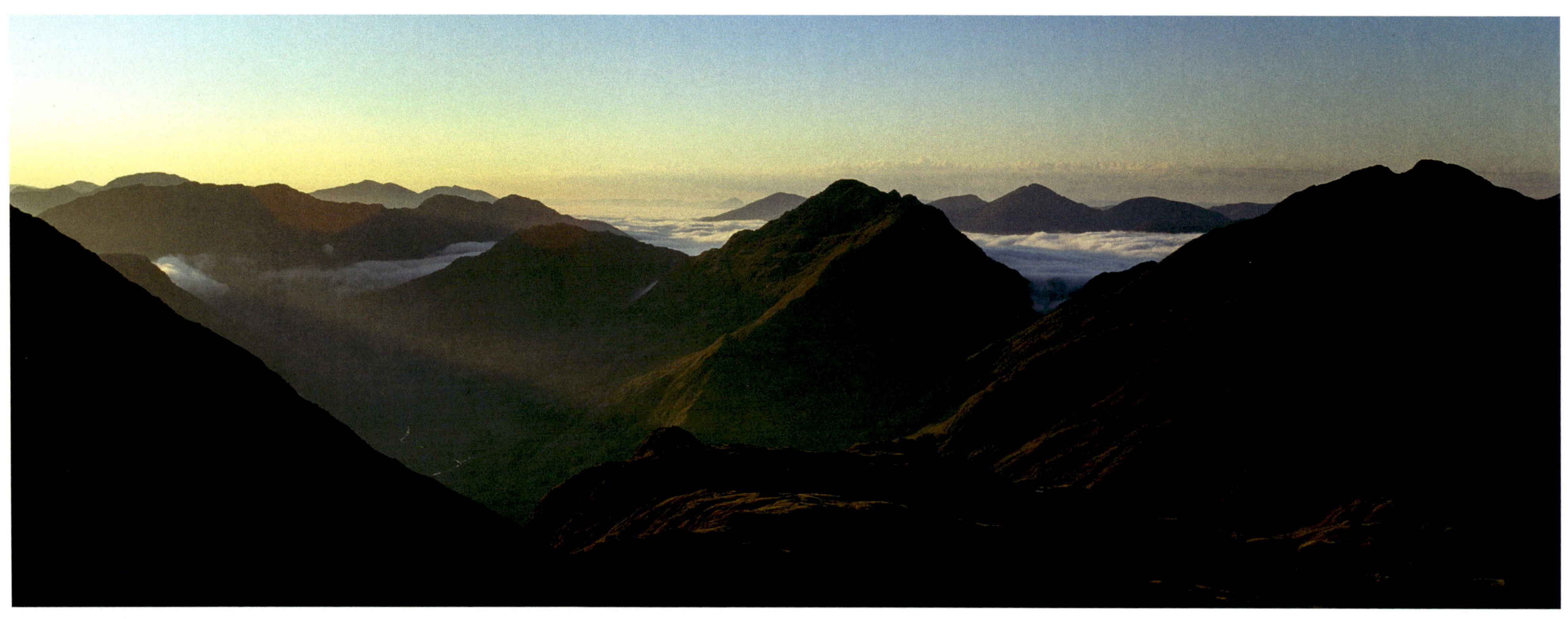

Glen Barrisdale, Knoydart
June 2013

After a long wait for the right weather window I finally
found myself deep in Knoydart witnessing a spectacular
summer sunrise. To add to the atmosphere, a significant
cloud inversion had developed overnight to cover much
of Lochaber and as the sun rose it illuminated the peaks
of this remote peninsula in the most wonderful light.

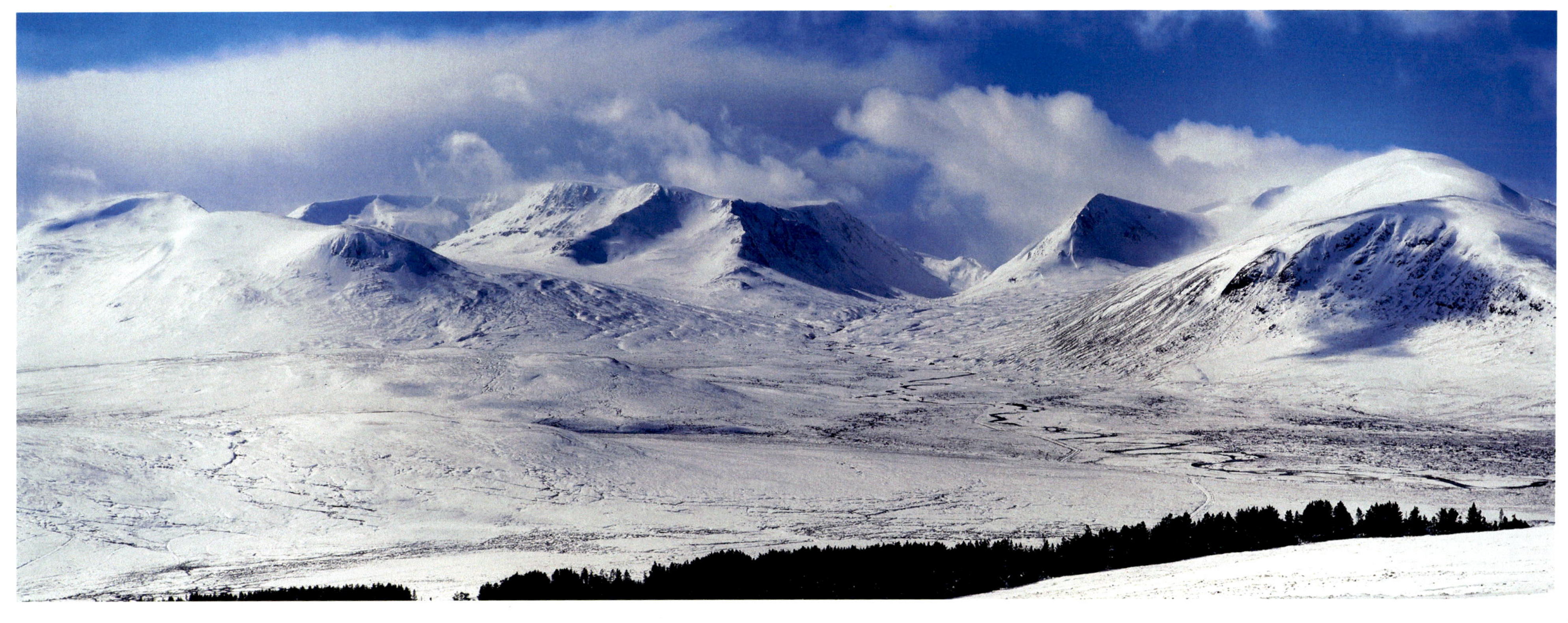

Ben Alder, Badenoch
April 2014

After a long approach through a number of heavy snow showers, I reached my elevated viewpoint just as the skies around me cleared. The front drifted slowly westward and left in its wake a wondrous winter landscape befitting this enigmatic mountain.

Slioch from the River Grudie
June 2017

The short River Grudie collects from the remote open
landscape of Flowerdale in Torridon and develops quickly
through the steep-sided Glen Grudie. Its lower course
then slows dramatically as it meanders through
well-established pockets of native pine woods, before
finally entering Loch Maree at the foot of Slioch.

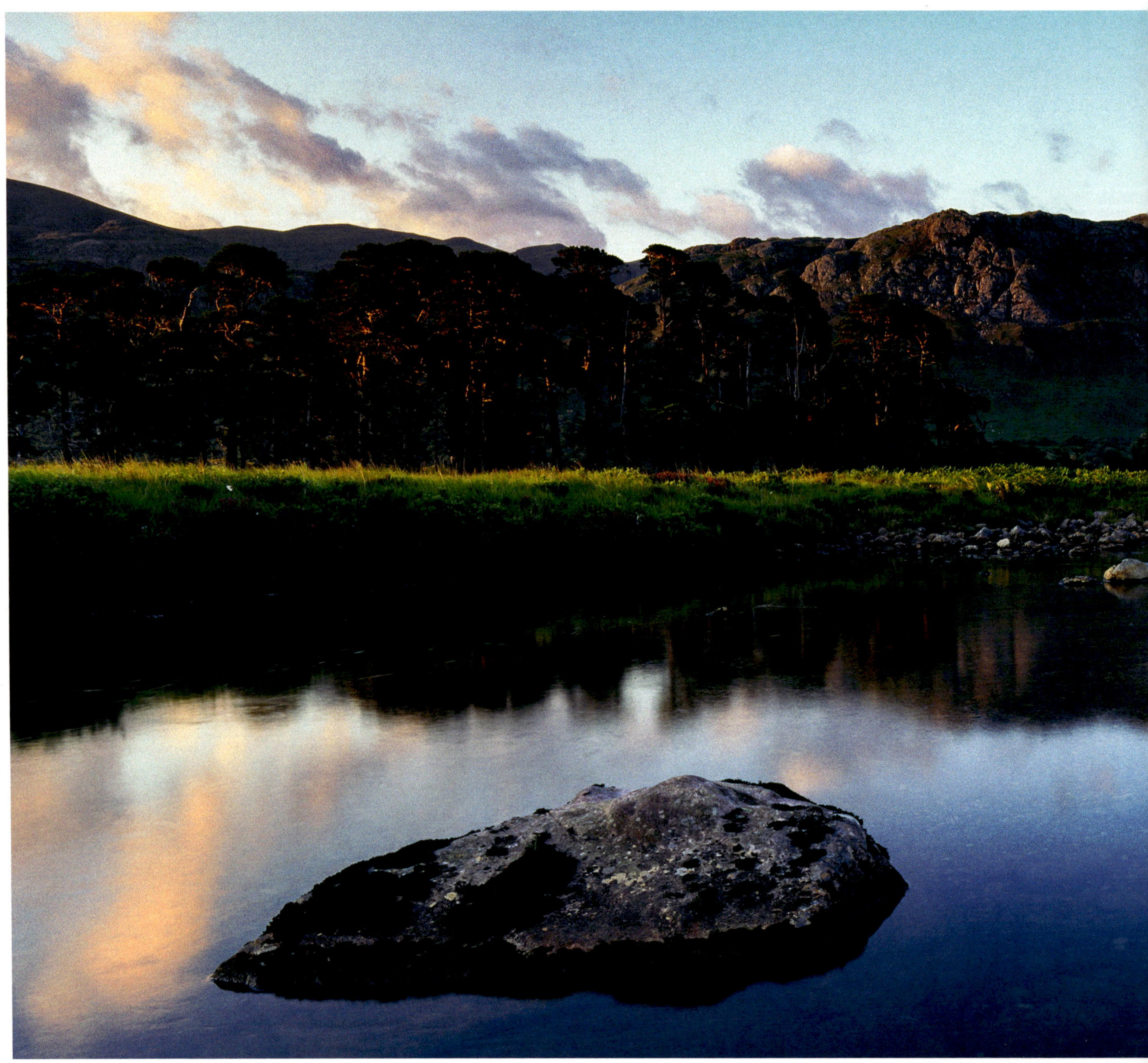

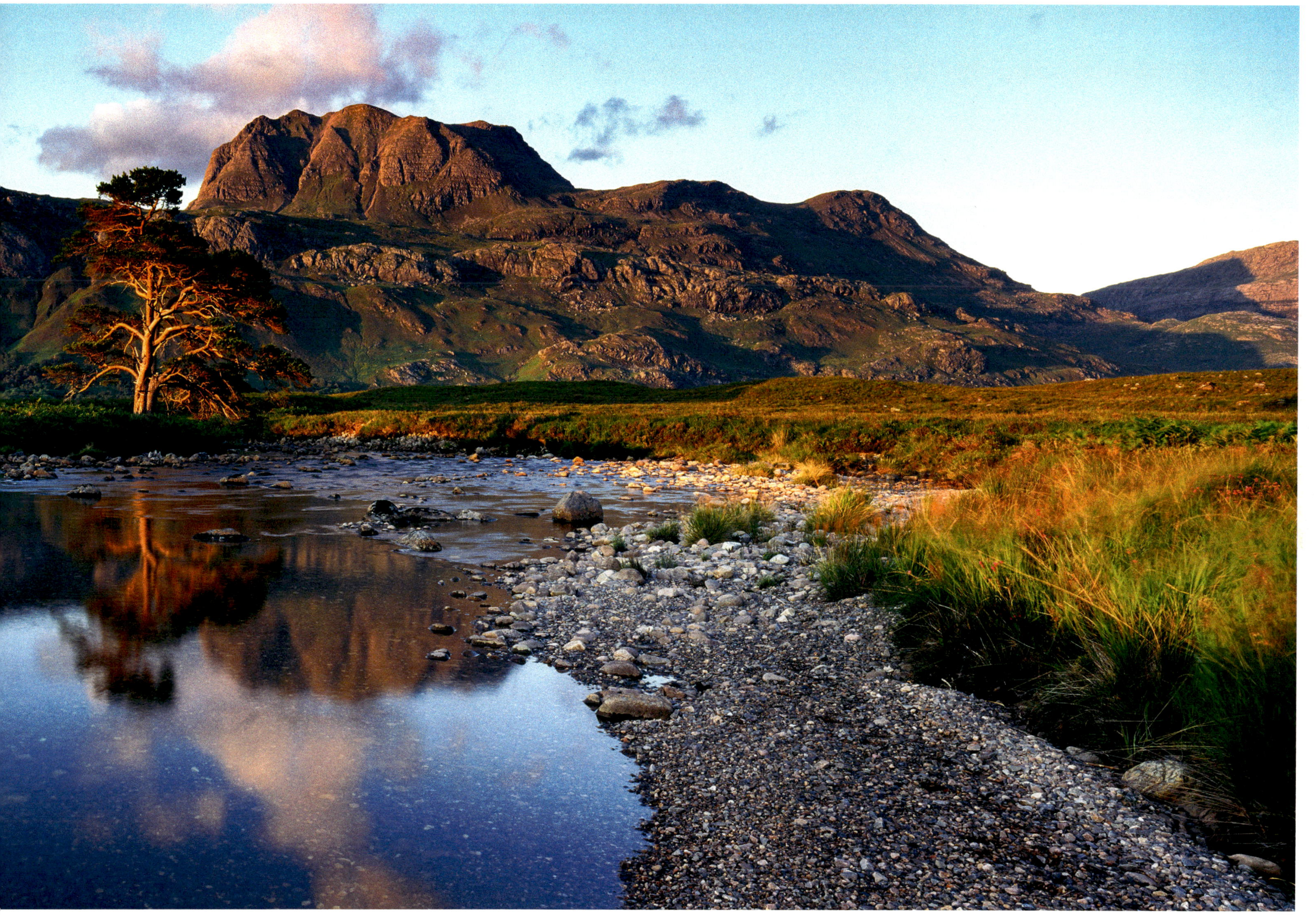

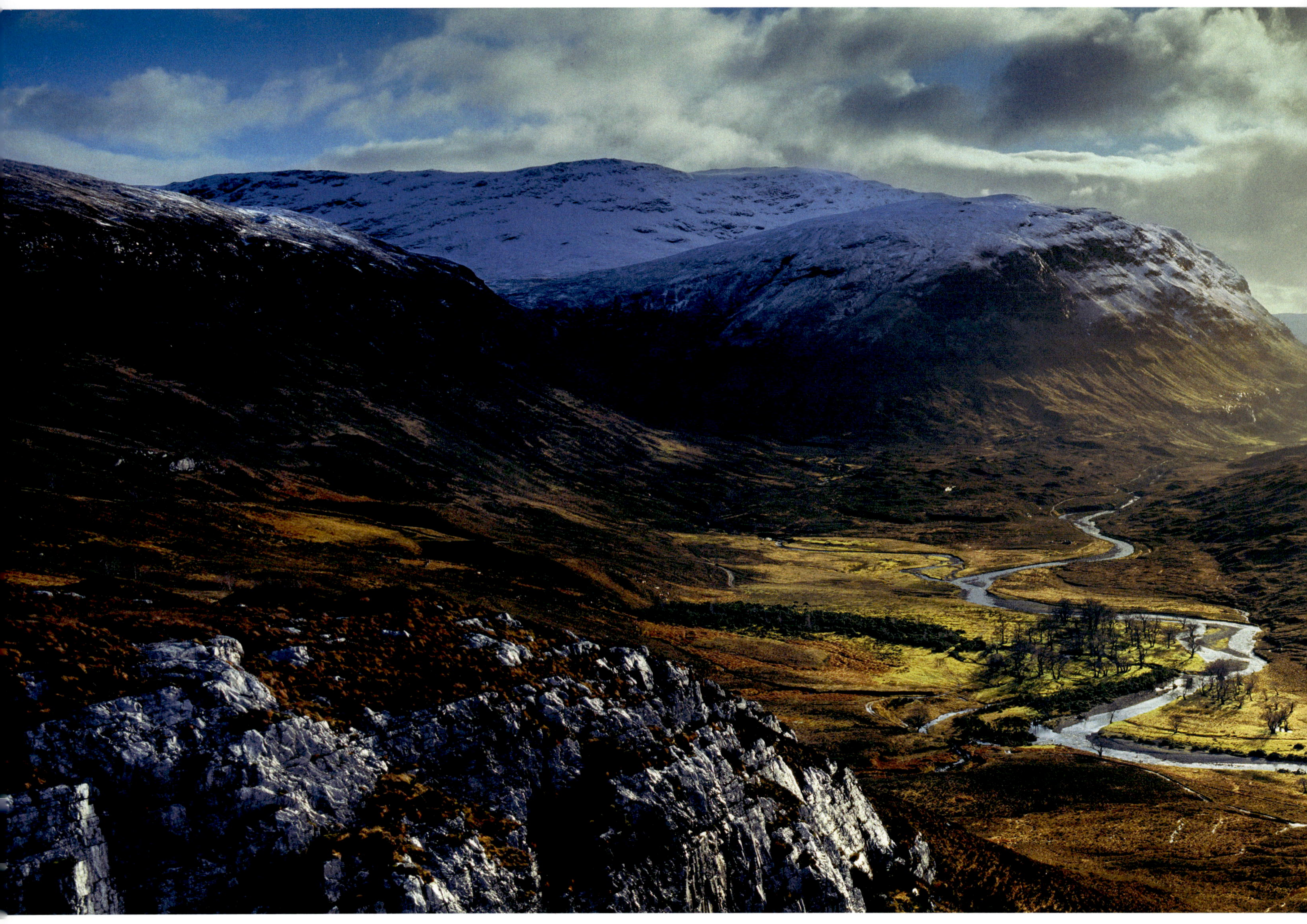

     WILD LIGHT

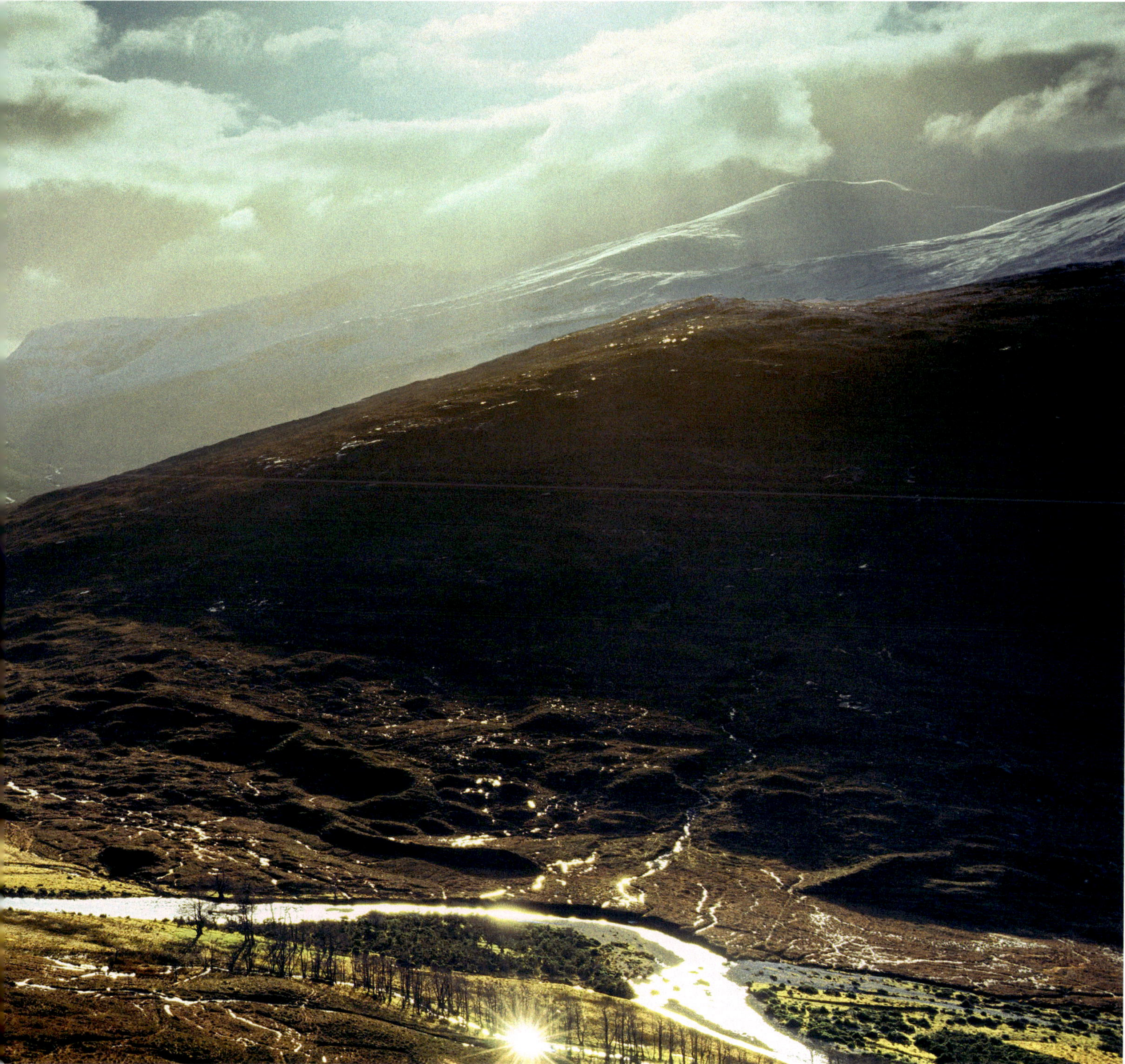

Strath na Sealga, Fisherfield
February 2016

The remote flat plain of Strath na Sealga in Fisherfield
is surrounded by big hills and steep slopes on all sides.
The confluence of burns and rivers that naturally meet
here meander their way north-west to Loch na Sealga
and eventually out to sea via Gruinard Bay.

Following Page
Stob Daimh, Ben Cruachan
March 2017

Starting out from Dalmally I could see the lower slopes
of Ben Cruachan sweeping up and disappearing into
an ominous blanket of low-lying cloud. With such
gloomy conditions overhead I already had my doubts,
but I decided to press on and made my way up and into
the cloud. At around 600 metres I hit the well-defined
snow line and hoped, with every step, that I would soon
emerge from the omnipresent murk. Eventually, I reached
the crest of the main ridge where the cloud miraculously
began to thin. As I finally breached the surface a whole
new world suddenly revealed itself.

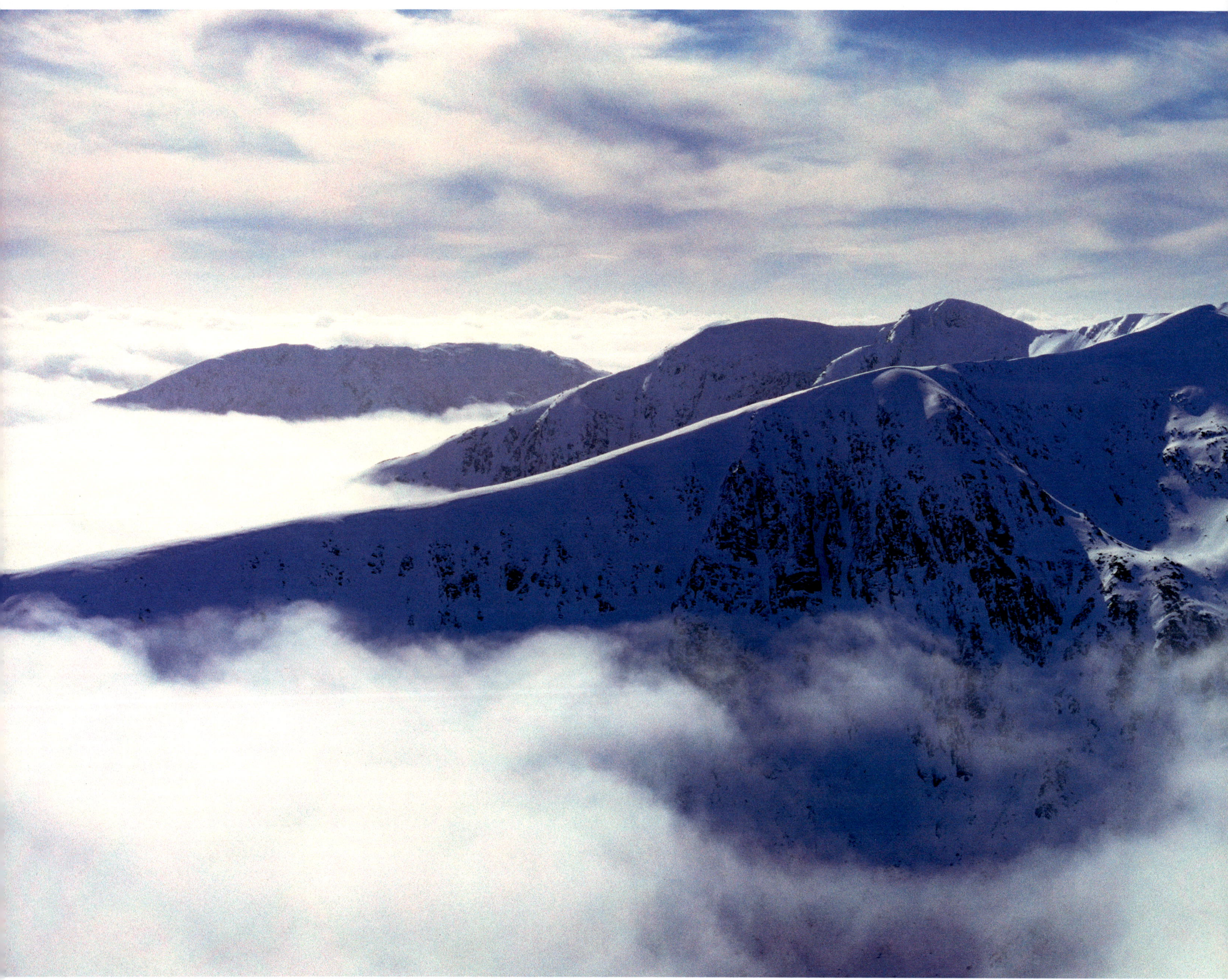

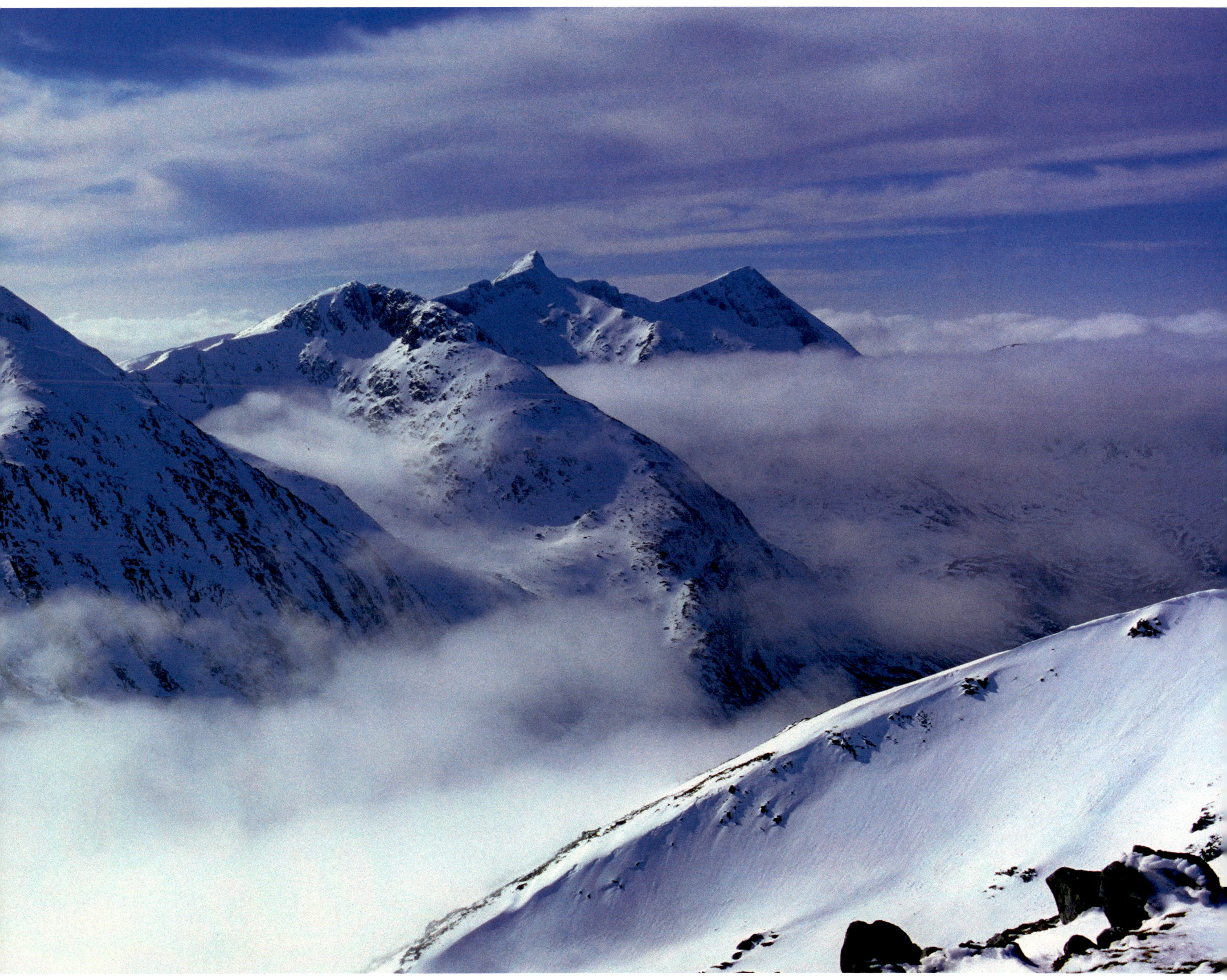

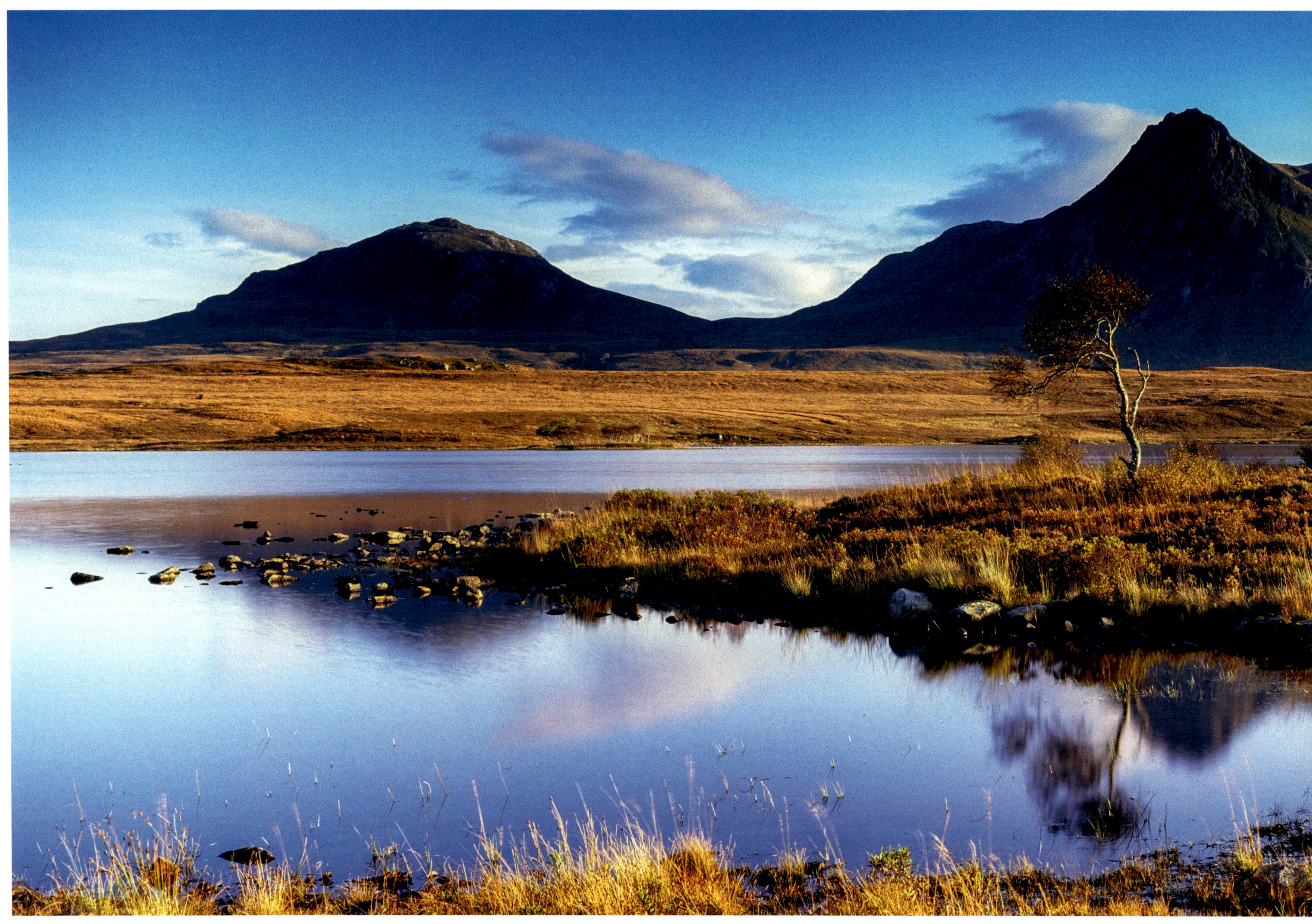

     WILD LIGHT

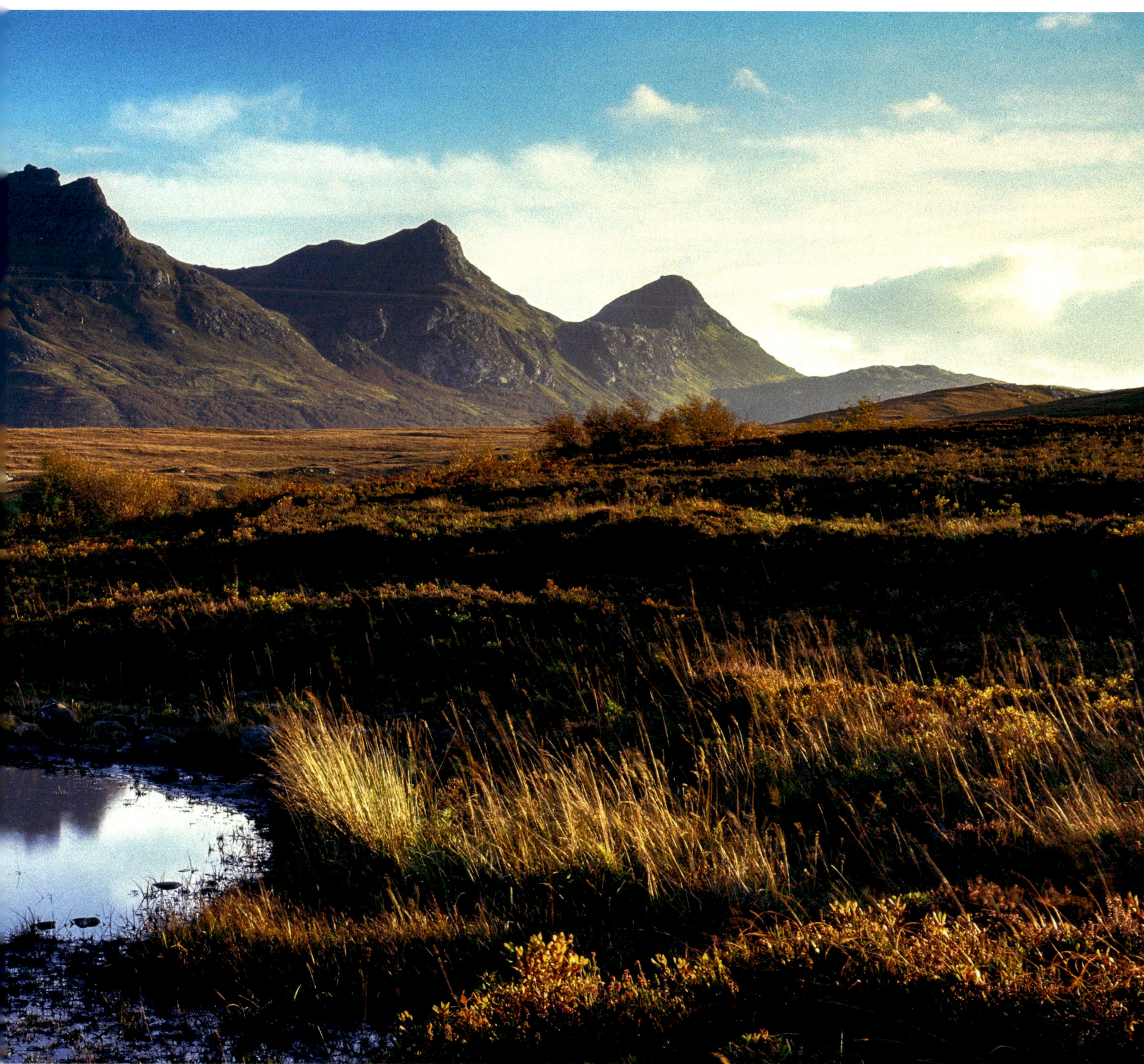

Ben Loyal, Sutherland
October 2011

Ben Loyal stands proud and isolated close to the
tidal estuary of the Kyle of Tongue. Its four distinct
granite peaks rise from the surrounding Flow Country
of north Sutherland and overlook the still waters of
Lochan Hakel from where this image was taken.

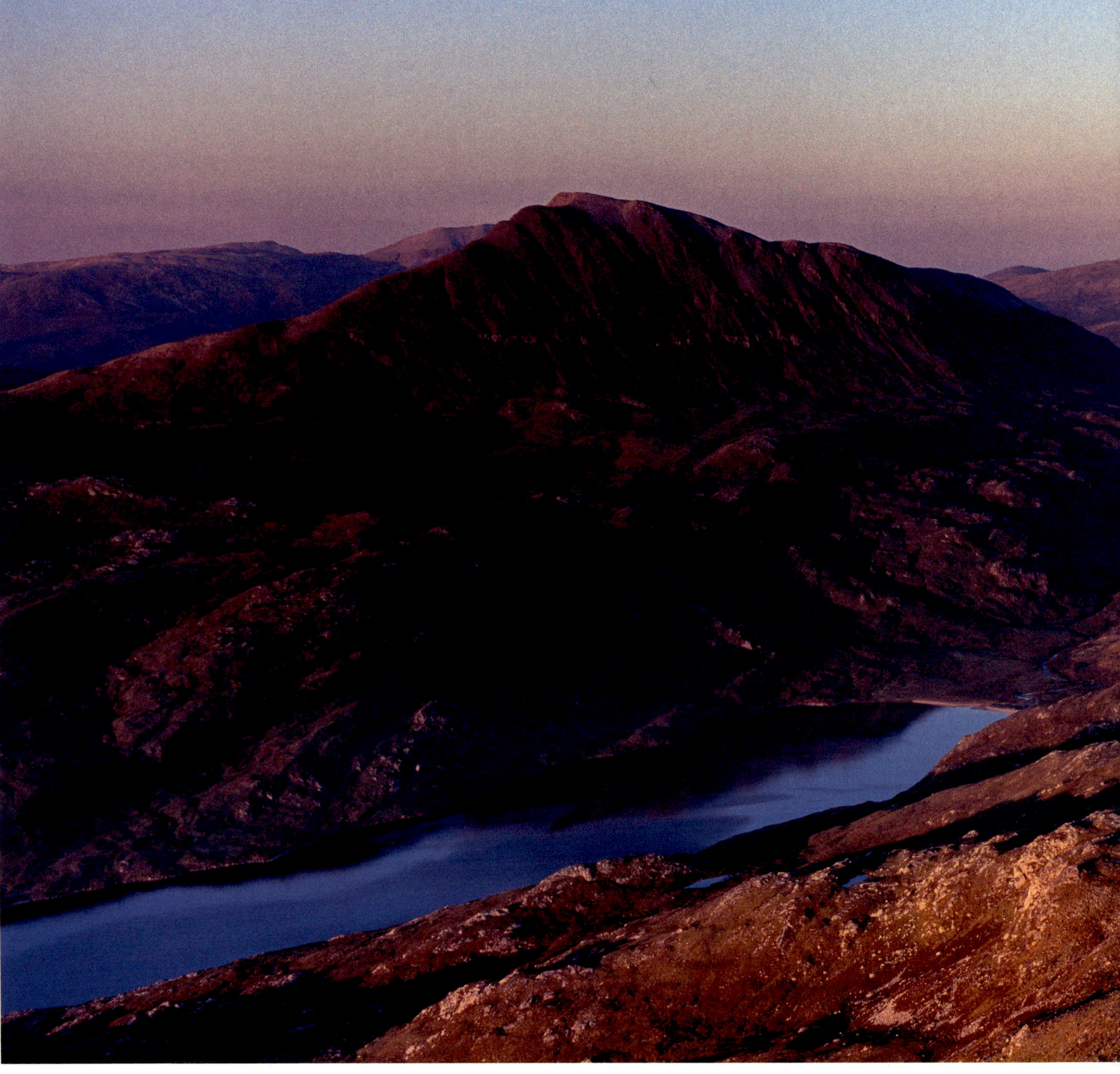

Suilven and Canisp, Assynt
May 2017

The sculpted flanks of Suilven were carved out by
Scotland's last retreating ice sheet nearly 12,000 years
ago – relatively recent in geological terms, as the
landscape upon which it resides is thought to be around
3 billion years old. Little wonder then that these iconic
survivors, known as inselbergs, are full of individual
character, making excellent photographic subjects.
This image is the view south-east from Suilven's highest
summit, Caisteal Liath. While waiting for sunset I watched
the colours change and the shadows extend, reaching
out into the oncoming dusk.

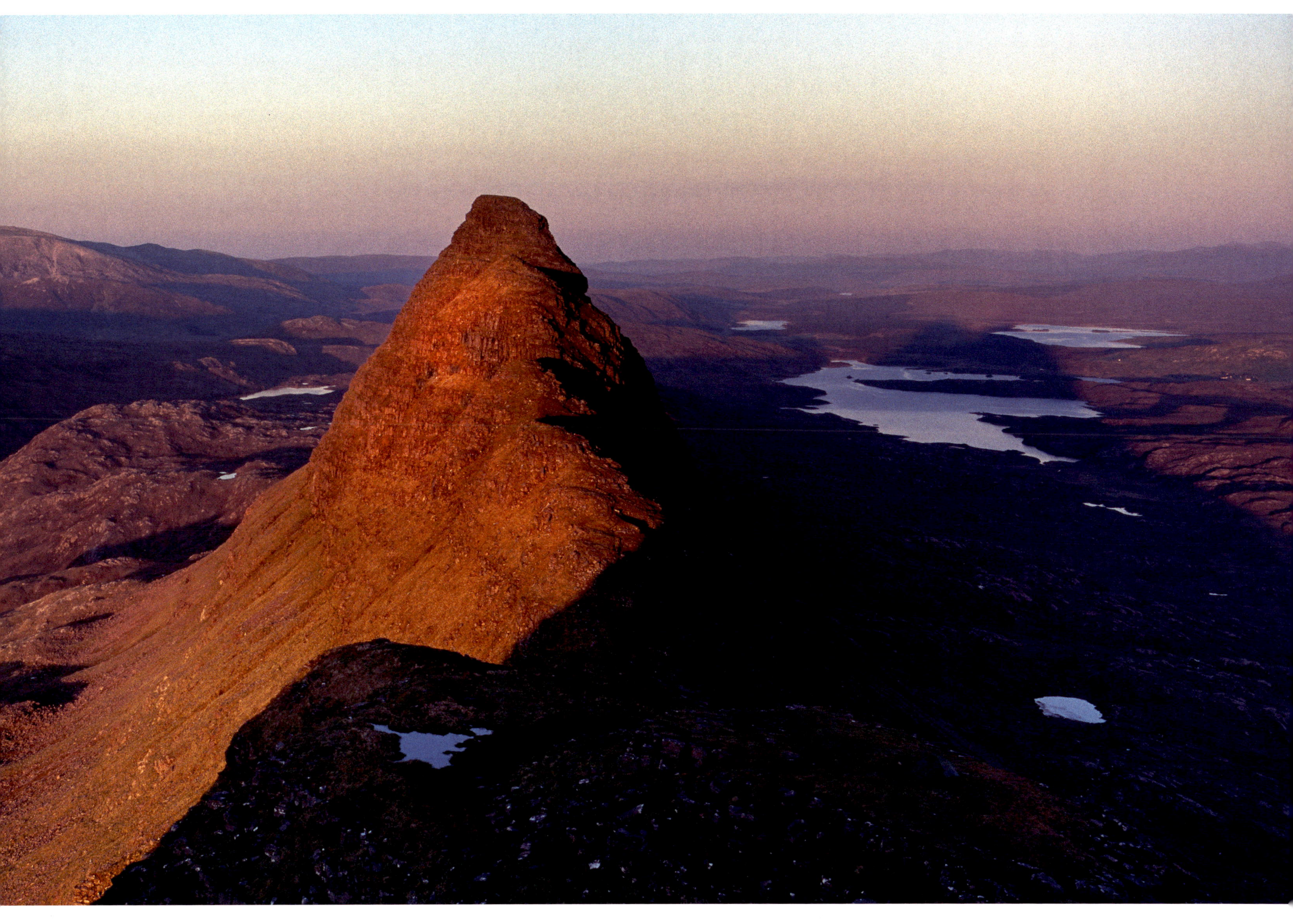

Springtime in Scotland can produce some massive dumps of snow in the mountains, even well into April. Generally, these events are quite different in nature to traditional winter falls: with the sun higher in the sky and raised freezing levels, the only significant accumulations tend to settle at higher altitudes and can disintegrate rapidly. In the wake of a colossal cold front which brought copious amounts of fresh snow to the Southern Highlands during mid-April 2018, I immediately made my way to Beinn Eunaich for the arduous 989-metre ascent. On the upper slopes, as suspected, the volume of loose, unconsolidated snow was extreme – waist deep on certain aspects – and I slowly battled on a step at a time using my walking poles as leverage to gain ground. This torturous race against the clock continued until eventually the summit cairn appeared, just poking above the pristine driven snow. I arrived rather unceremoniously on my hands and knees, exhausted but relieved. With time running out I took a series of images as the sun set and the landscape transformed.

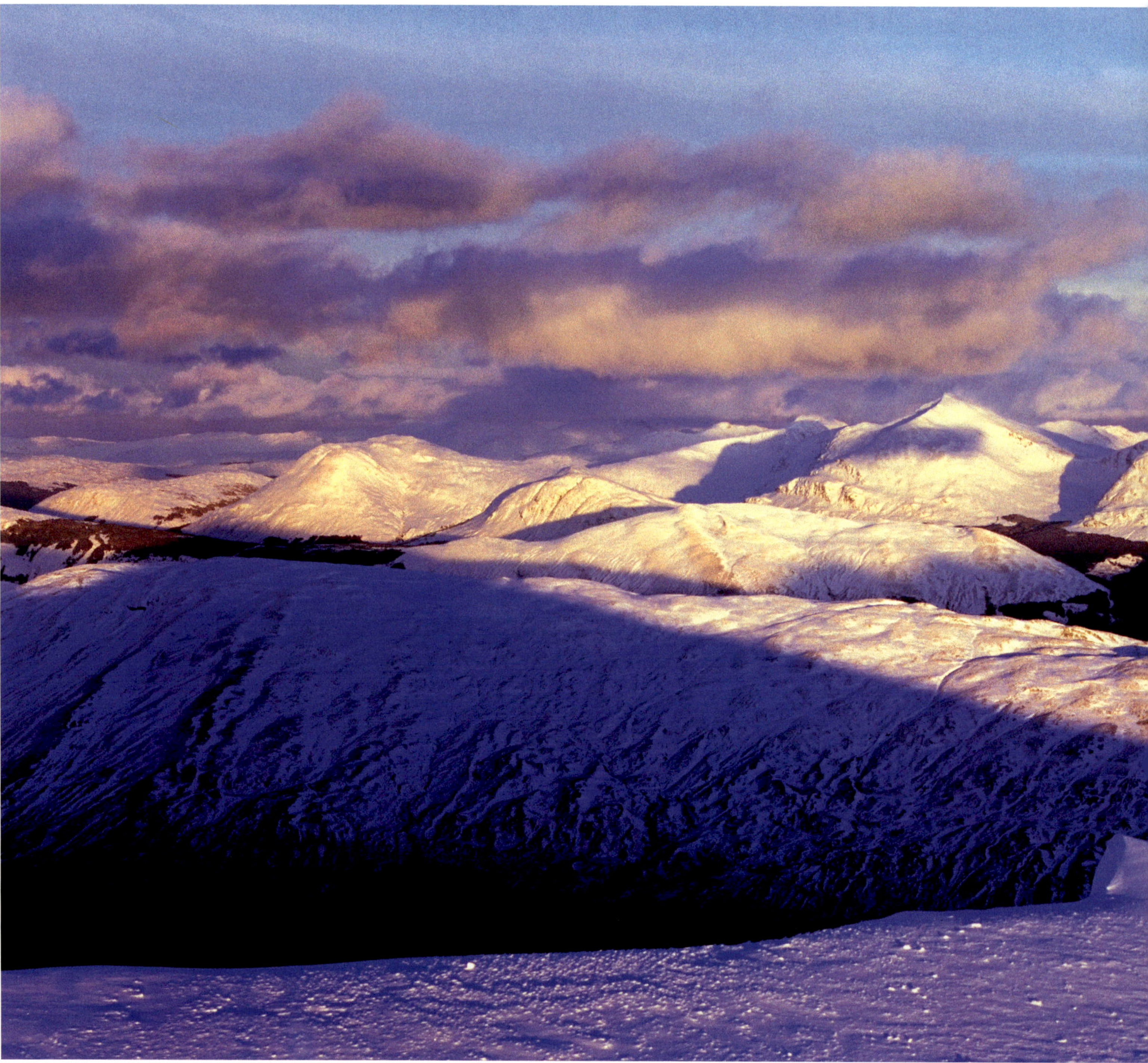

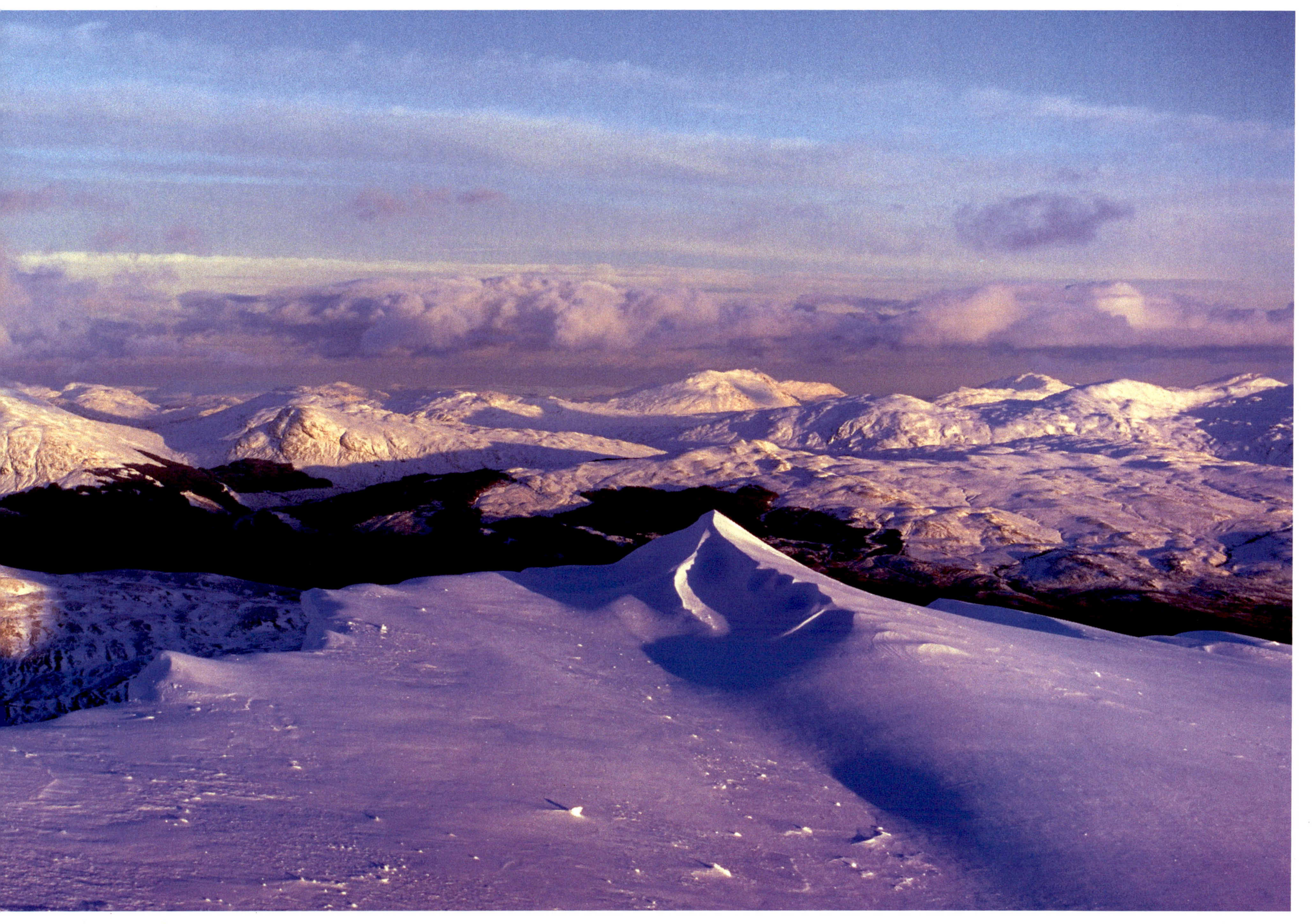

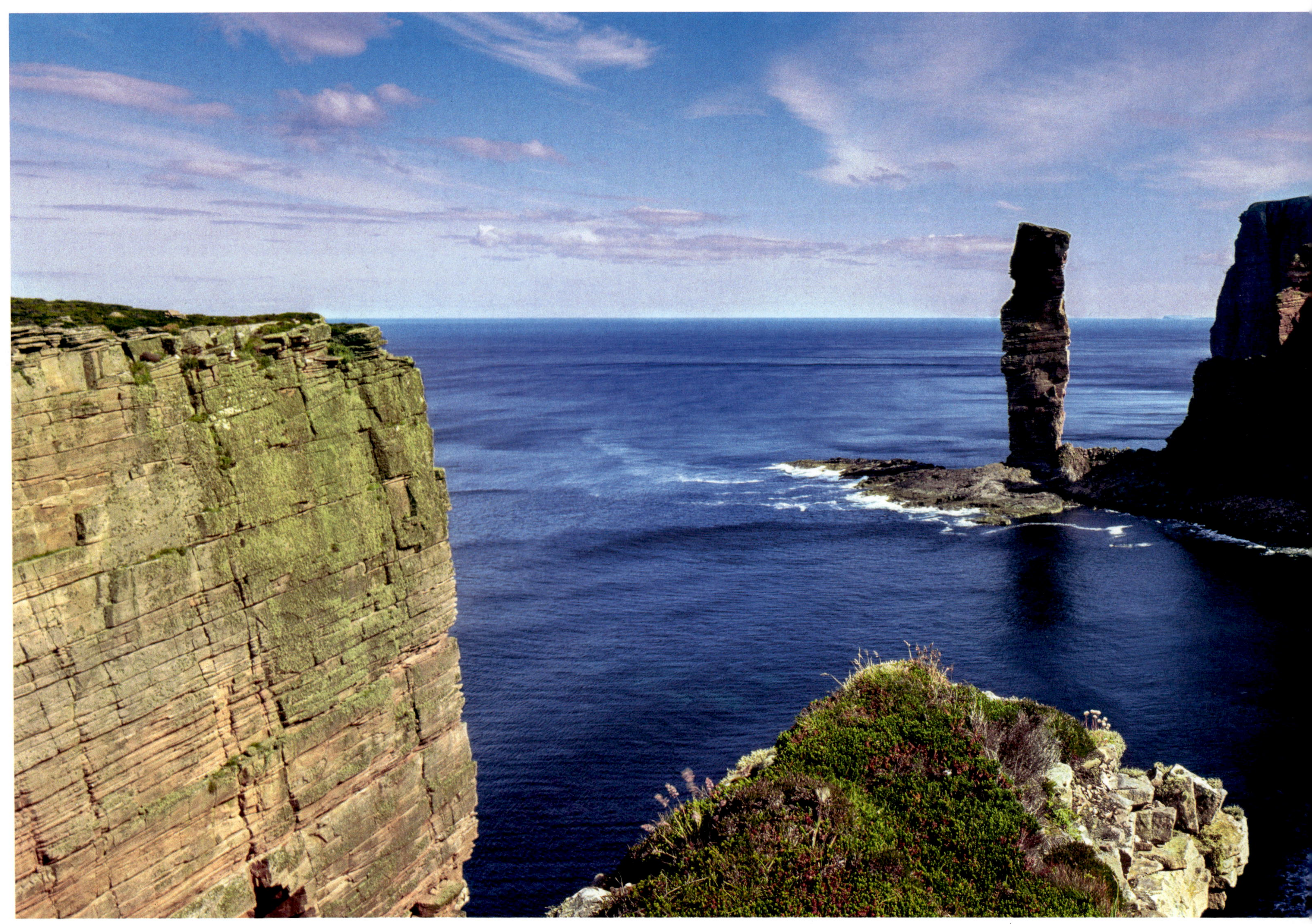

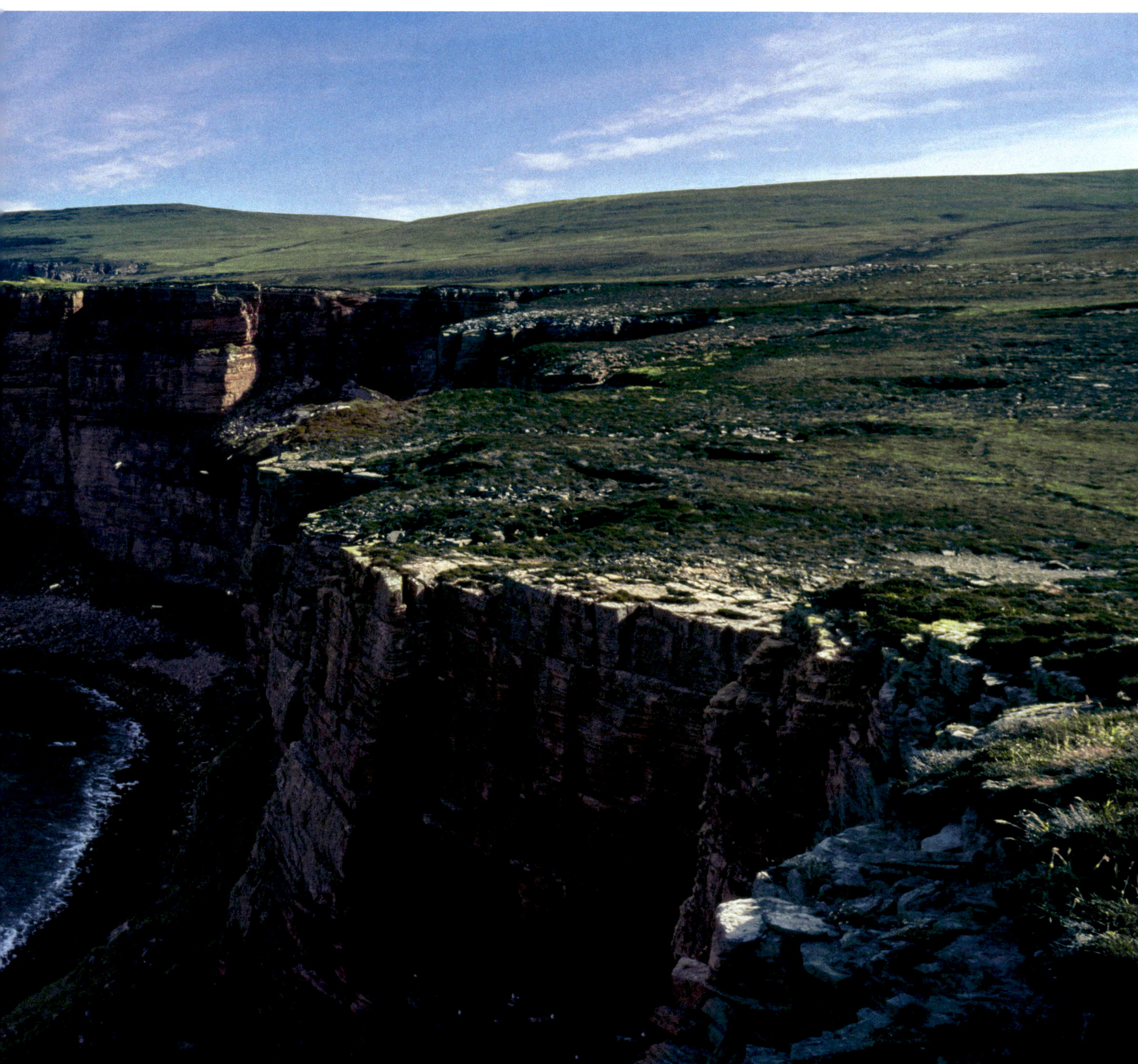

The Old Man of Hoy, Orkney
July 2014

The Old Man of Hoy is a needle of ancient Orcadian
sandstone that rises 137 metres from the Atlantic.
It is one of the tallest sea stacks in Scotland and
until relatively recently – around the late eighteenth
century – the exposed structure formed a huge sea
arch that has since been separated by the power of
natural coastal erosion.

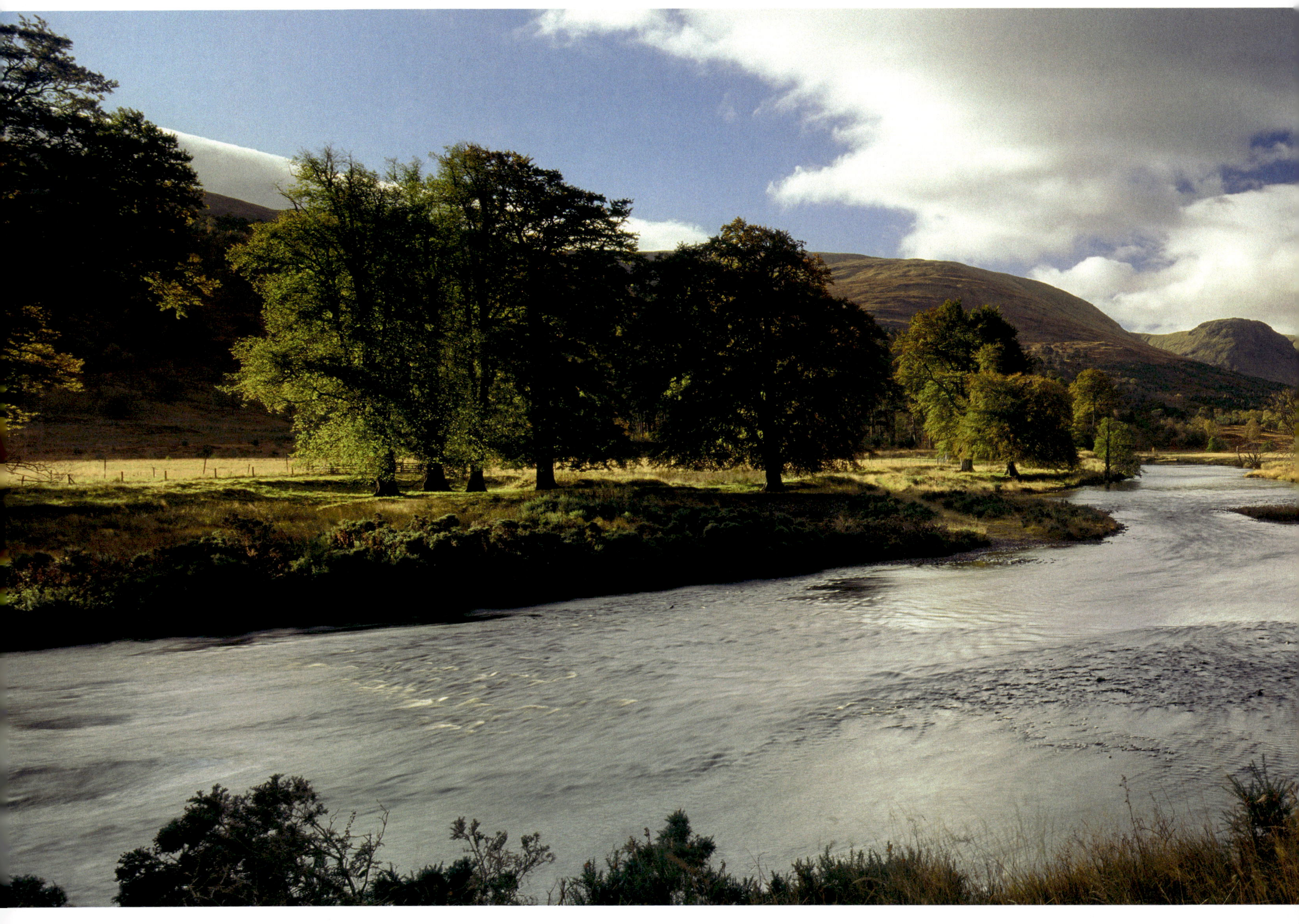

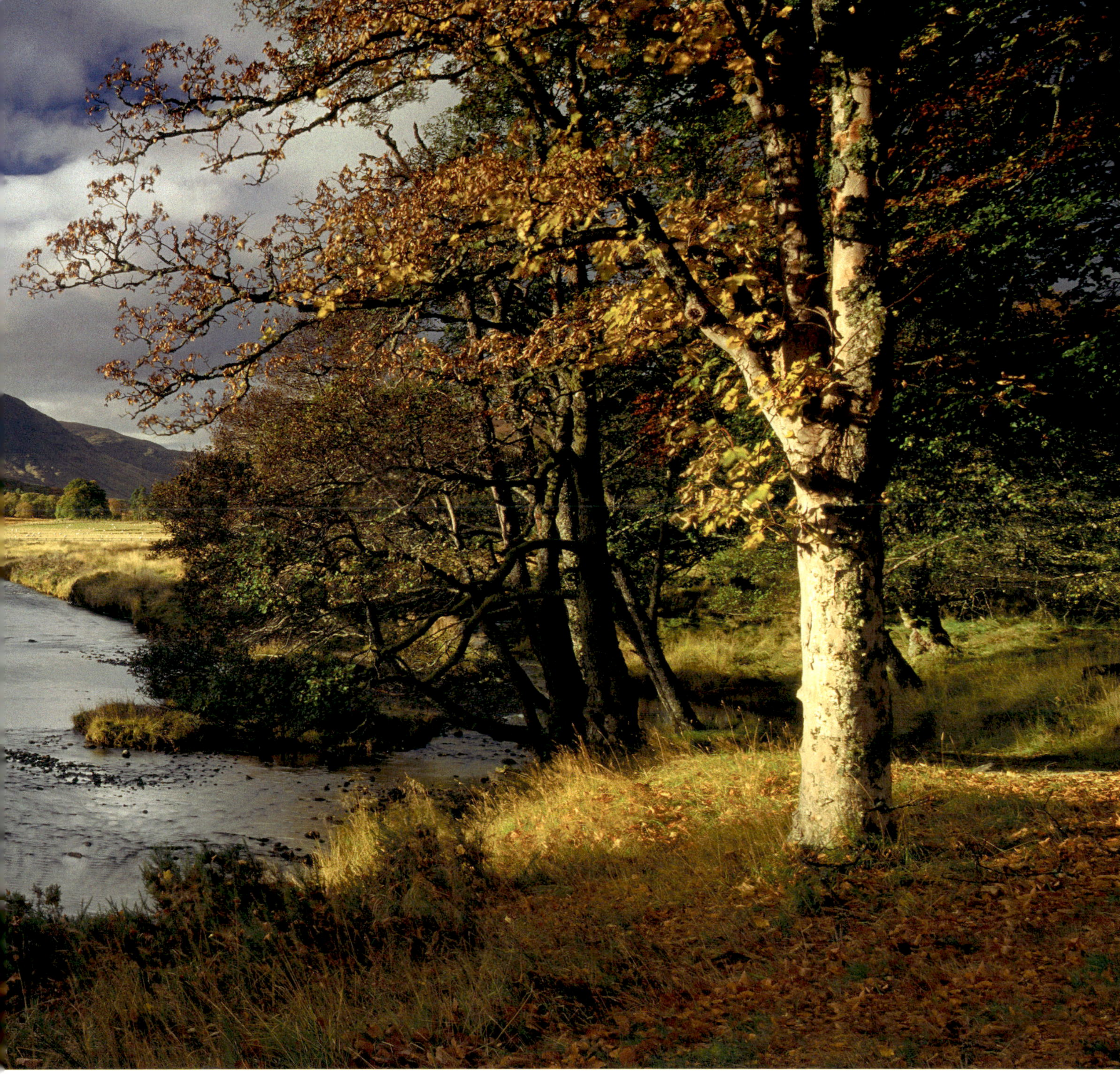

The River Lyon, Glen Lyon
October 2012

The River Lyon rises from Loch Lyon and runs for some
thirty miles before its confluence with the Tay at the Appin
of Dull. Glen Lyon is one of the quieter, less frequented
glens of central Scotland and is often described as
Scotland's longest, loneliest and loveliest glen.

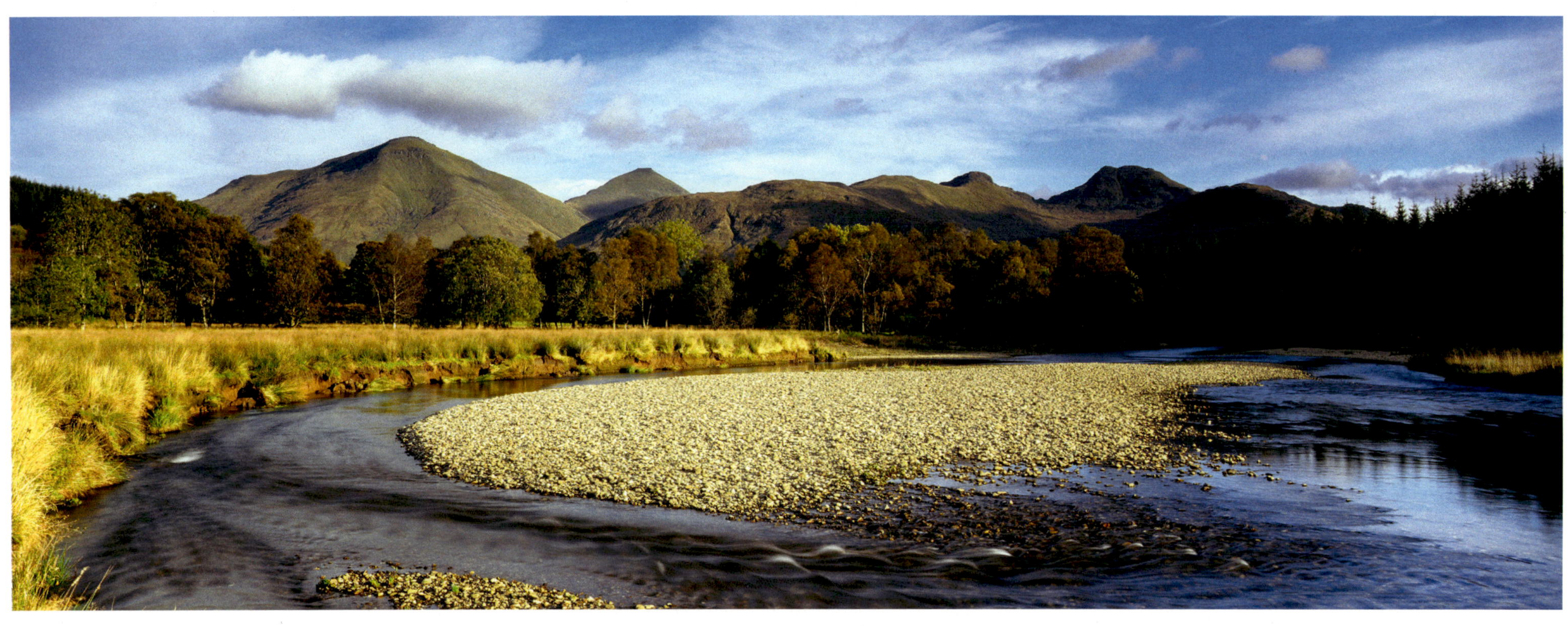

The River Fillan, Stirling
September 2012

From humble beginnings, the waters of the River Fillan
slowly meander eastwards and eventually merge to
form the mighty River Tay. At approximately 120 miles
long the Tay is Scotland's longest river and continues
all the way to the east coast where it becomes tidal
and forms the Firth of Tay.

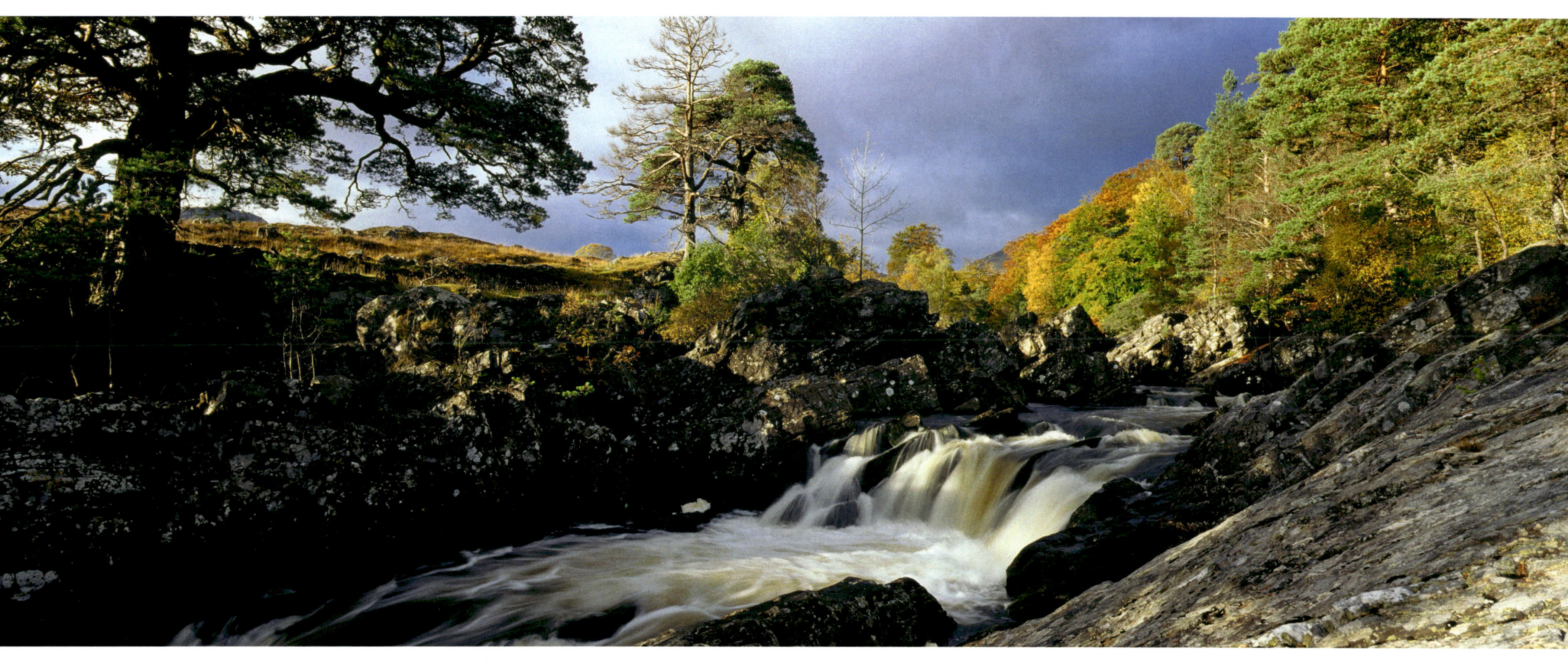

Glen Lyon
October 2012

The upper reaches of the River Lyon drop through
a series of beautiful waterfalls and woodland
gorges before eventually joining the Tay. These rich
microcosms are home to a healthy mix of native oak,
ash, hazel, elm and the emblematic Caledonian pine.

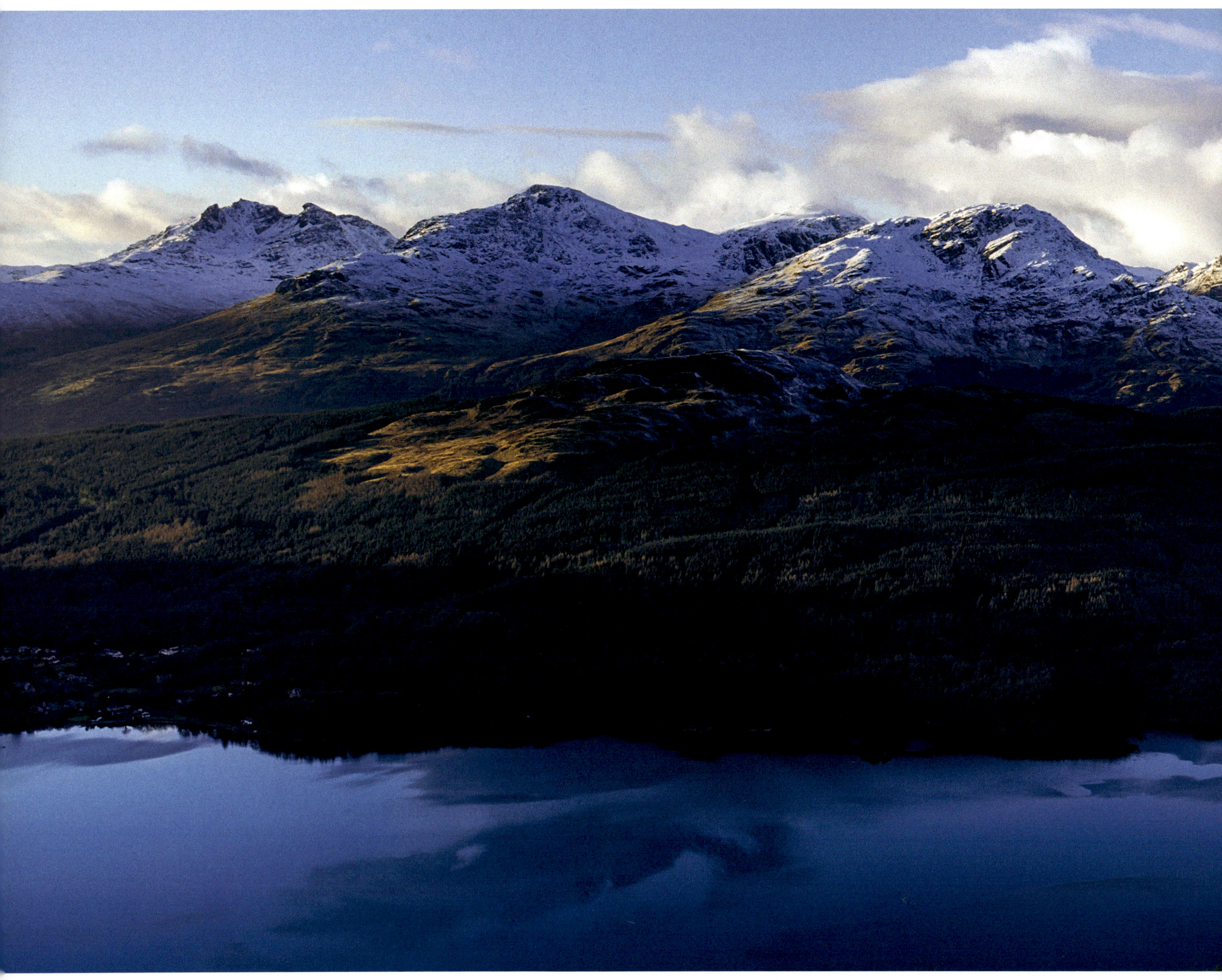

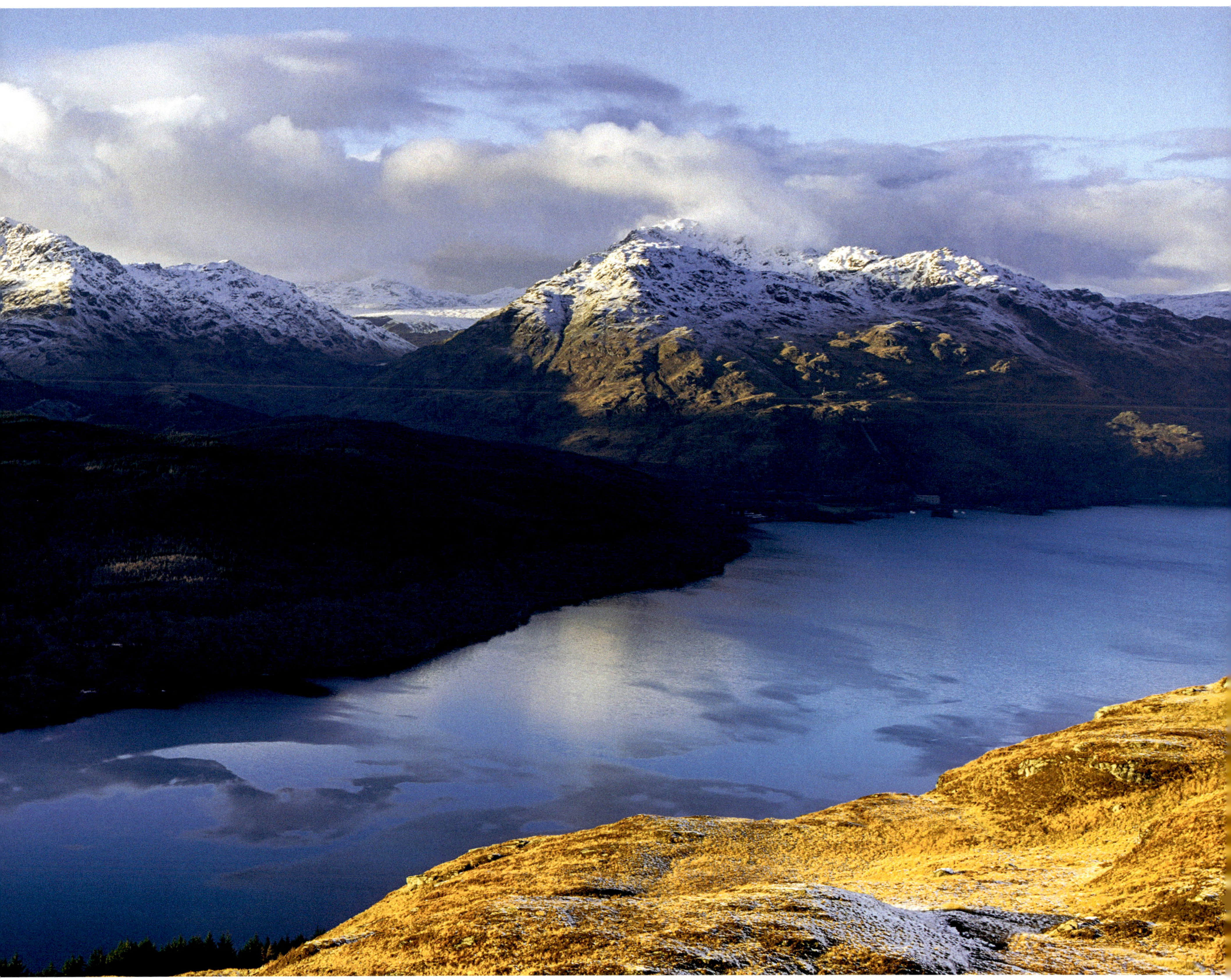

Loch Lomond and the Arrochar Alps
December 2012

High above the eastern shore of Loch Lomond
I had the perfect viewpoint towards these magnificent
mountains. Collectively known as the Arrochar Alps,
this compact group contains no less than five Munros
and eight Corbetts, the most impressive of which
is Ben Arthur, commonly known as The Cobbler
and seen here on the left.

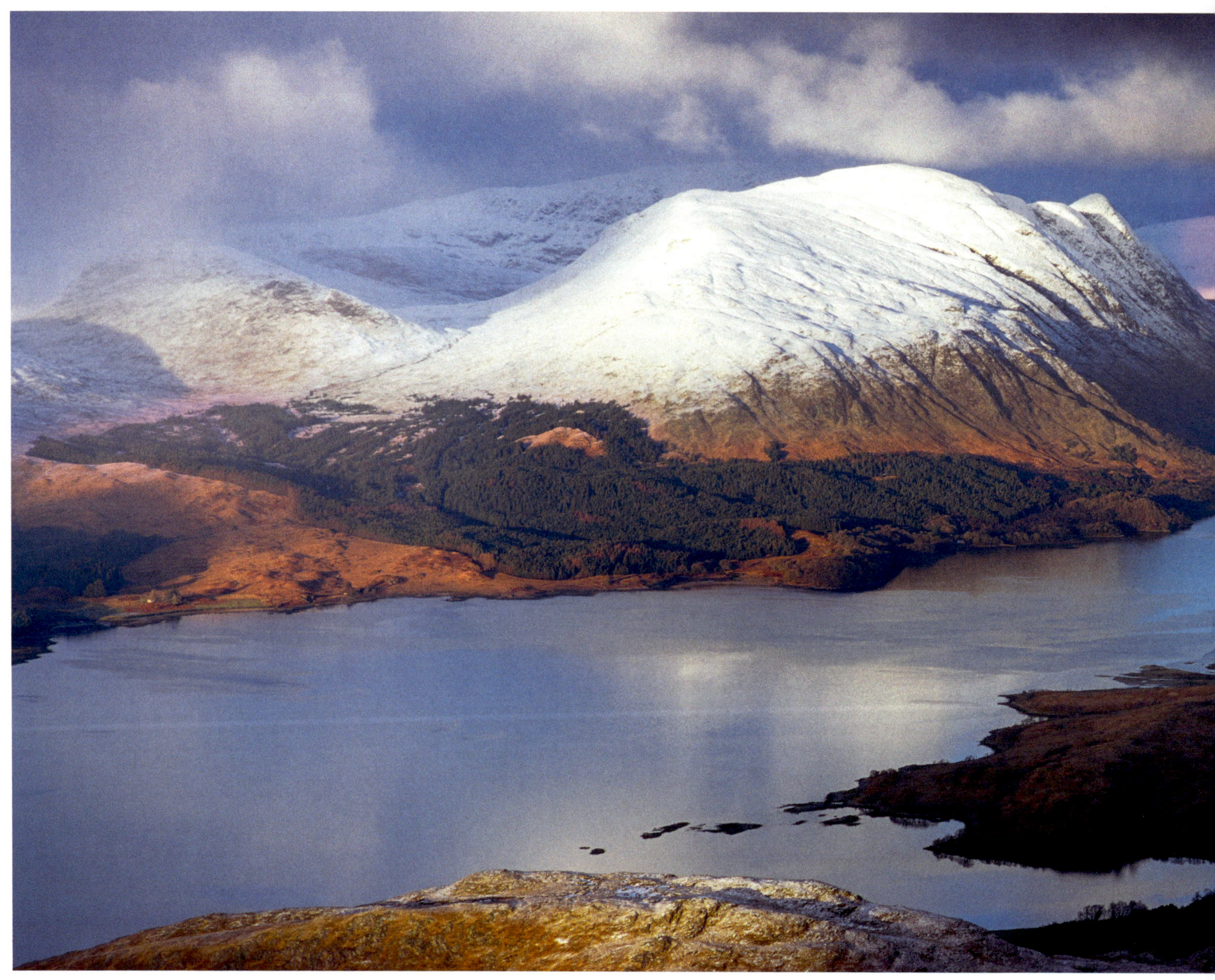

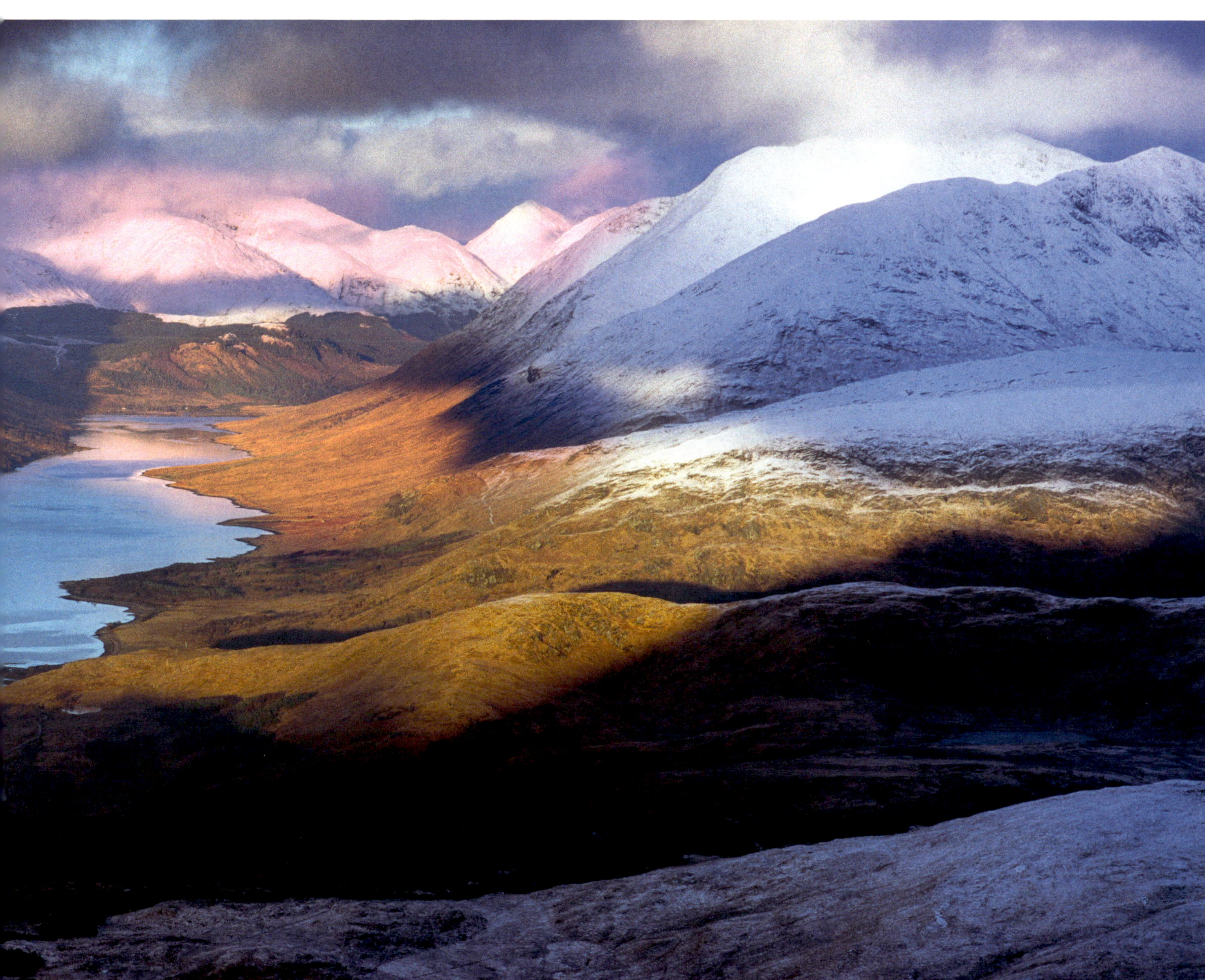

Loch Etive
December 2017

Having explored the area surrounding Loch Etive
extensively over the years, one summit had
remained unclimbed: the inconspicuous Meall Copagach.
Tucked in behind the looming mass of Ben Cruachan,
I had deduced from various surveys that the outlook
from here would provide an excellent vantage point.
This particular day was one of light winds but heavy
showers, and as sunset approached the cloud began
to build and any remaining patches of clear sky were
now few and far between. On the horizon the darkening
sky looked grim with a foreboding temperament.
But I was in luck; the sun eventually found a way
through the burgeoning cloud bank and transformed
the scene before me.

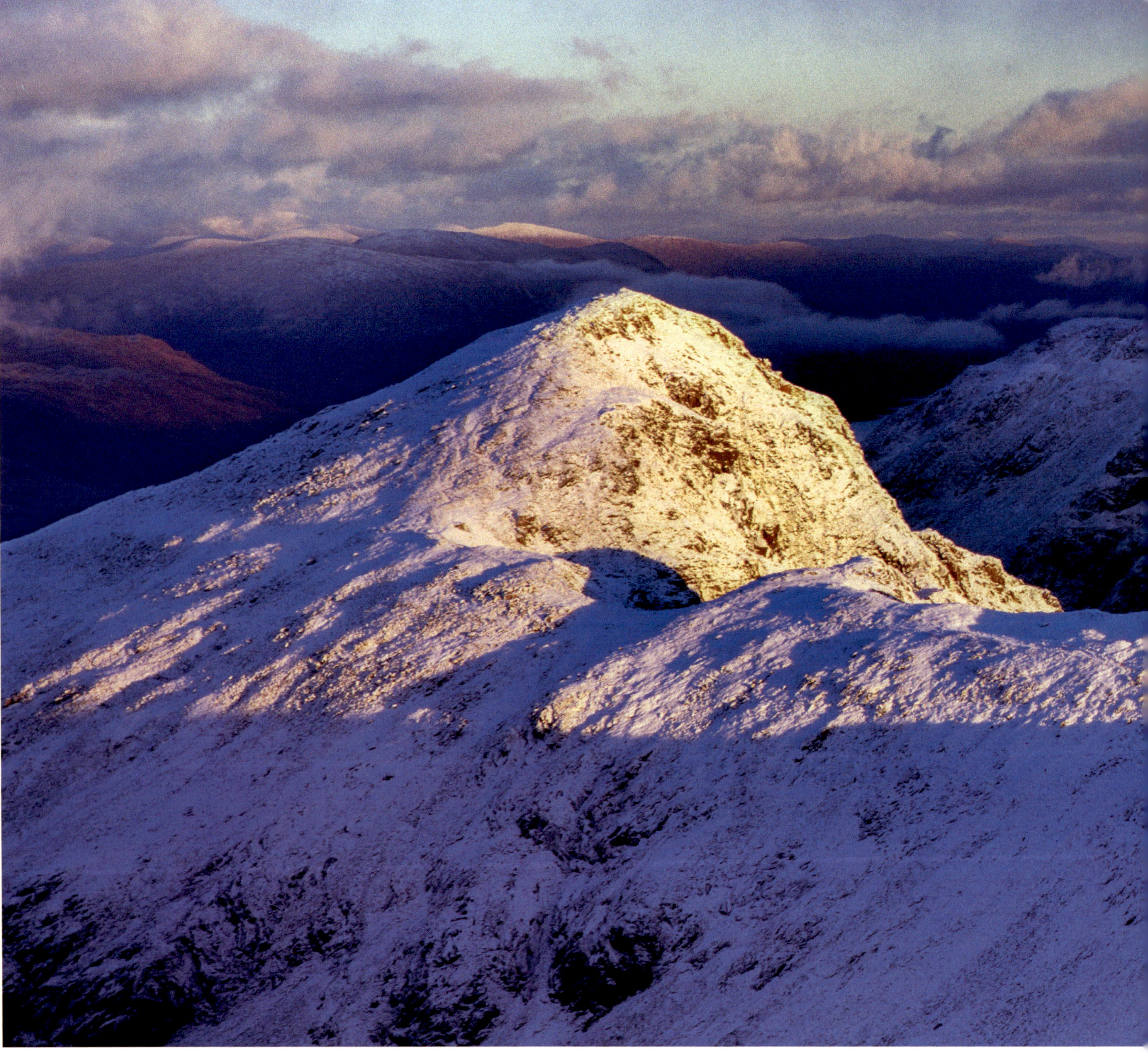

Aonach Eagach, Glen Coe
December 2017

The Aonach Eagach needs little introduction to most.
This precarious ridge links the two Munros of Meall Dearg
and Sgorr nam Fiannaidh to form the steep northern
aspect of Glen Coe. It has a fearsome reputation and
in winter offers a true mountaineering expedition.
Fortunately for this image, I didn't need to traverse the
ridge itself; I made my approach from the west via a
straightforward ascent of Sgorr nam Fiannaidh. As it
was Boxing Day I had the view to myself; conditions
were superb and fresh snow had settled overnight which
helped emphasise the stunning mountain architecture
in the warm midwinter light.

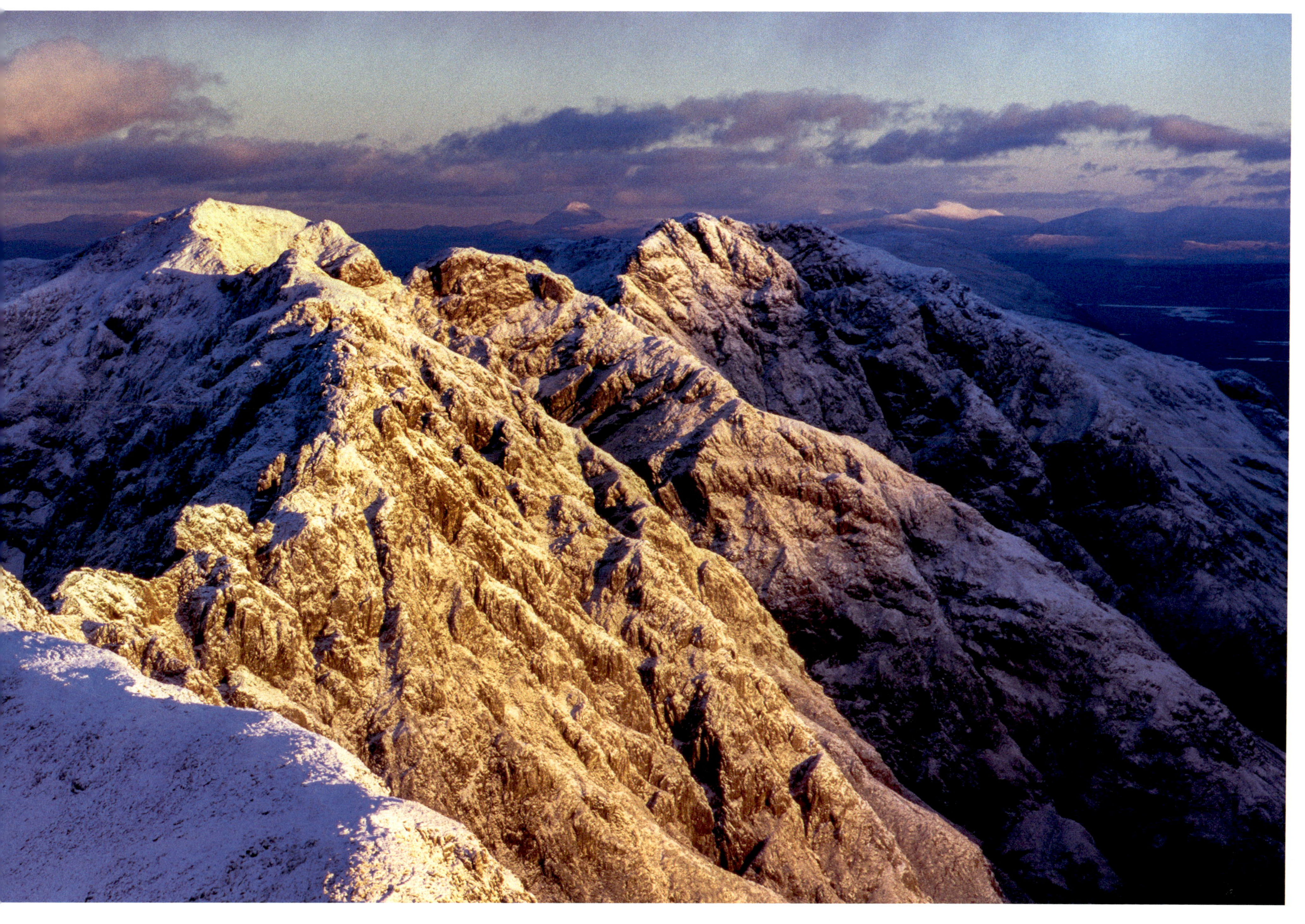

Sandwood Bay, Sutherland
October 2012

Sandwood Bay is one of the most beautiful and
isolated beaches in the British Isles. This pristine coastal
environment has everything: big waves, sea cliffs, sand
dunes and the landmark sea stack of Am Buachaille.

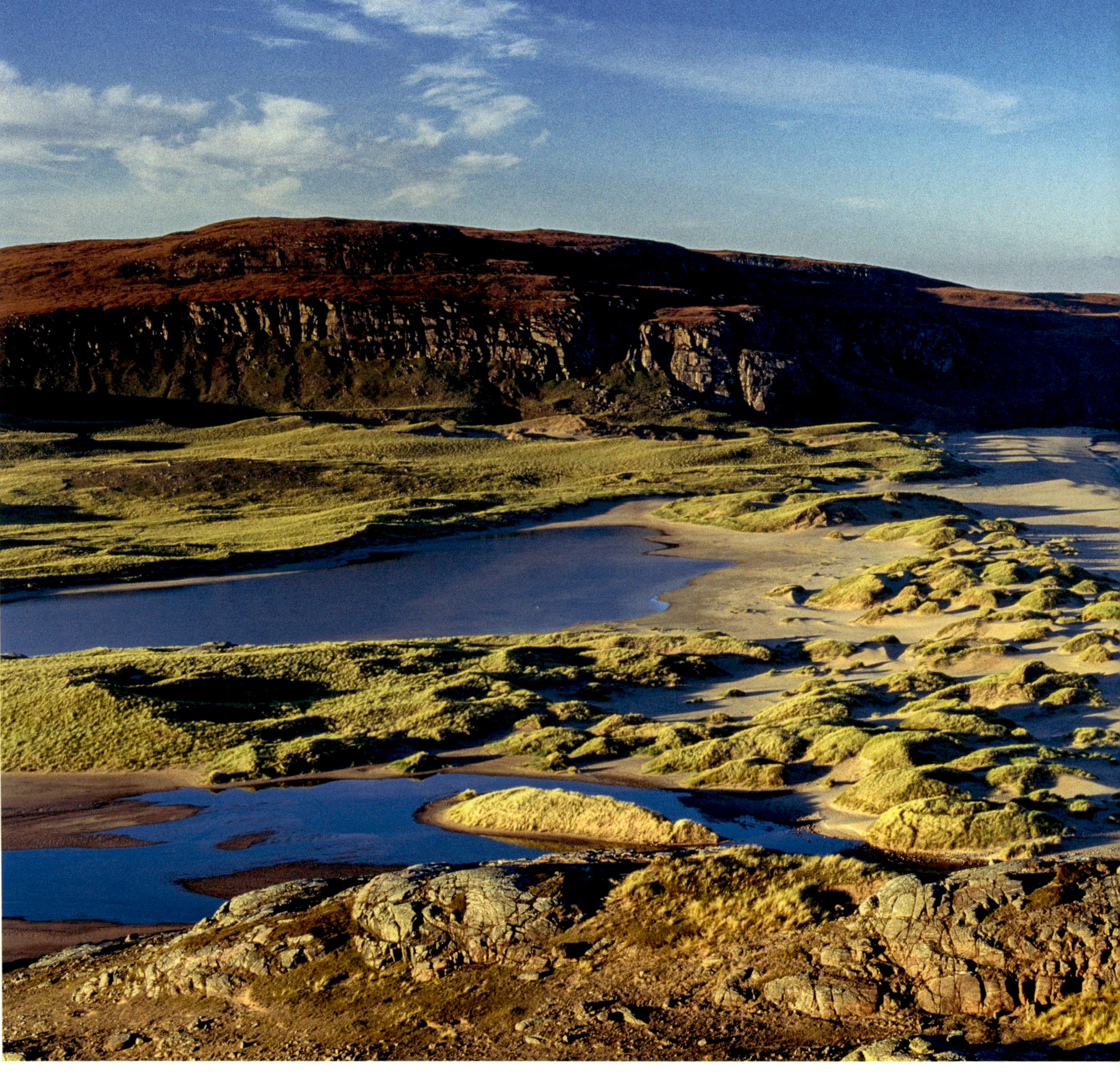

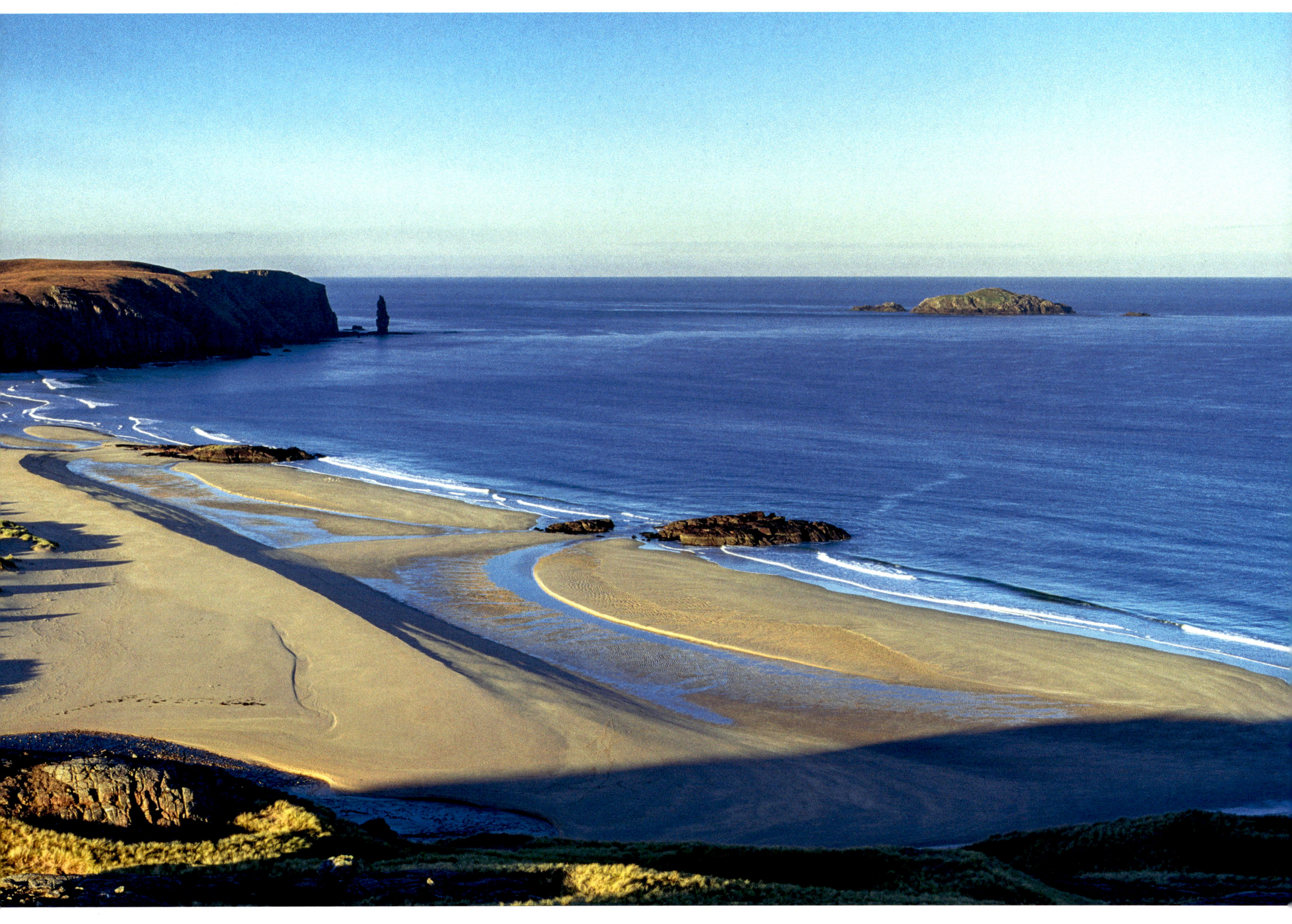

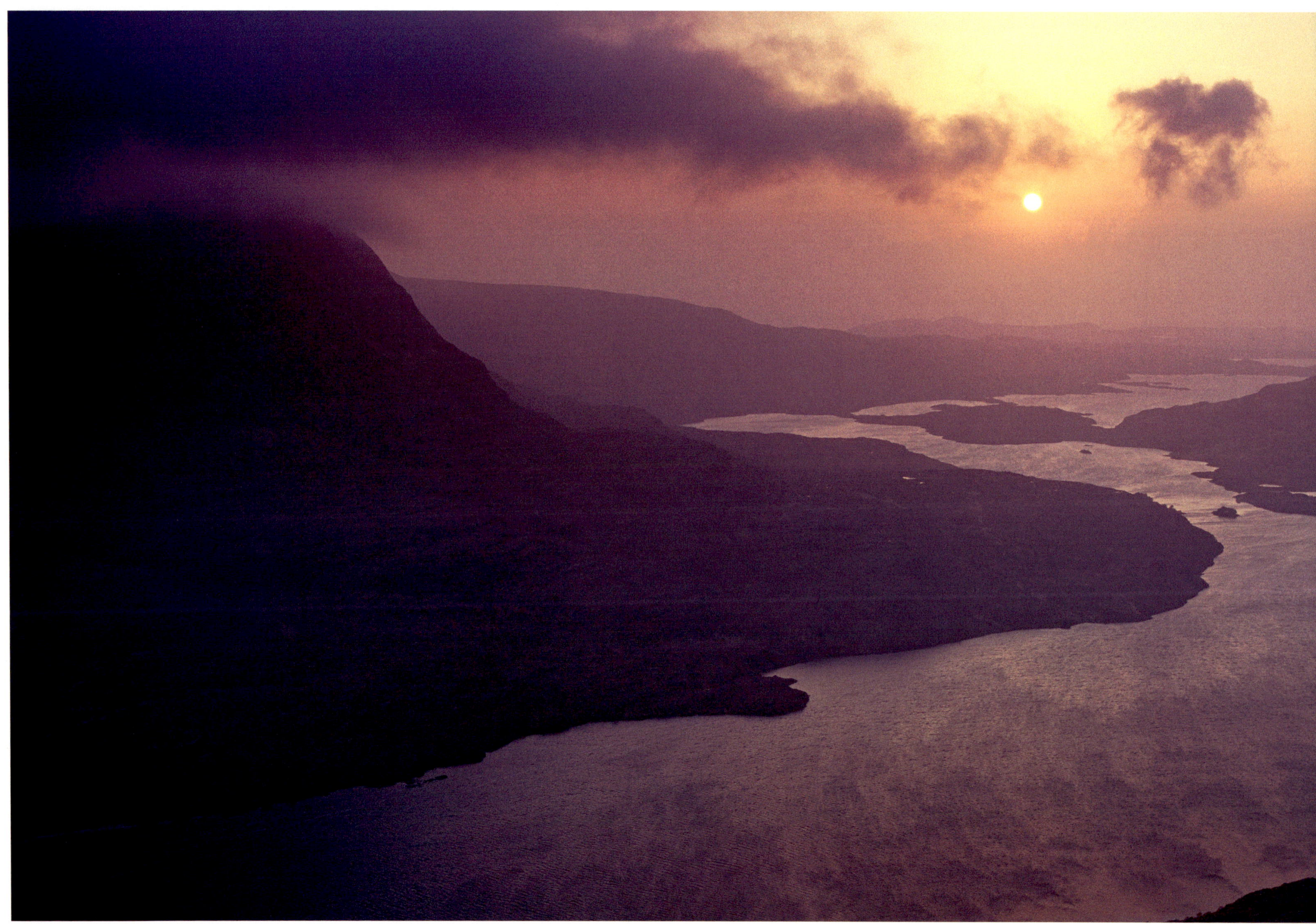

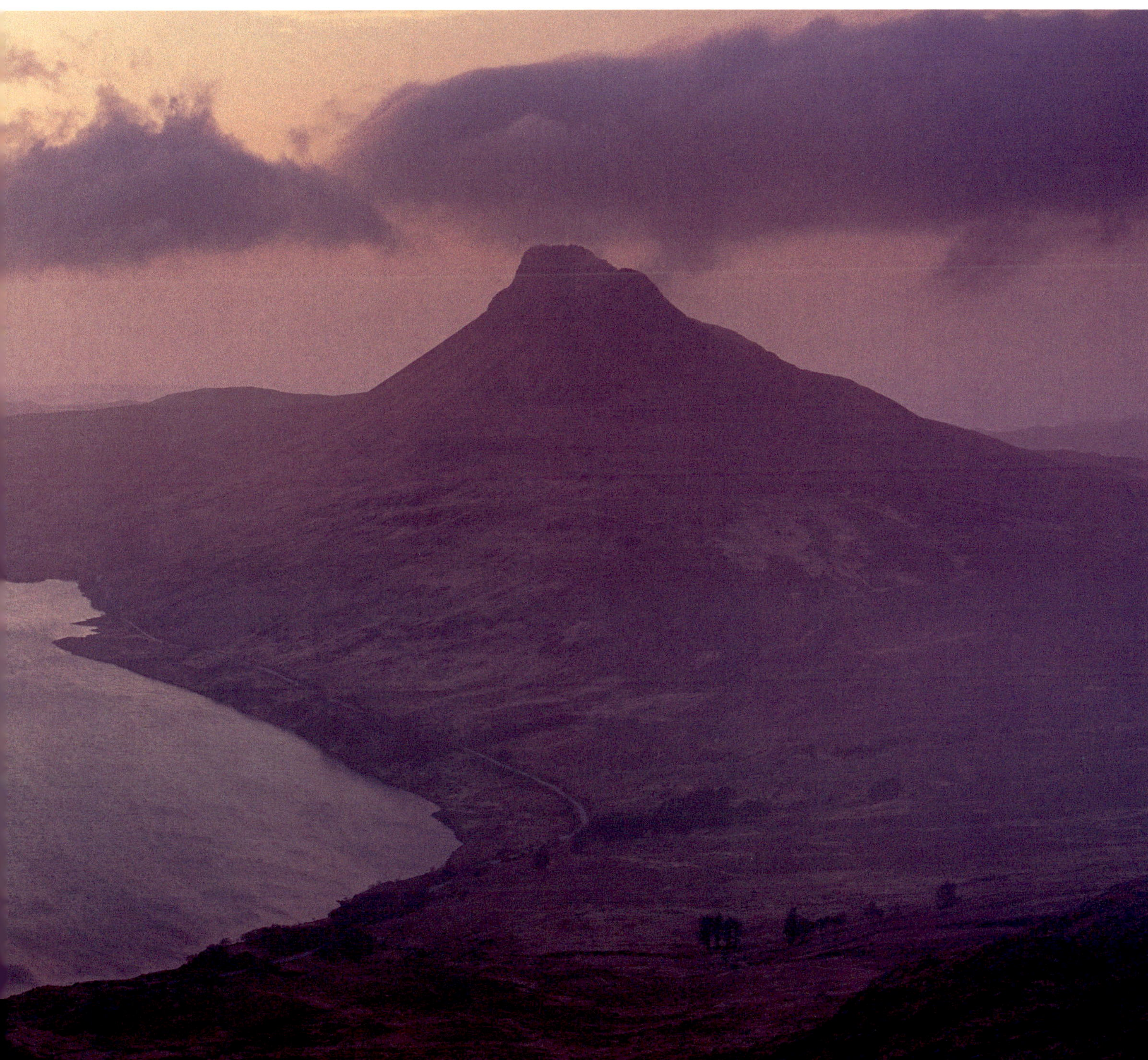

Loch Lurgainn, Inverpolly
April 2018

At the cloud-capped summit of Cùl Beag the forecasted
winds were as savage as predicted. I hastily retreated
from this hostile environment to find a safer alternative
that would provide some much-needed shelter but
still offer the view I had sought from the top. Descending
out of the cloud I carefully navigated the complex
sandstone cliffs that make up the north-western face
and eventually found a small sanctuary just below
the cloud base. I set up to capture the sunset;
the pattern of eddies in the waters of Loch Lurgainn
are indicative of the wind speed even at lower levels.

Ben Vorlich, Loch Lomond
January 2018

Ben Vorlich, the most northerly member of the Arrochar
Alps, offers some excellent views towards Ben Lomond
and beyond to the famous waters of Loch Lomond.
After a long and steep ascent from Inveruglas, I lingered
on the summit and looked on as the last group of
climbers disappeared down the rugged spine before me.
Alone, I waited for the sun to set and watched as the
snow-covered landscape absorbed the last rays of
intense winter light before starting my own descent
into the darkness.

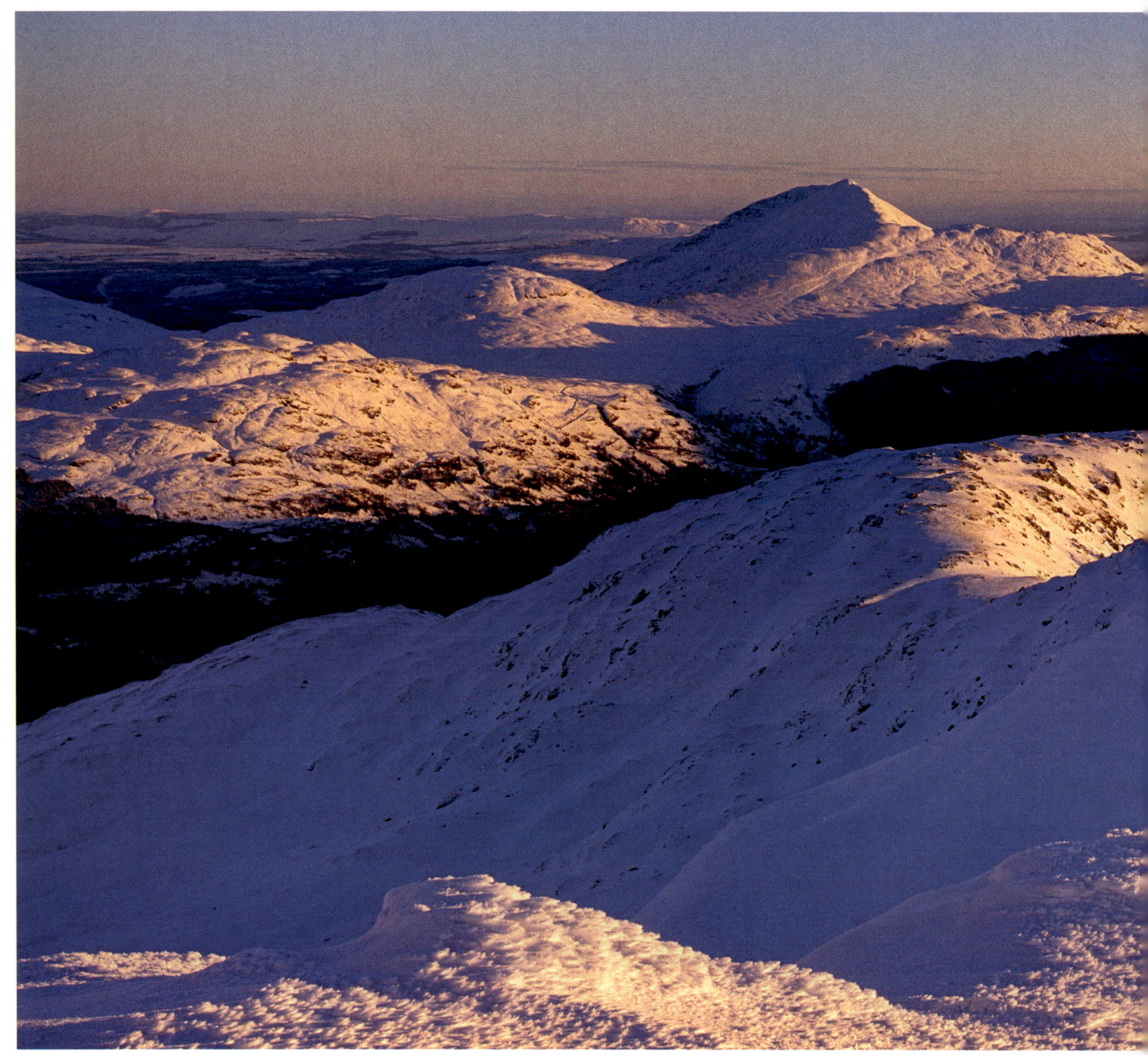

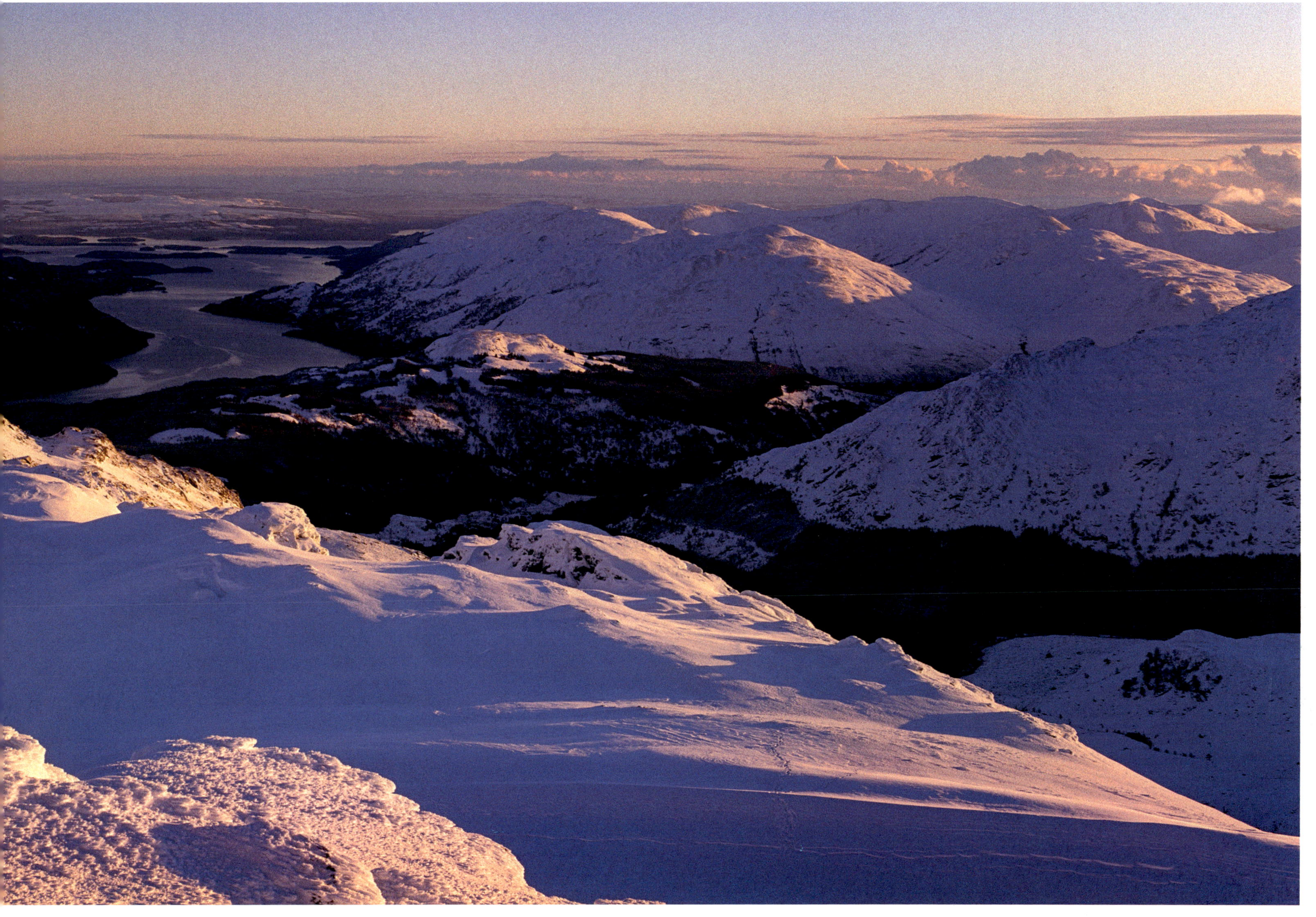

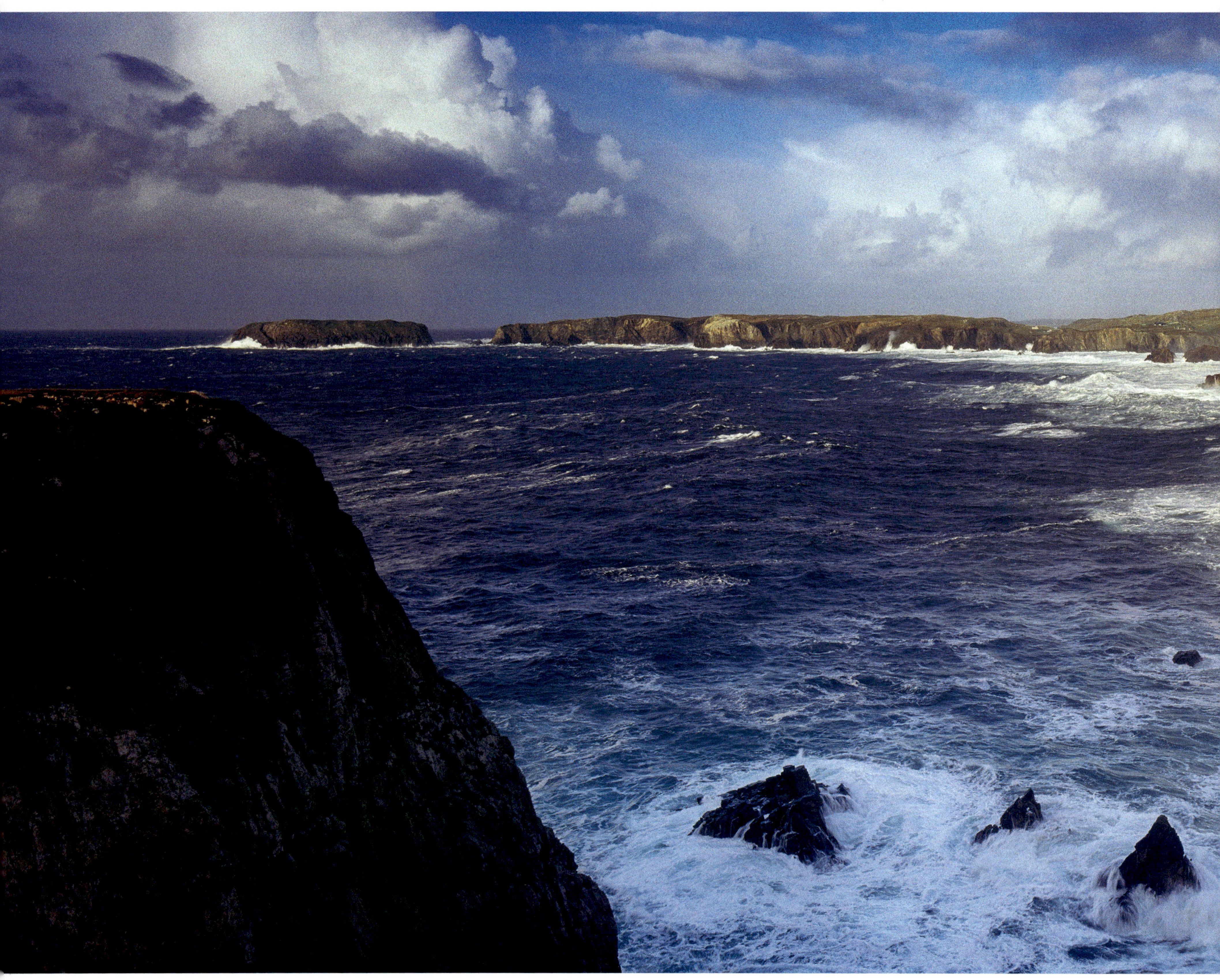

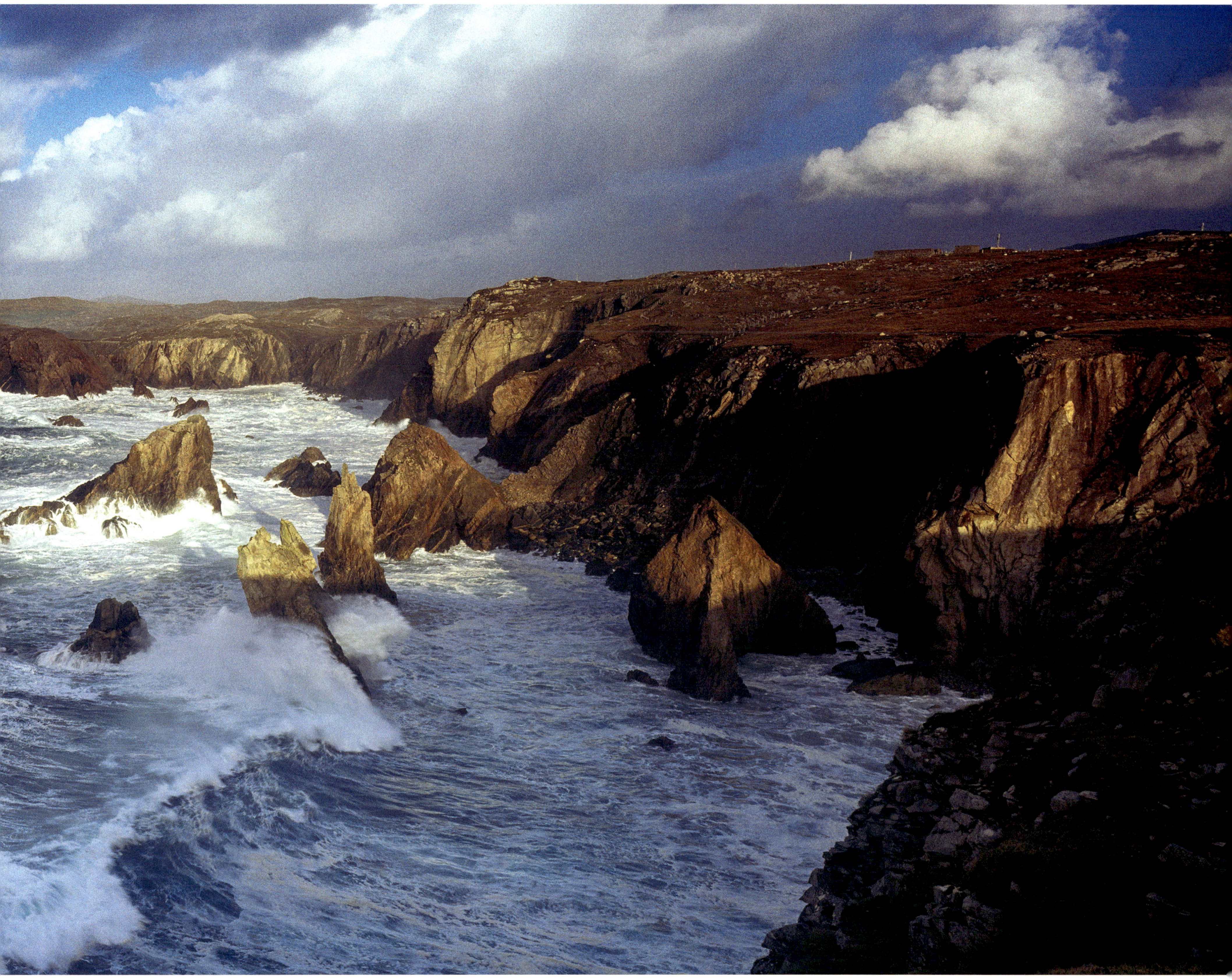

Mangurstadh, Isle of Lewis
November 2013

Perched high on the sea cliffs overlooking the west coast of Lewis I positioned myself as safely as possible amid the volatile storm conditions. This was an extreme environment to be working in and I tried to make the photograph with every element at its best.

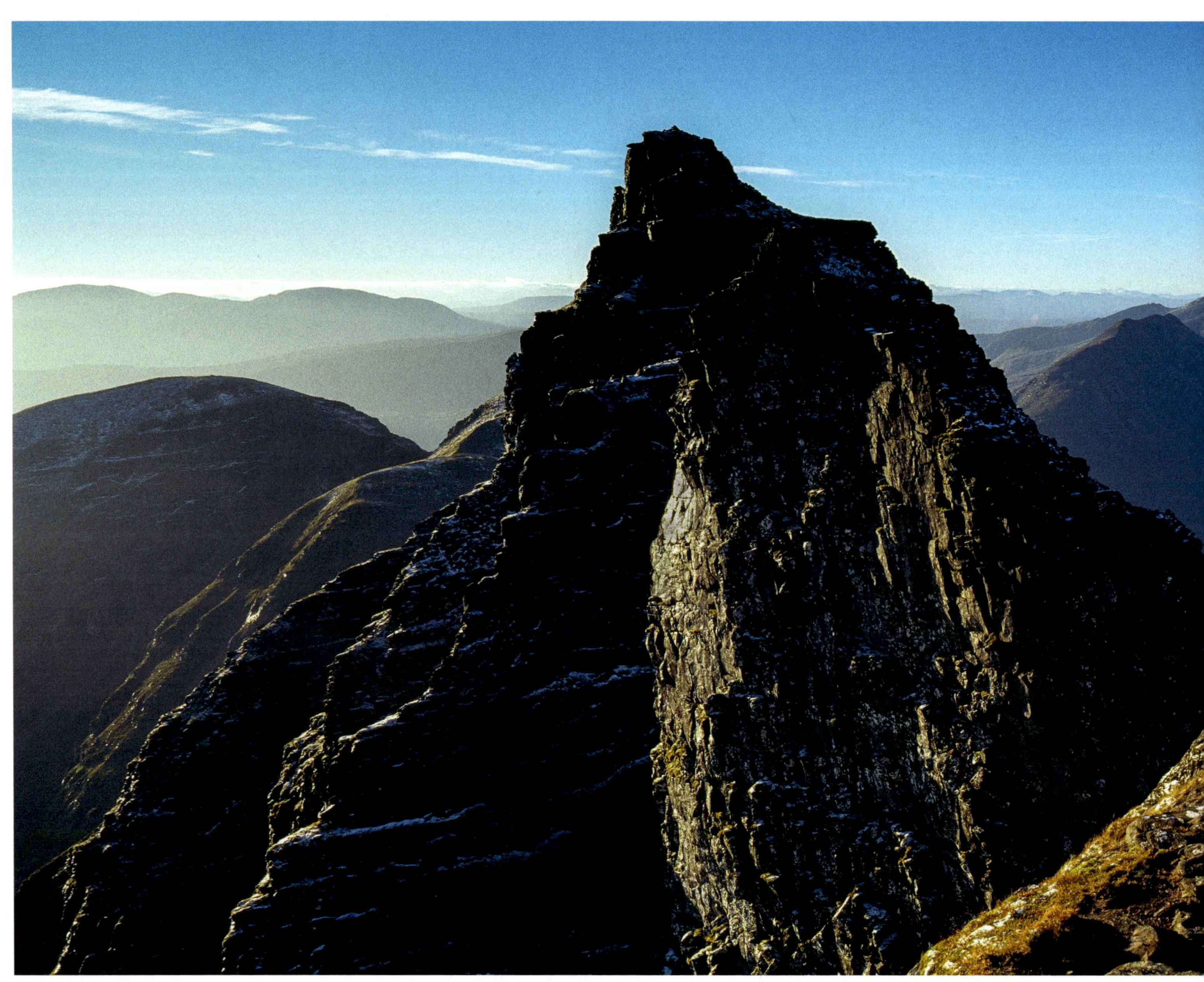

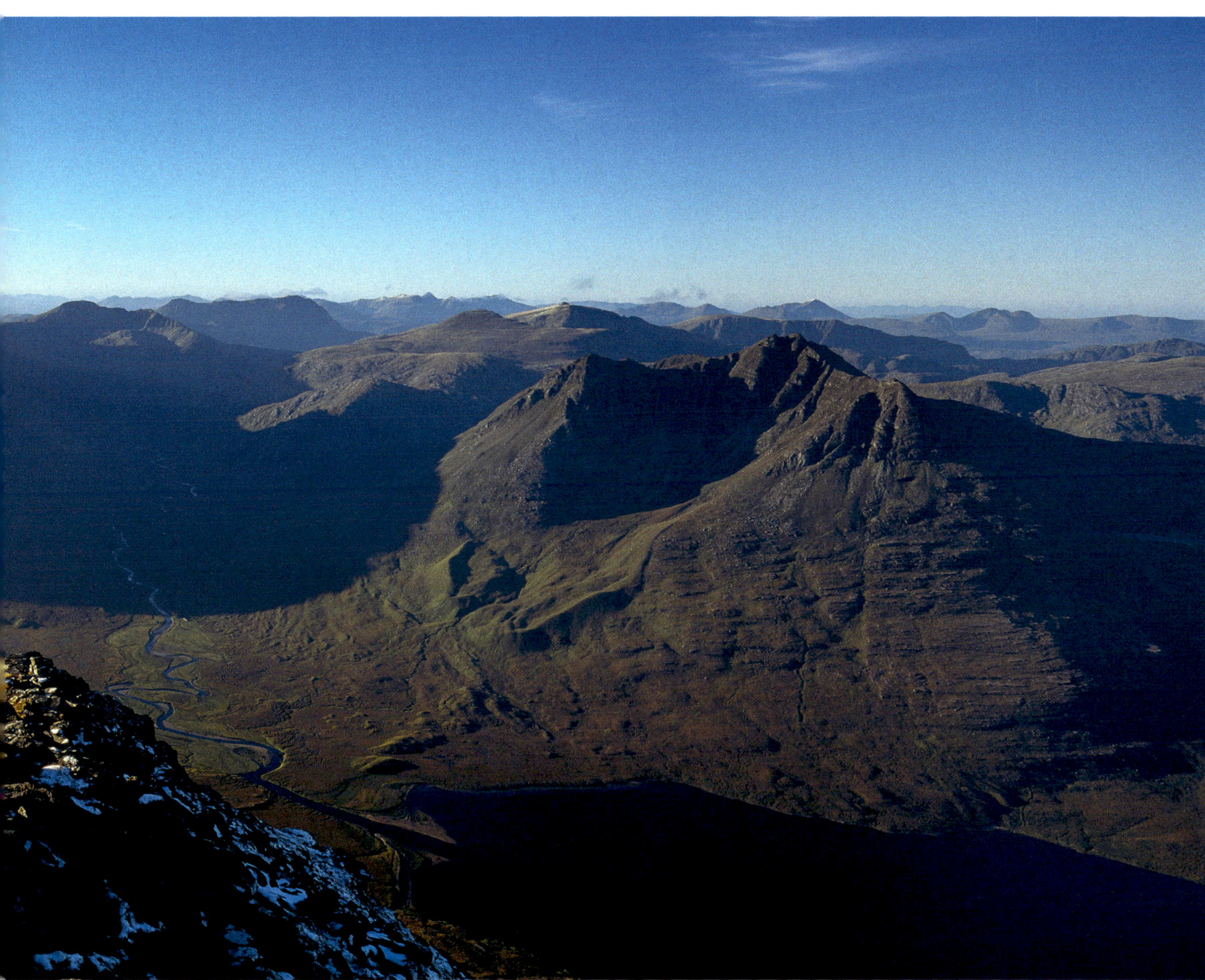

Lord Berkeley's Seat, An Teallach
October 2013

For walkers doing a full traverse of An Teallach,
the overhanging rock spire affectionately named
Lord Berkeley's Seat marks the start of a grade-3
scramble across the infamous Corrag Bhuidhe Buttress.
This section of the mountain forms an exciting
600 metres of airy ridge walking with extreme
exposure and expansive views across Fisherfield.

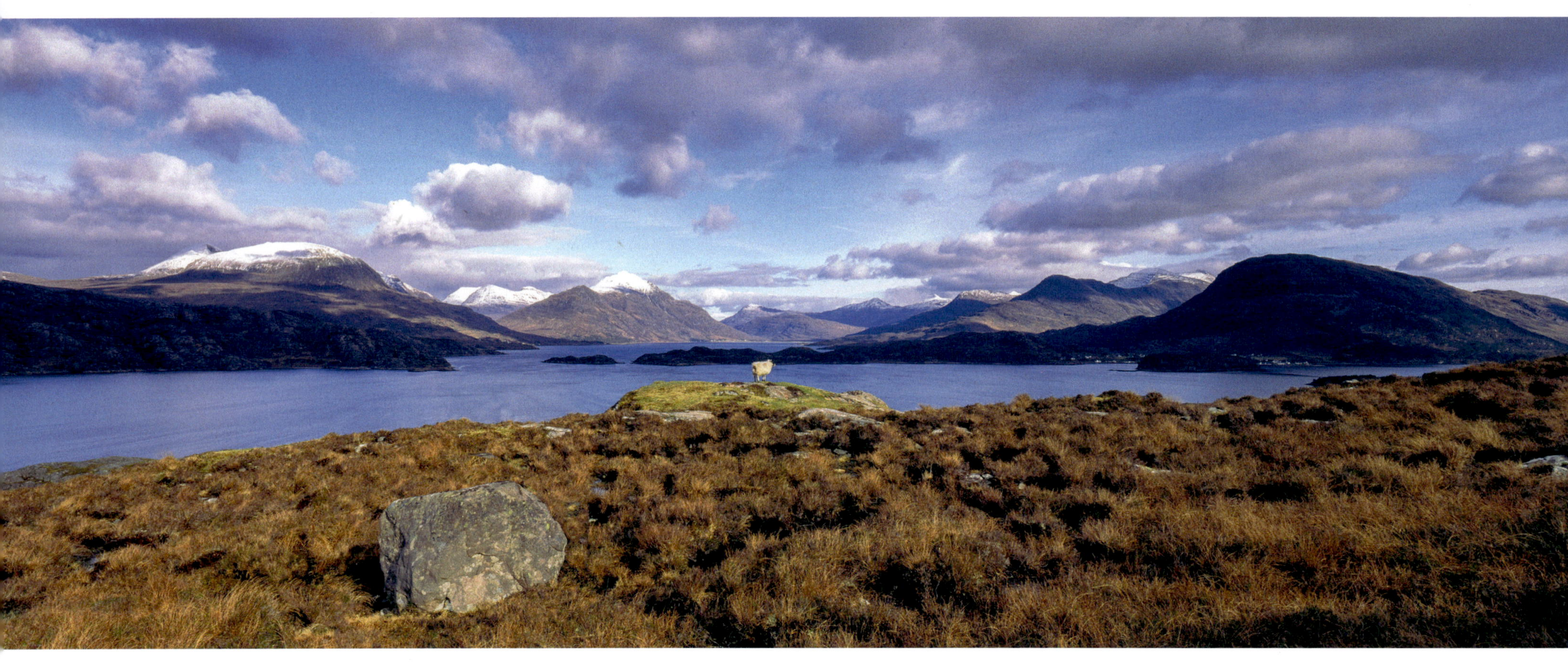

Torridon
March 2012

Loch Torridon is one of the largest tidal sea lochs on the
west coast of Scotland. Stretching for over fifteen miles
into the heart of the Torridon mountains, it is actually
composed of three individual but connected bodies of
water: the outer Loch Torridon, the middle basin of Loch
Shieldaig and the inner body of Upper Loch Torridon.

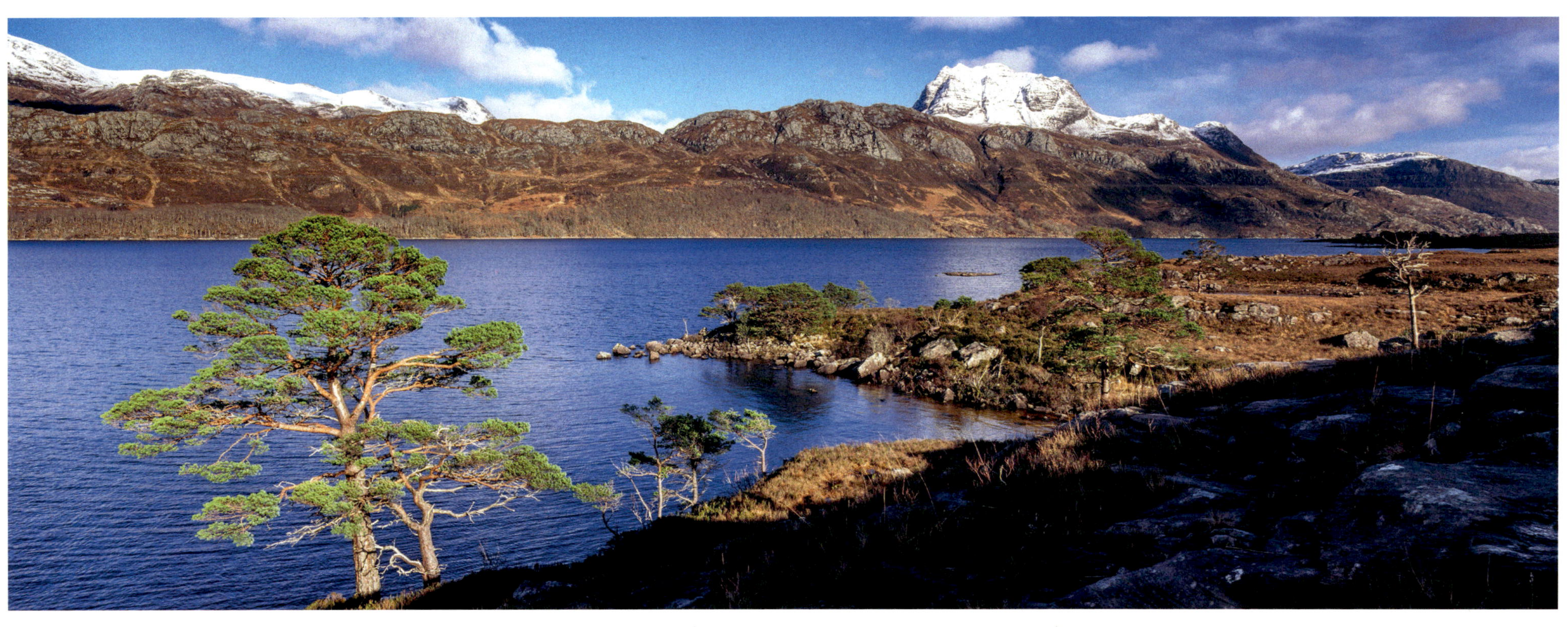

Slioch from Loch Maree
March 2016

From the wooded shores of Loch Maree, the majestic walls of Slioch rise almost vertically to form a seemingly impenetrable fortress of Torridonian sandstone. Despite this imposing impression, Slioch is a relatively straight-forward prospect by means of an excellent path that cuts through a vast corrie hidden from view on the eastern side of the mountain.

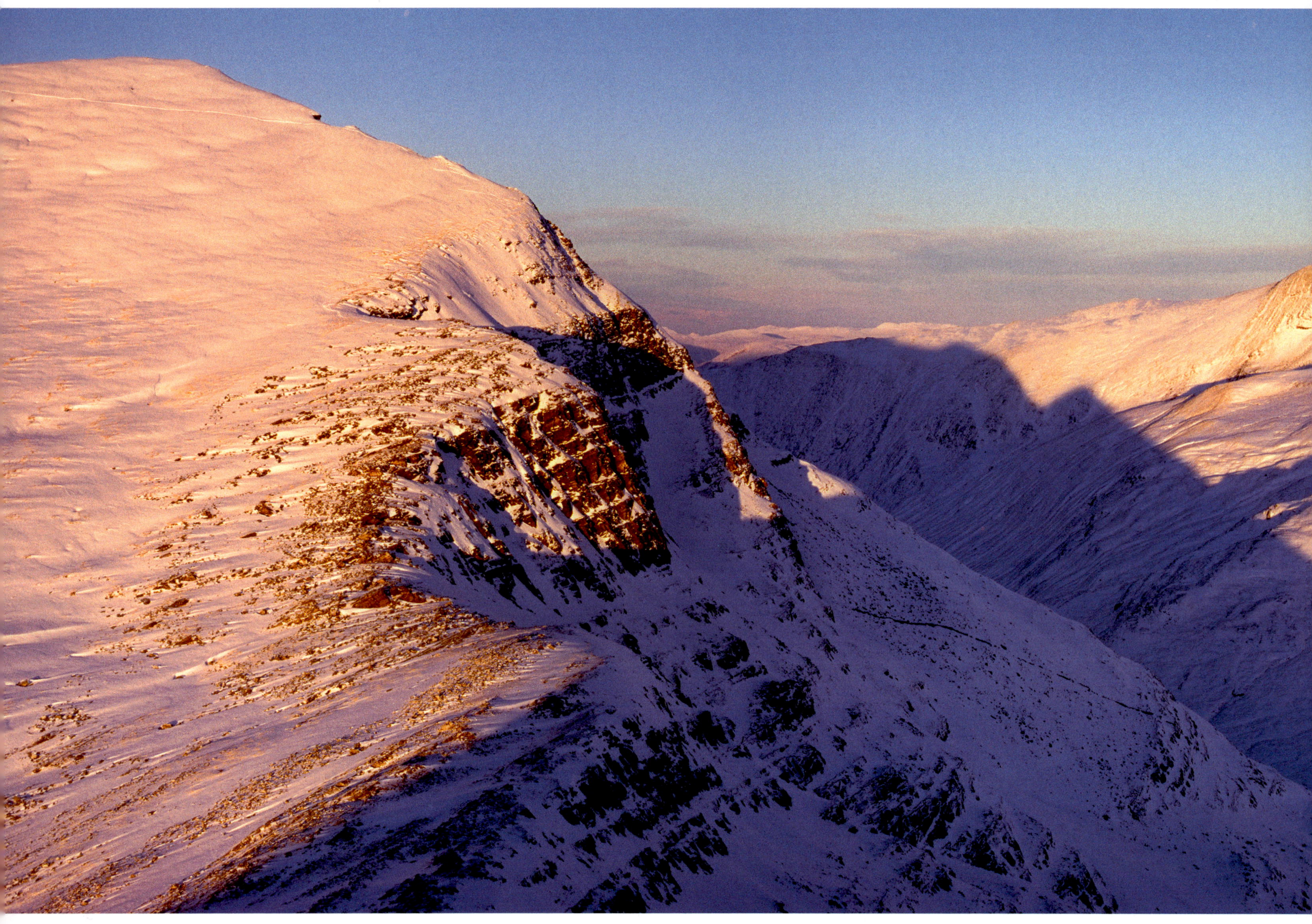

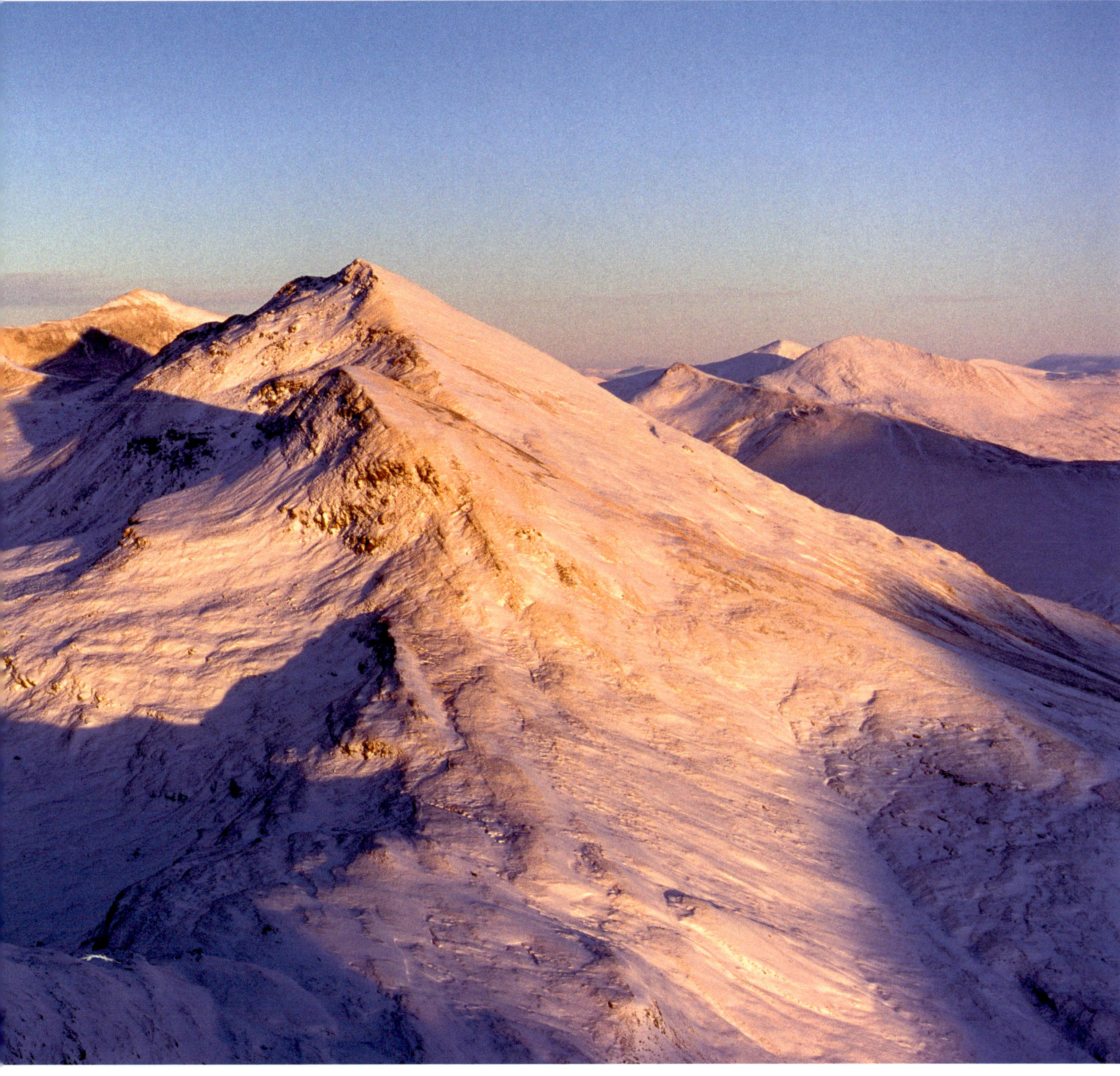

Sgùrr Choinnich Beag, Glen Nevis
December 2017

Sgùrr a' Bhuic lies deep in the heart of Glen Nevis and forms a subsidiary peak of the great Aonach Beag. It's a peak that can be easily lost amongst its more renowned neighbours, but it does provide an excellent viewpoint of the fine high-level ridge that links Sgùrr Choinnich Beag and Sgùrr Choinnich Mòr to the Grey Corries far to the east.

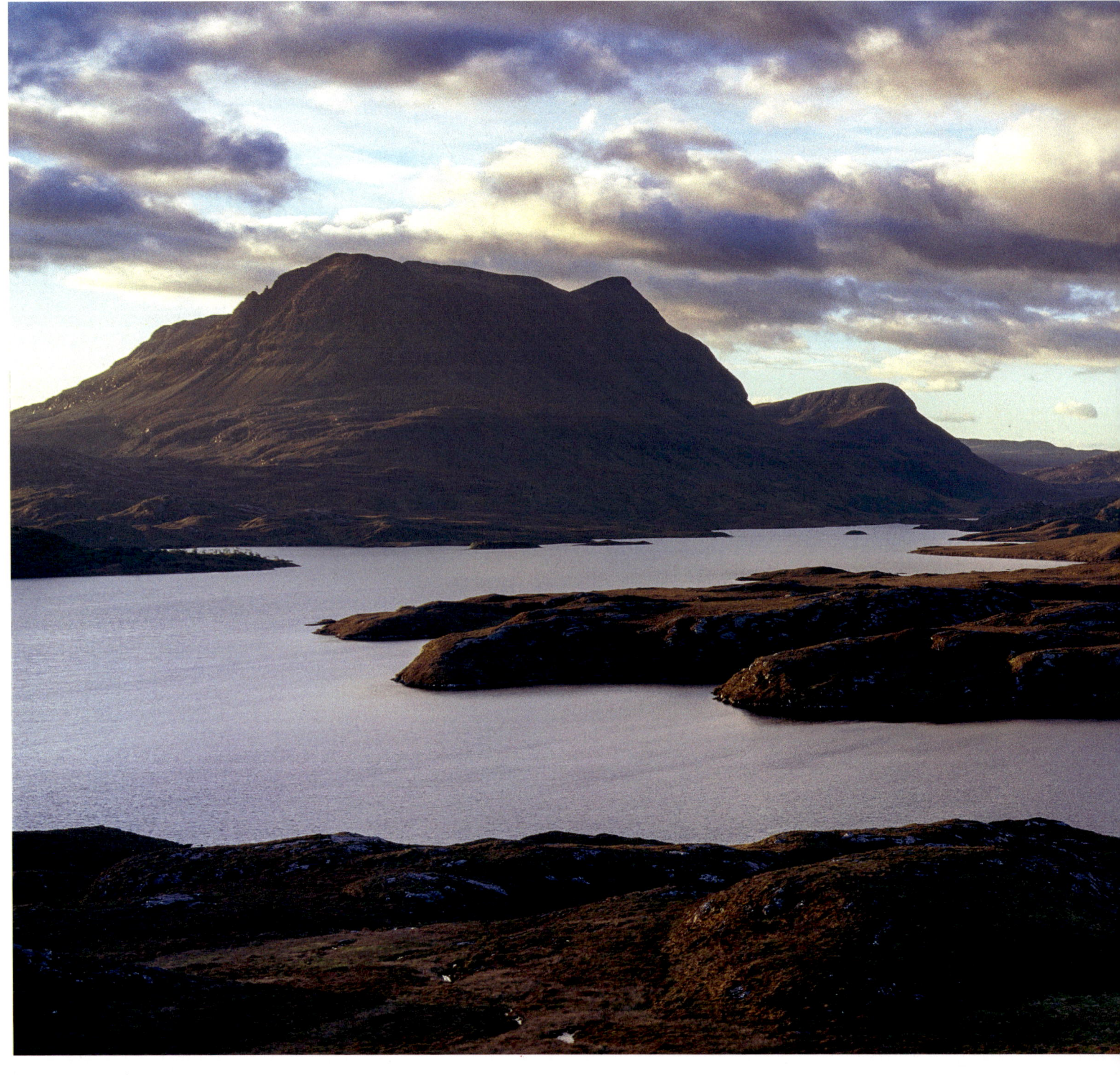

Loch Sionascaig, Inverpolly
May 2011

Amongst the blanket bog and moorland of Inverpolly lies the rugged shoreline of Loch Sionascaig. Its deep freshwater basin is fed by the numerous streams and falls collected from the slopes of Cùl Mòr, Cùl Beag and Stac Pollaidh, and it is reputed to be one of the best trout lochs in the Highlands.

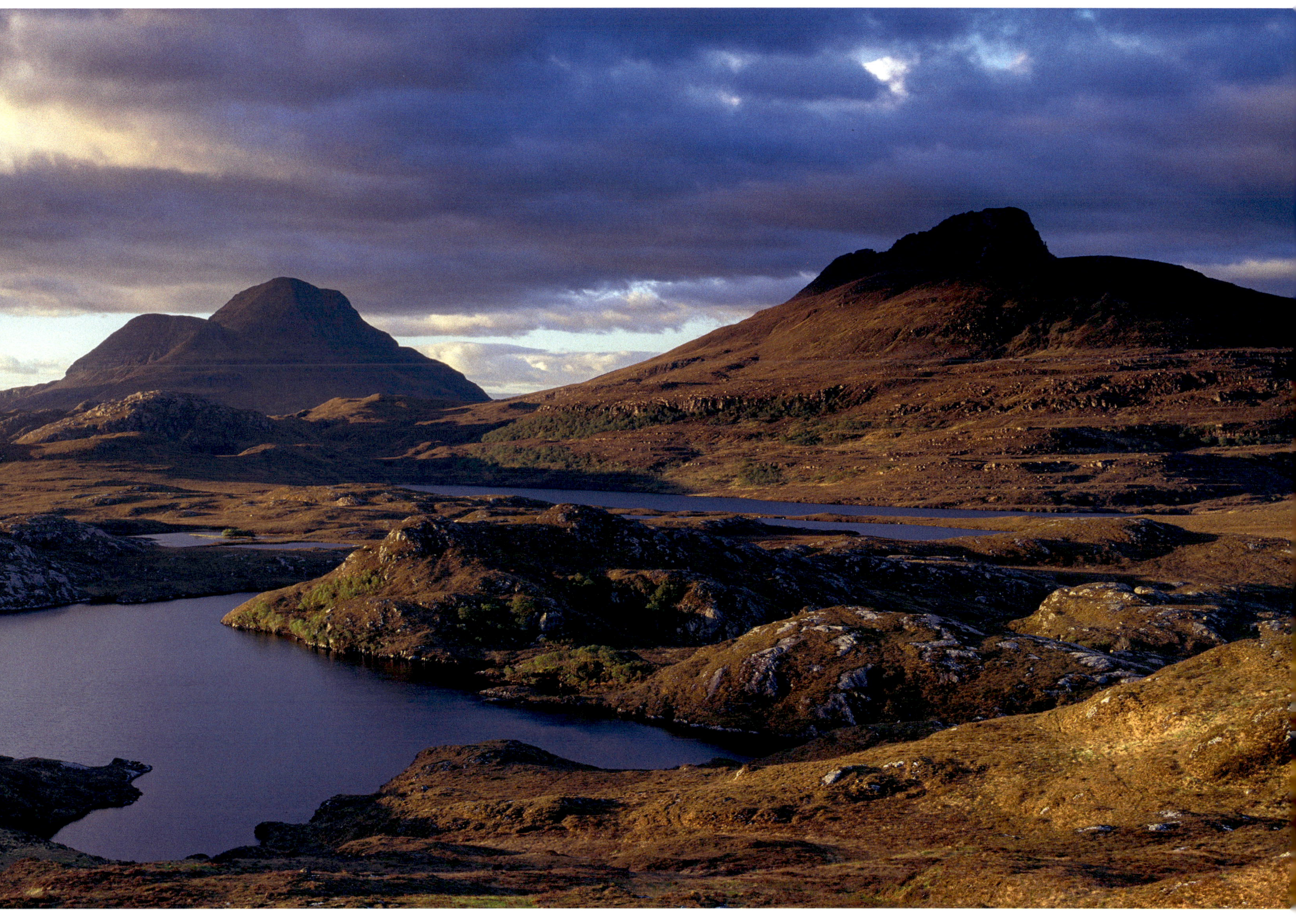

Beinn an Dòthaidh and Beinn Dòrain, Loch Tulla
January 2016

From the shores of Loch Tulla the last light of a perfect
winter's day ignites the trees and landscape around the
Bridge of Orchy. As it reached its peak I desperately
willed the wind to drop for long enough to settle the
water for an added reflection of Beinn an Dòthaidh
and Beinn Dòrain.

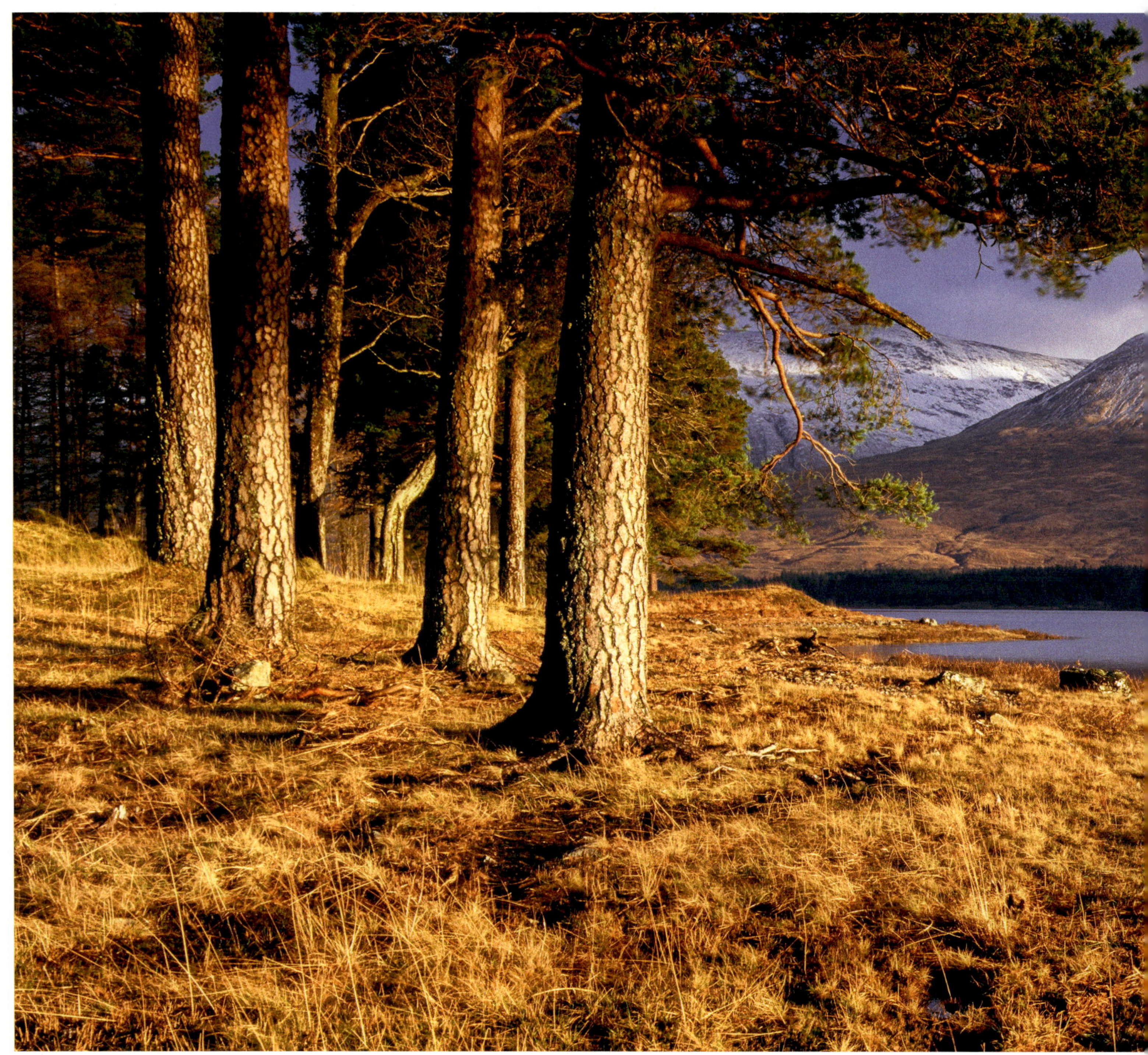

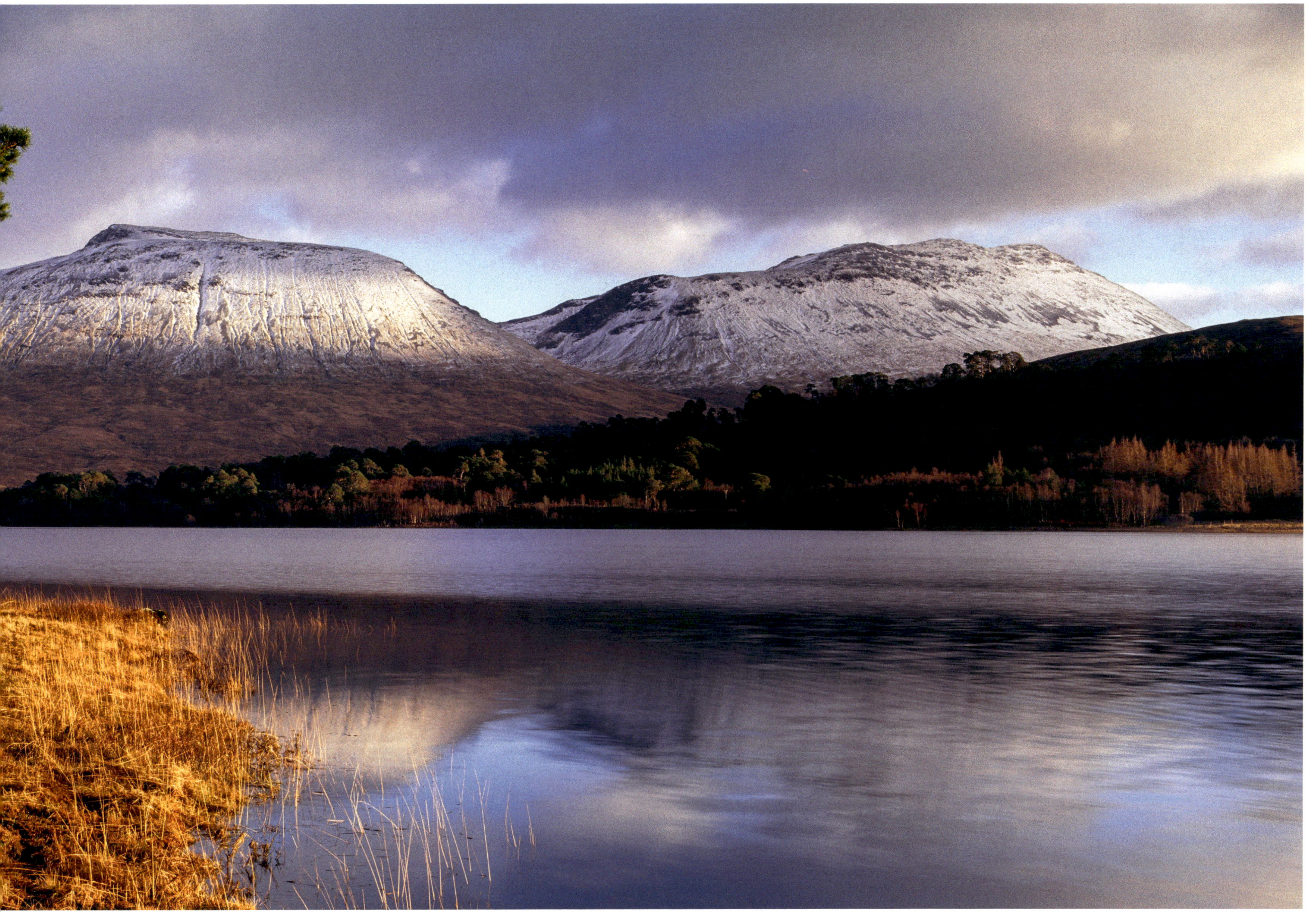

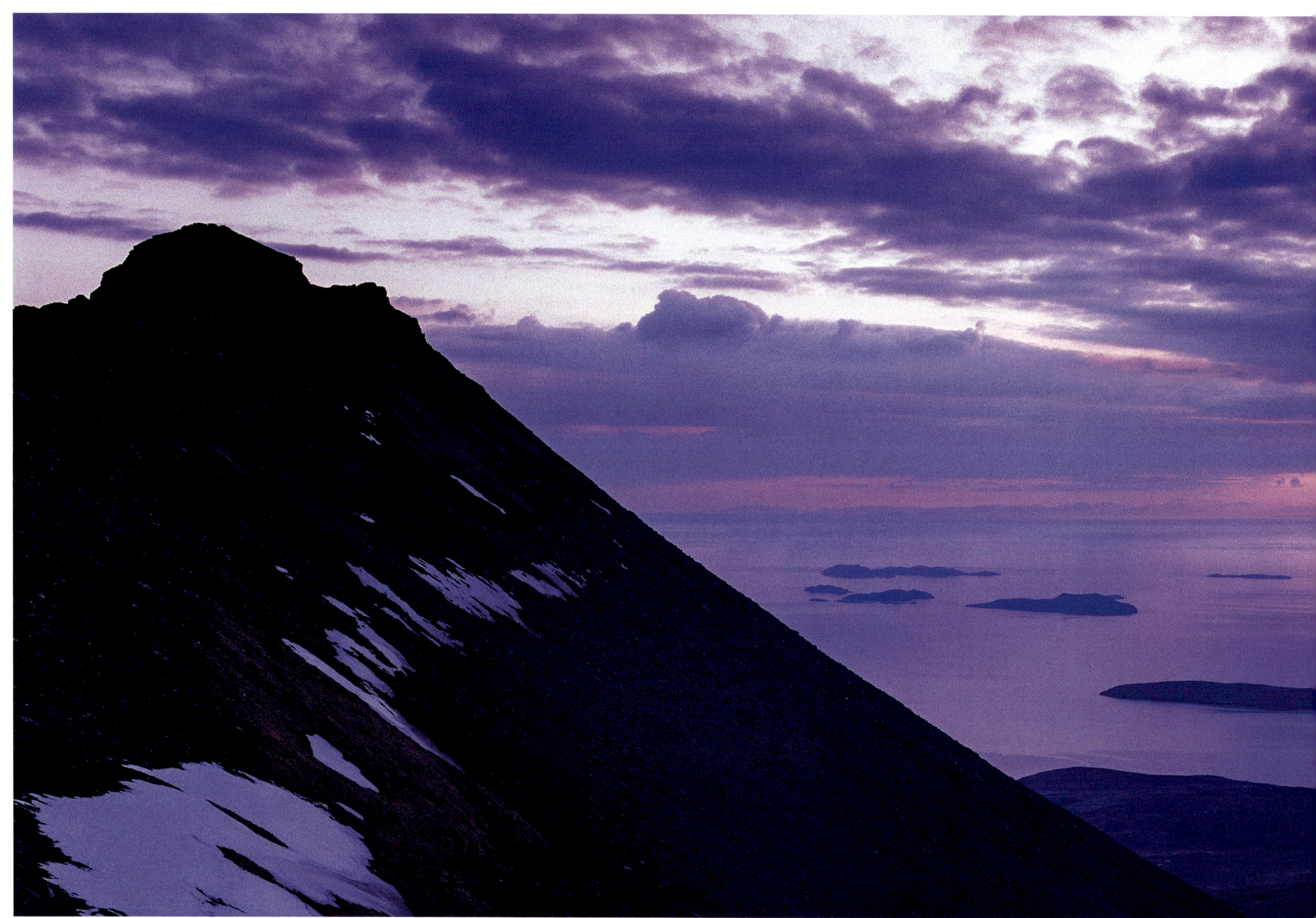

    WILD LIGHT

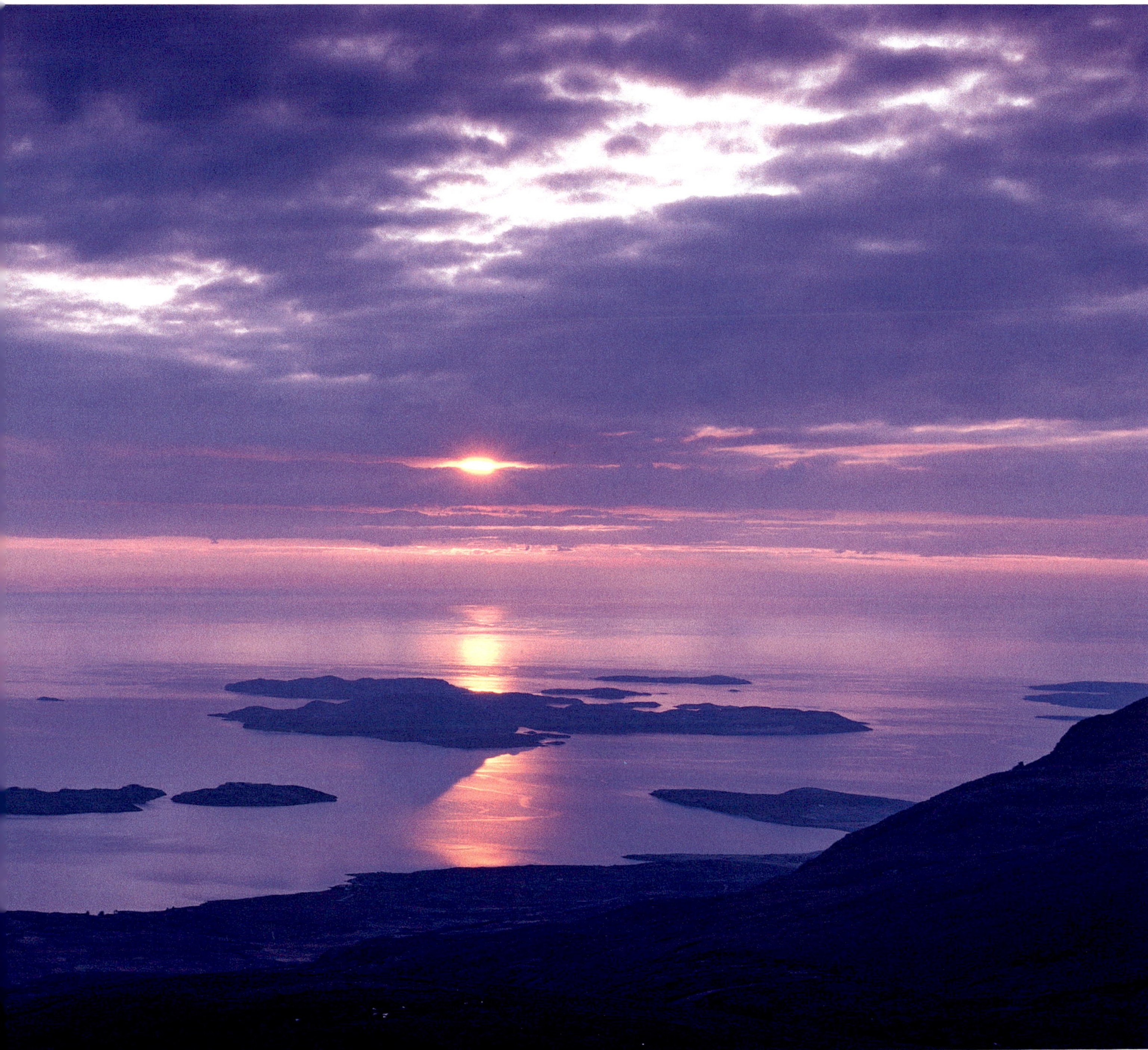

The Summer Isles, Coigach
April 2017

Photographed here from the summit of Ben More
Coigach, the Summer Isles is a compact group of
twenty or so islands and skerries spread over thirty
square miles. The largest, Tanera Mòr, is now officially
uninhabited. It is thought to be the inspiration for the
fictional pagan island of 'Summerisle' in the 1973
cult horror film *The Wicker Man*.

Torridon, Wester Ross
June 2017

Despite its imposing appearance, Beinn Alligin is actually a fairly straightforward prospect. Thanks to its natural horseshoe formation, the two principal summits can be easily gained in a single traverse that offers stunning views of the north-western seaboard and beyond to Wester Ross. Looking east from the summit of Sgùrr Mòr the warm evening light is in sharp contrast to the depth of shadow in the glen below, an indication of just how steep-sided and dramatic this landscape can be.

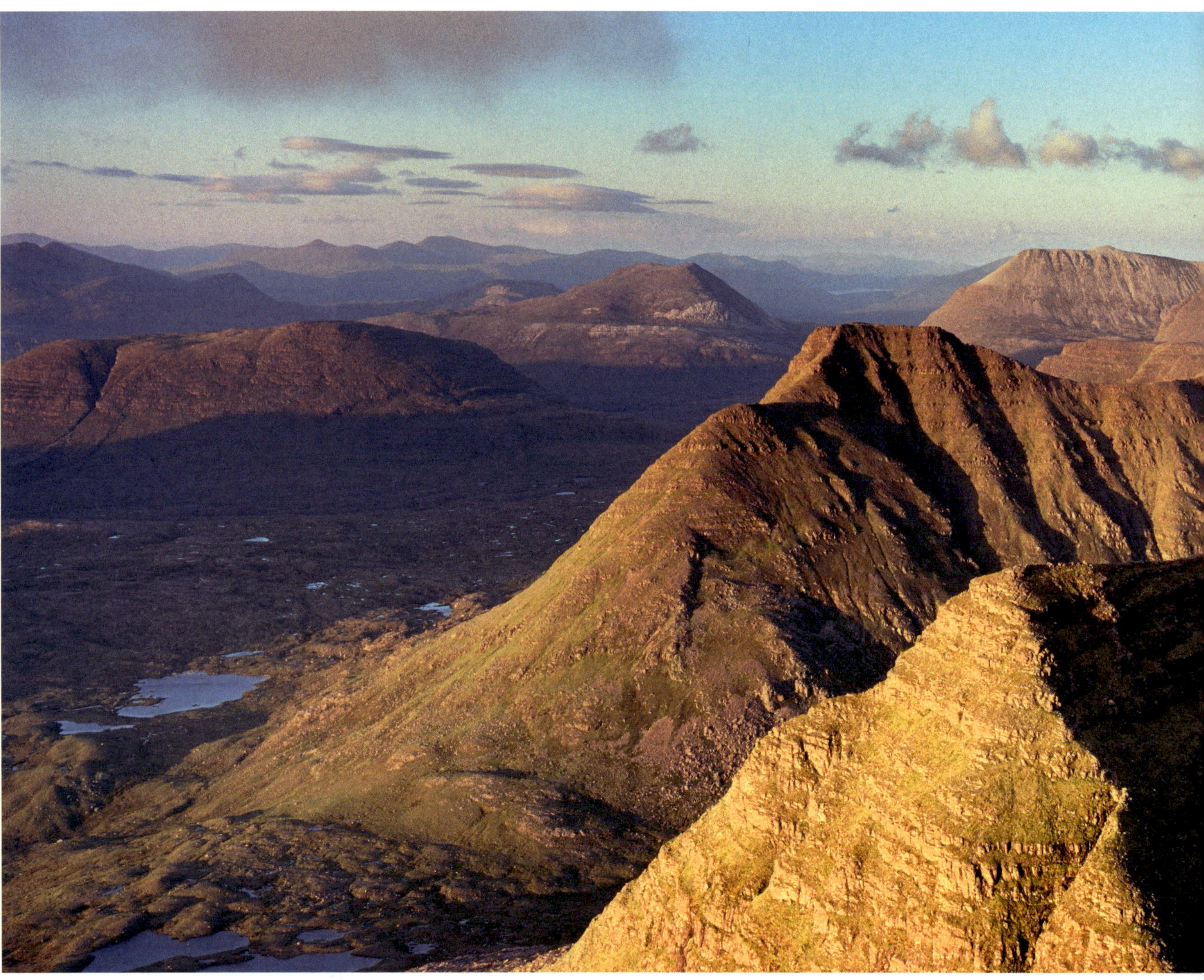

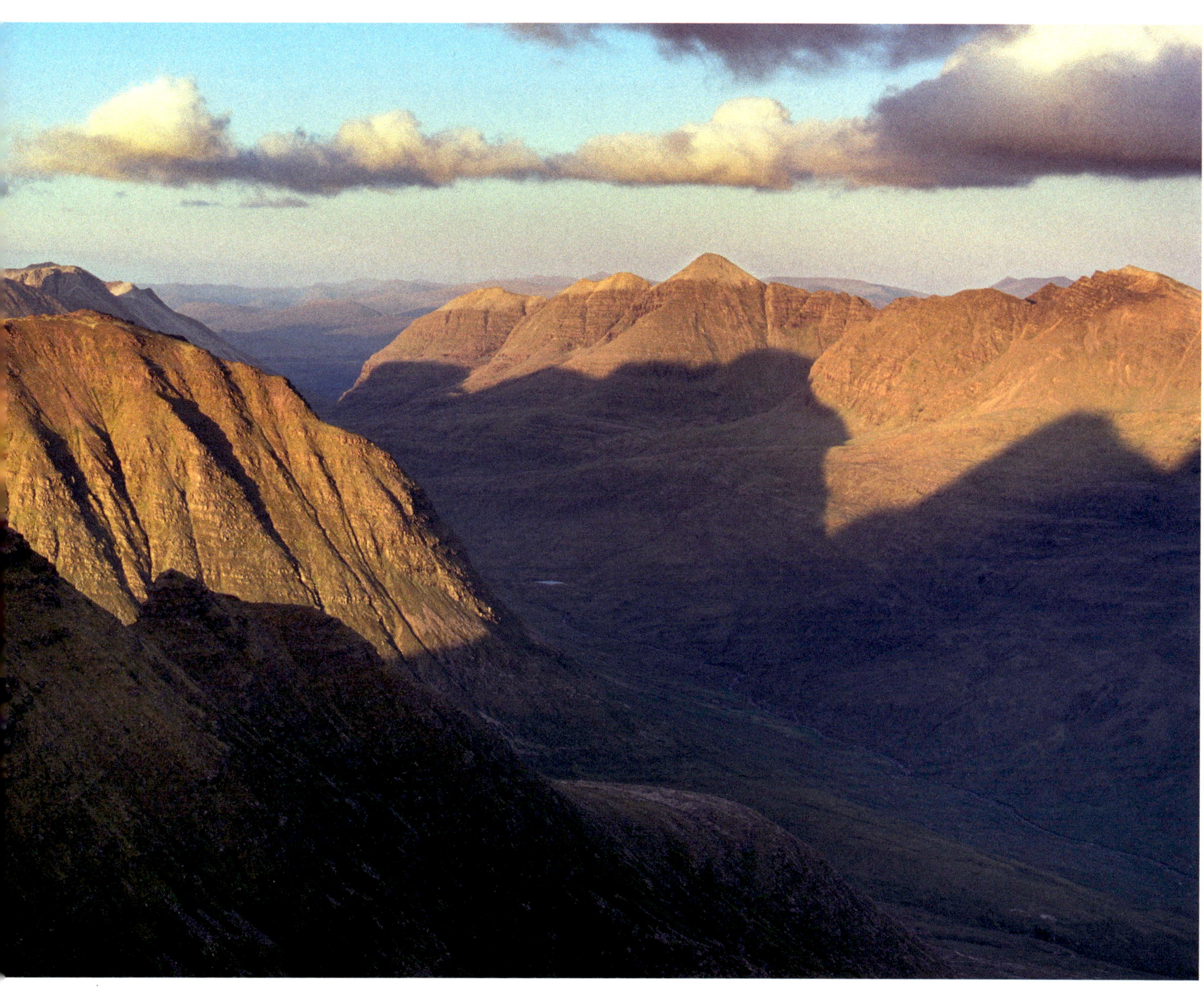

Following Page
Glen Luibeg, Braemar
December 2012

Thanks to their unique underlying geology,
the expansive tracts of the Cairngorms make for
a completely different environment to the vertical lines
and ridges so prevalent in the west. The deeply scoured
glens and rounded tops around Braemar are a classic
example of the profound effect that glacial erosion
has had on this granite landscape.

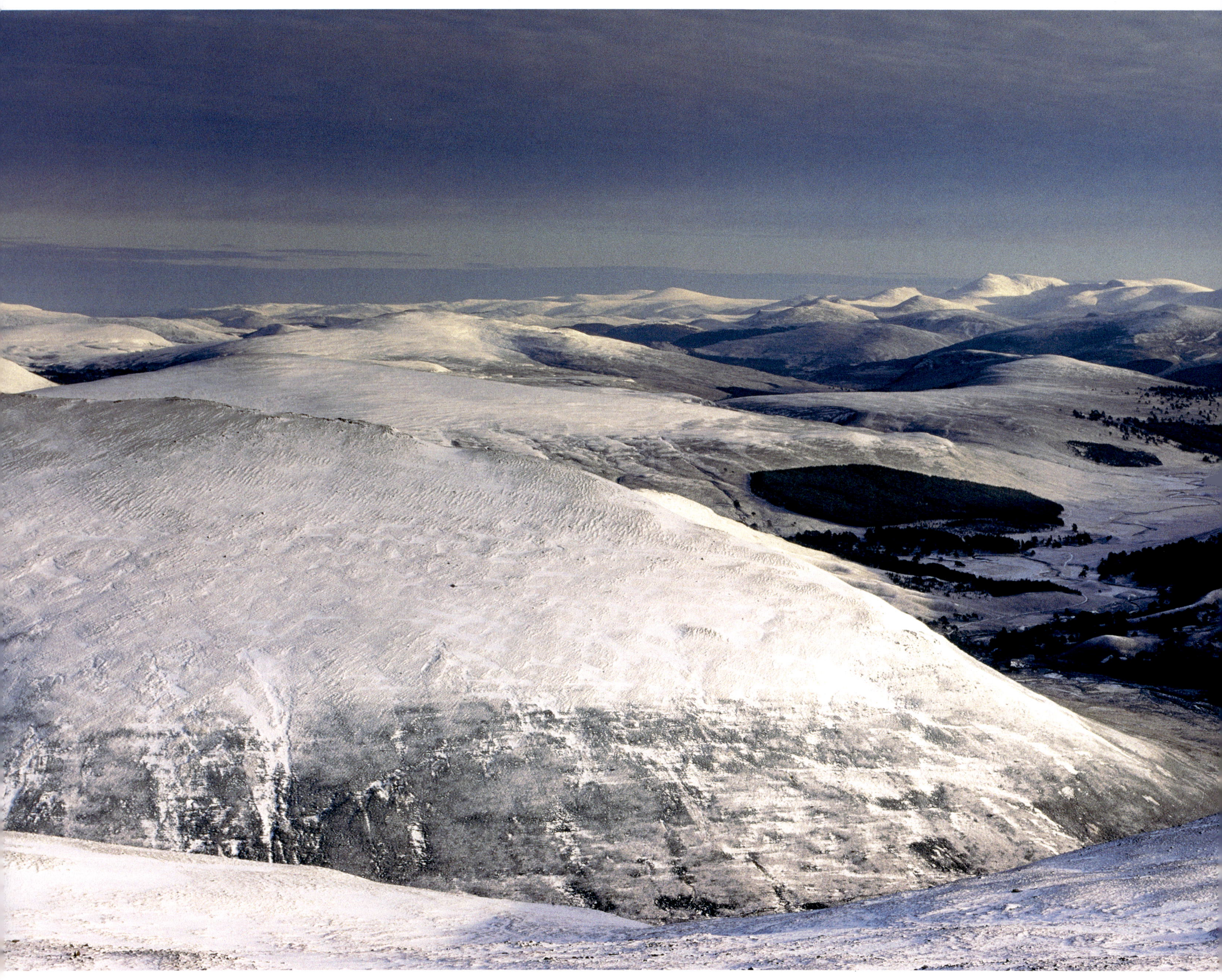

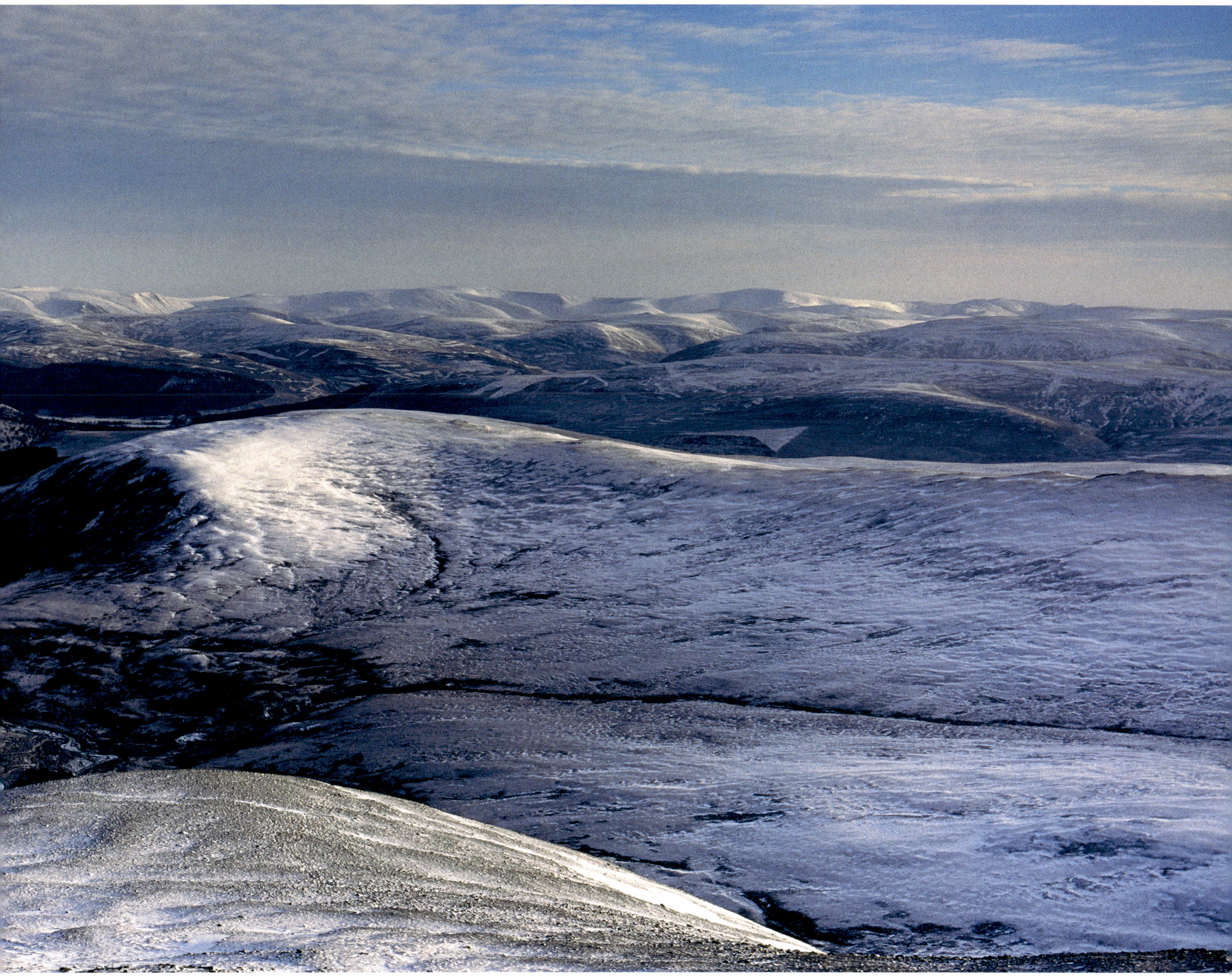

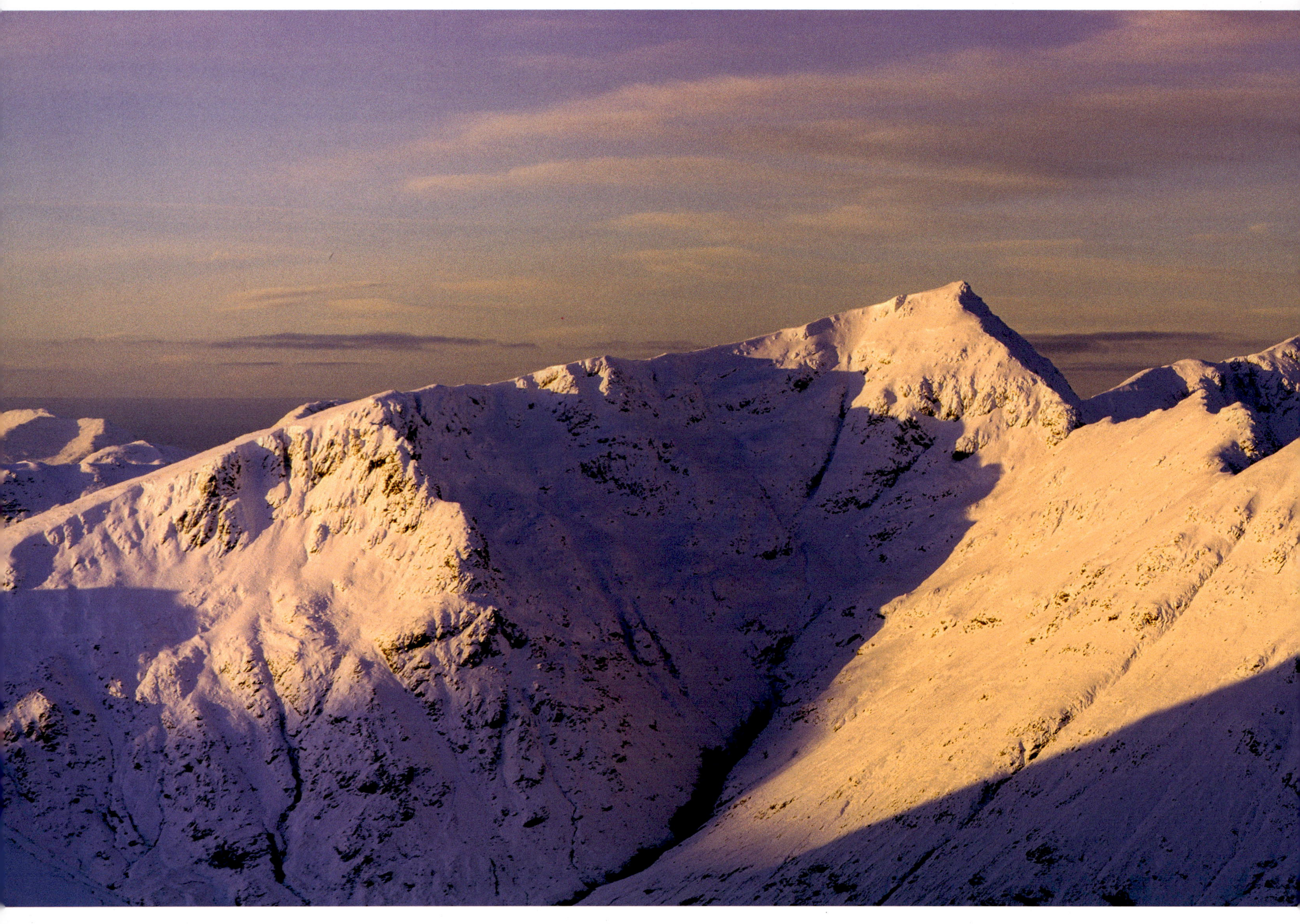

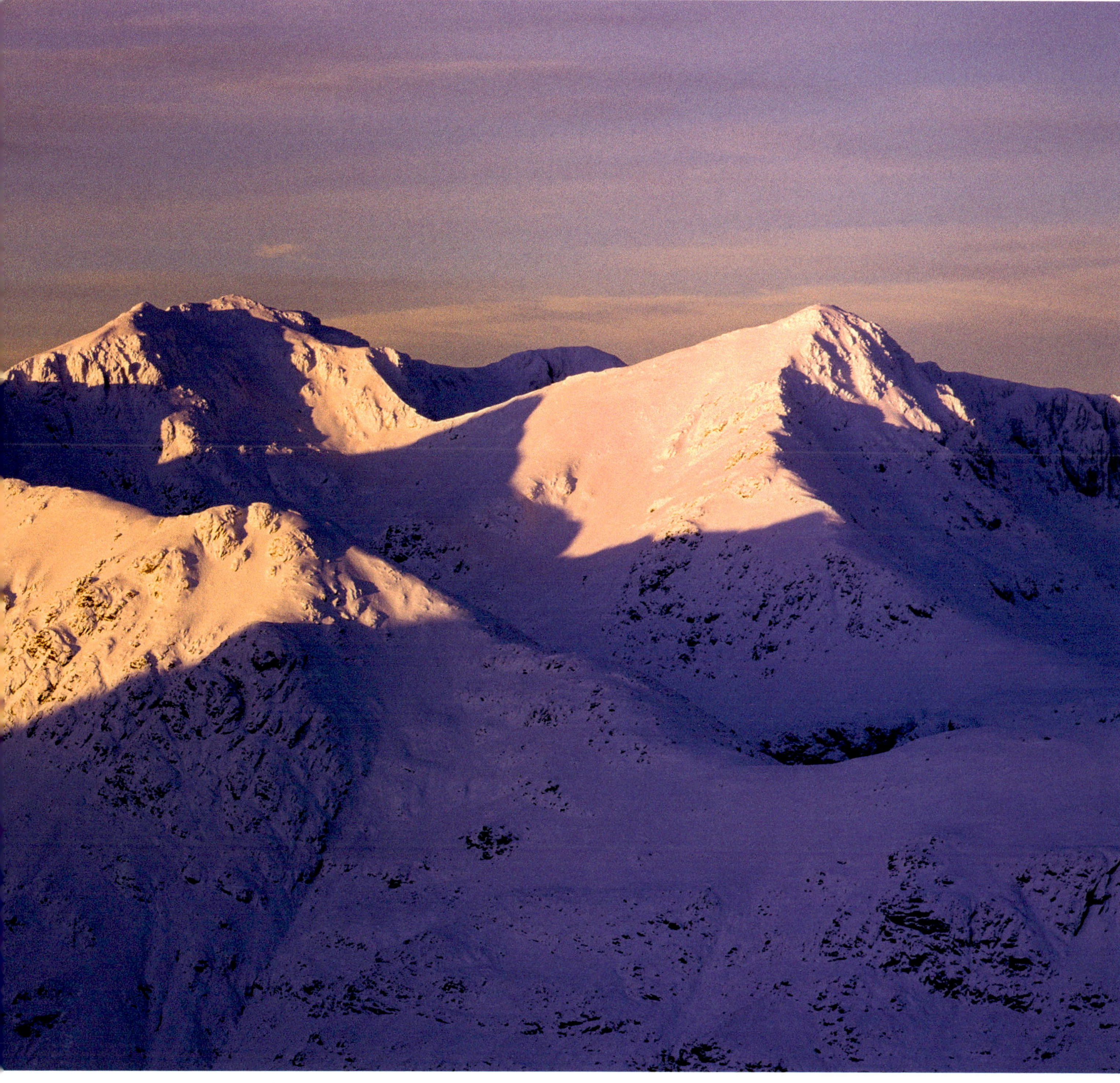

Bidean nam Bian, Glen Coe
January 2017

With stable weather firmly in charge, the midwinter sun rose clear into a beautiful morning sky. Fresh snowfall from the previous two days had rejuvenated the soaring mountains of Glen Coe, their steep riven flanks perfectly emphasised by the first light of dawn.

Stac Pollaidh, Inverpolly
May 2016

Although not eminent in height compared to the
other peaks of Coigach and Assynt, Stac Pollaidh
is still a favourite for many. Its characteristic profile is
indicative of the mountains in the North West Highlands,
thanks to the unique geology of weathered Torridonian
sandstone upon a bed of ancient Lewisian gneiss.

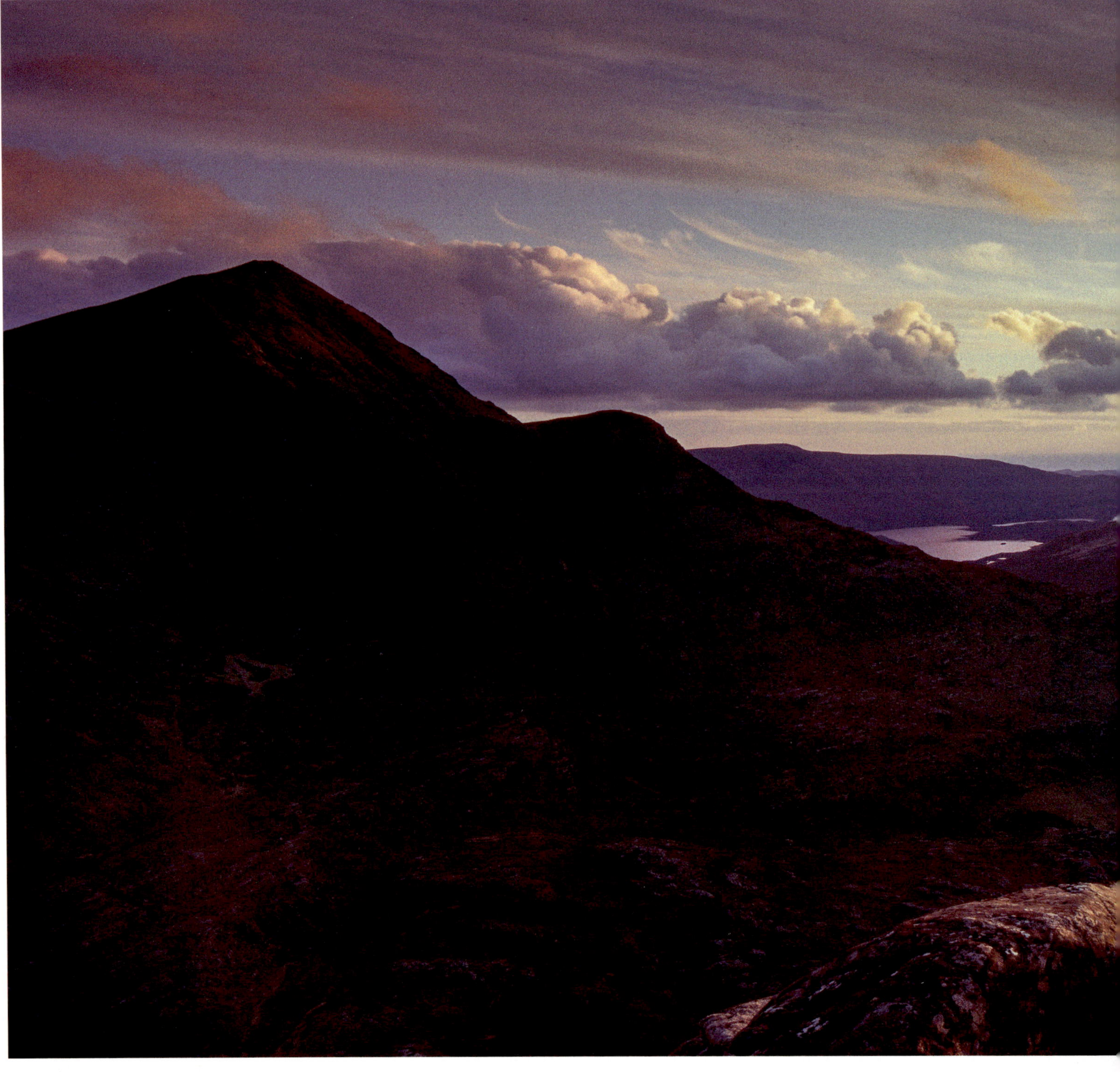

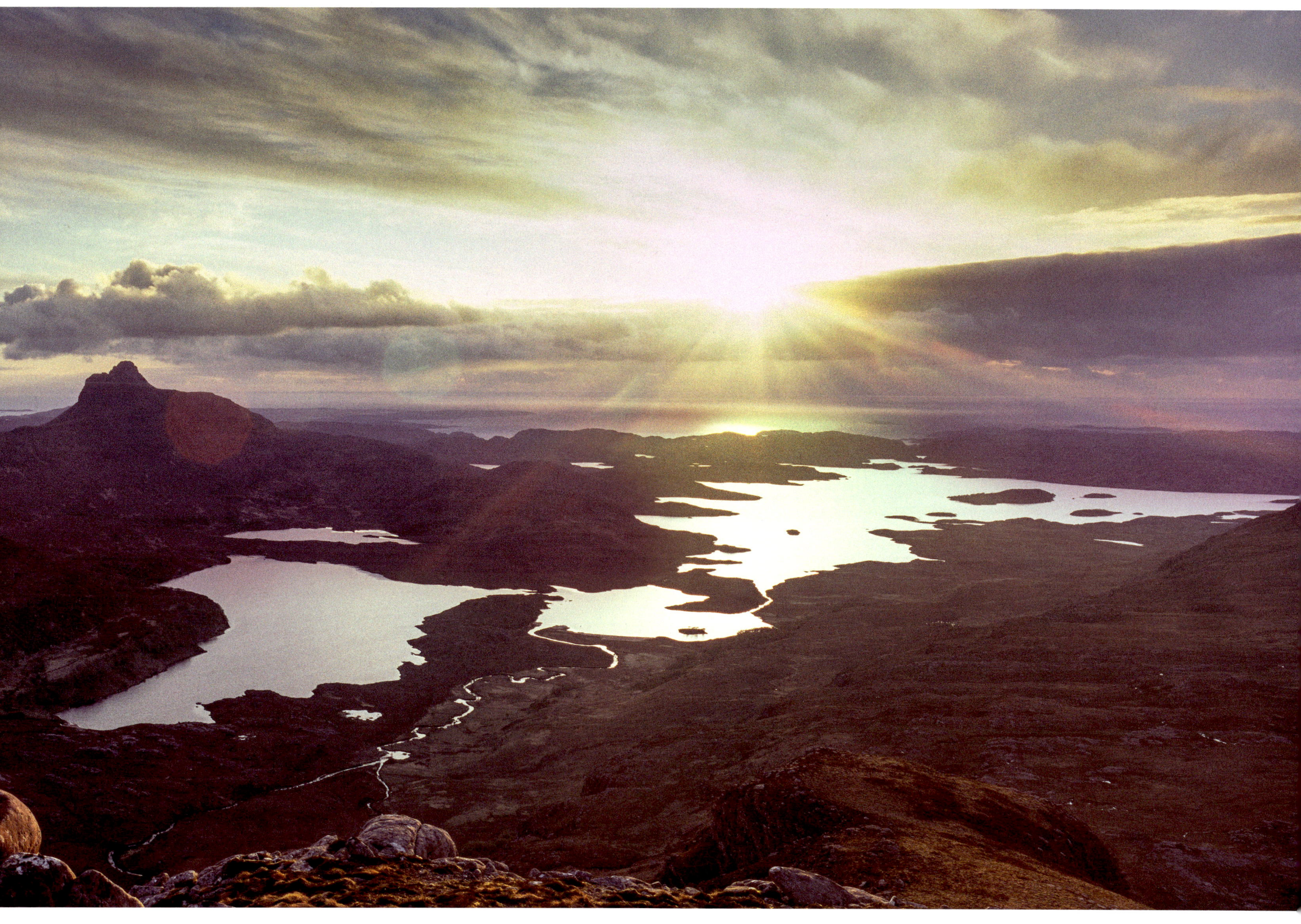

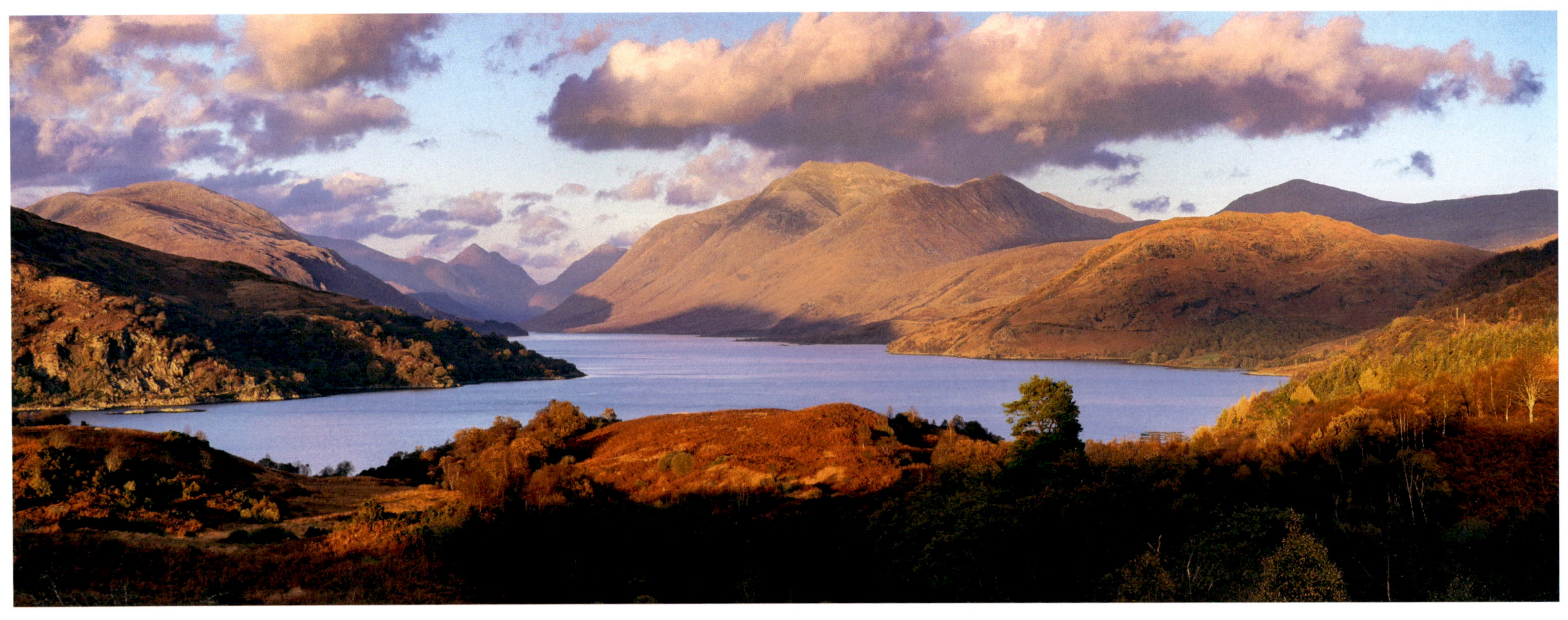

Loch Etive, Argyll and Bute
October 2014

Loch Etive is a place I enjoy returning to throughout the year. Since discovering this viewpoint many years ago I had wanted to shoot an image as the autumn colours reached their peak. On the last day of October the forecast looked promising and I headed off once again to this familiar patch. With excellent visibility and light winds, I waited until the sun was low in the sky before making the exposure.

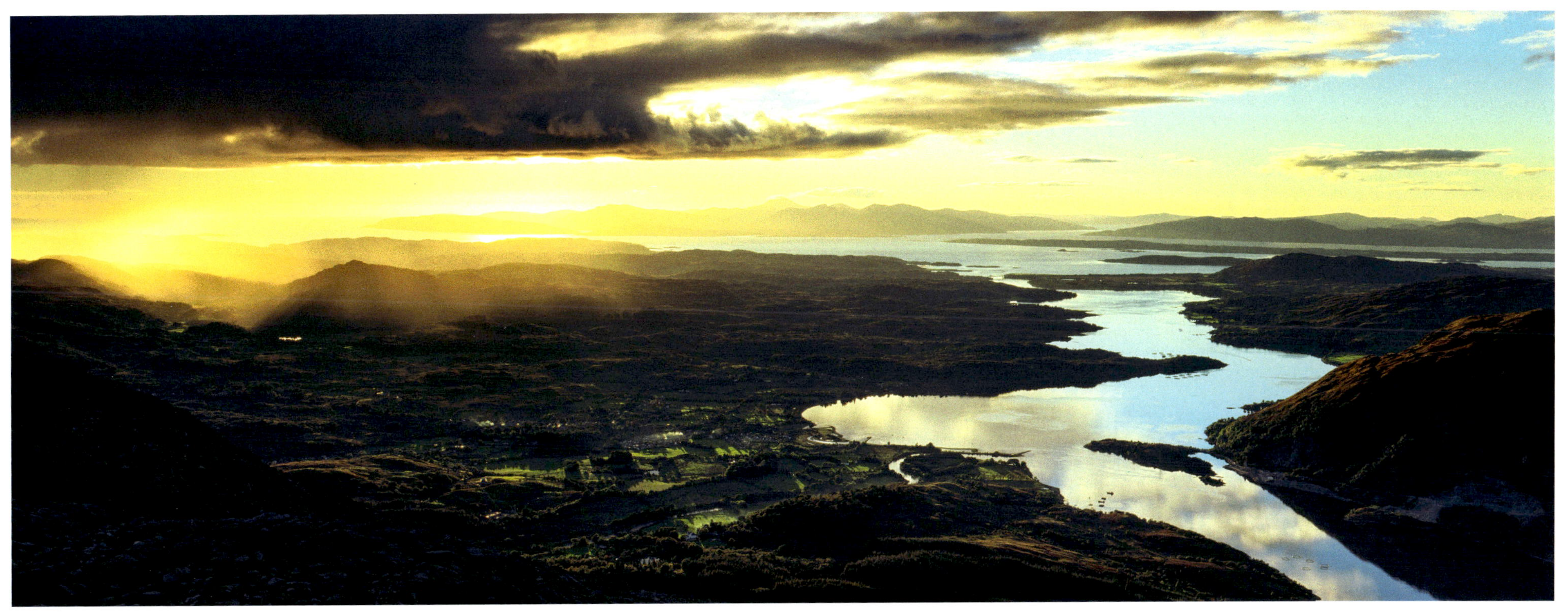

Loch Etive, Argyll and Bute
October 2016

High above the still waters of Loch Etive I was relieved
to see this mass of cloud pass just to the north of
my location. As it slowly tracked its way across the
landscape I watched mesmerised while it unleashed
a flood of biblical proportions in a deluge that was
beautifully backlit by the setting sun.

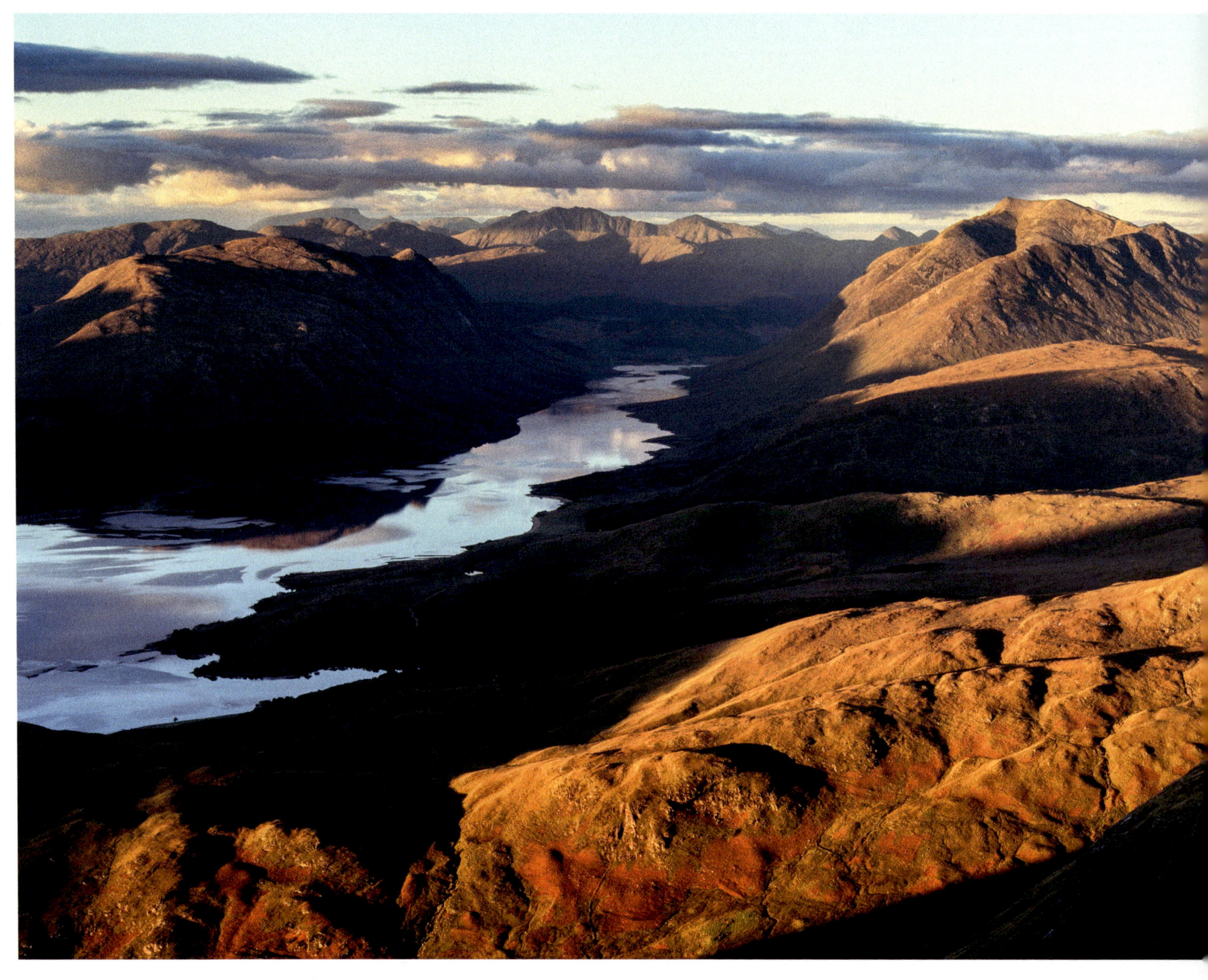

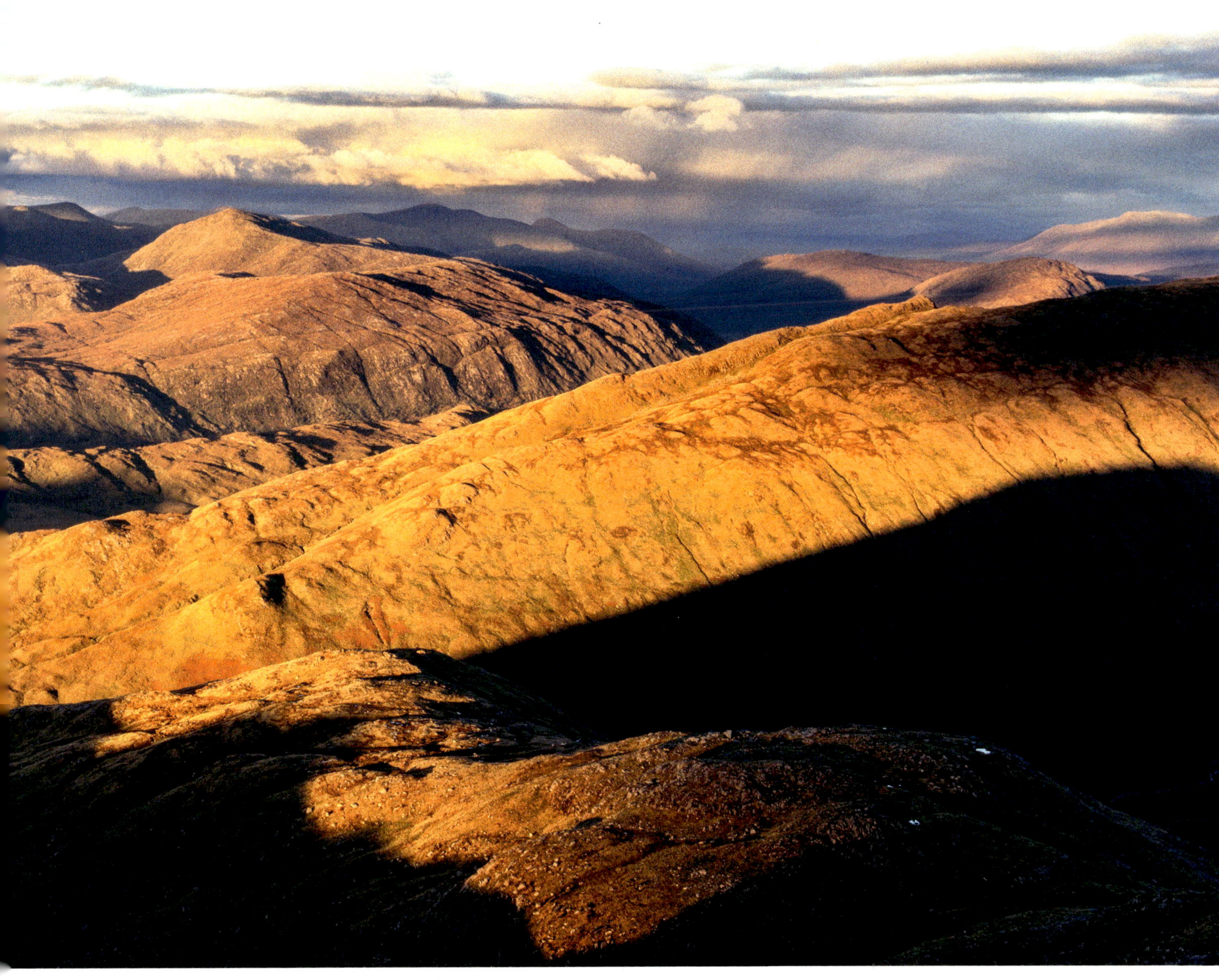

Lorn, West Highlands
October 2016

High above Glen Noe the last of the autumn light catches the tops of Ben Starav and the surrounding mountains of Glen Coe. The visibility was so good I could clearly make out the distinctive whaleback profile of Britain's highest mountain, Ben Nevis, from a distance of twenty-six miles away.

The Cobbler, Arrochar
February 2017

The delicate pink 'Belt of Venus' appears shortly
before sunrise. Also known as the anti-twilight arch,
this phenomenon separates the earth's shadow from the
approaching sunlight of dawn. The effect is most visible
low on the western horizon and particularly around the
antisolar point – the part of the sky directly opposite the
sun. I wanted to time this event with a full moon setting
over the distinctive profile of The Cobbler, a conjunction
which happens only a couple of times a year.

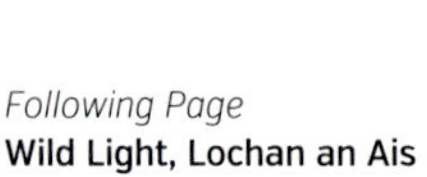

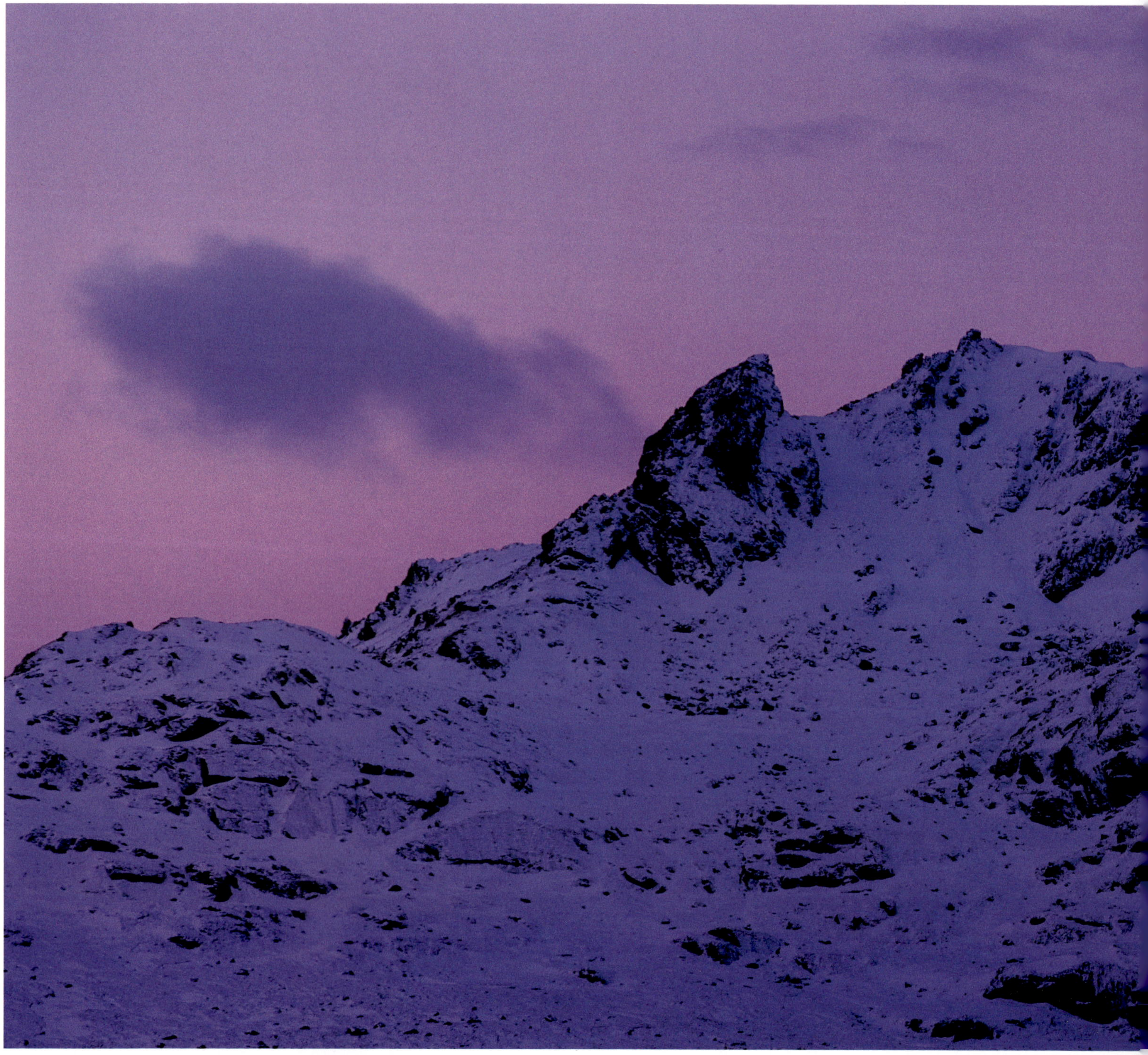

Following Page
Wild Light, Lochan an Ais
May 2016

From the thinnest slither of clear sky comes the most
intense burst of light imaginable. These wonderful
moments are rare in the landscape and I had to
concentrate hard in order to capture the event.
Fortunately, I had some film preloaded which spared
enough time for me to set up and capture the dying
light of the setting sun. As the rain poured down I could
think of no better conditions to show the unmistakable
profile of these unique mountains of the North West.

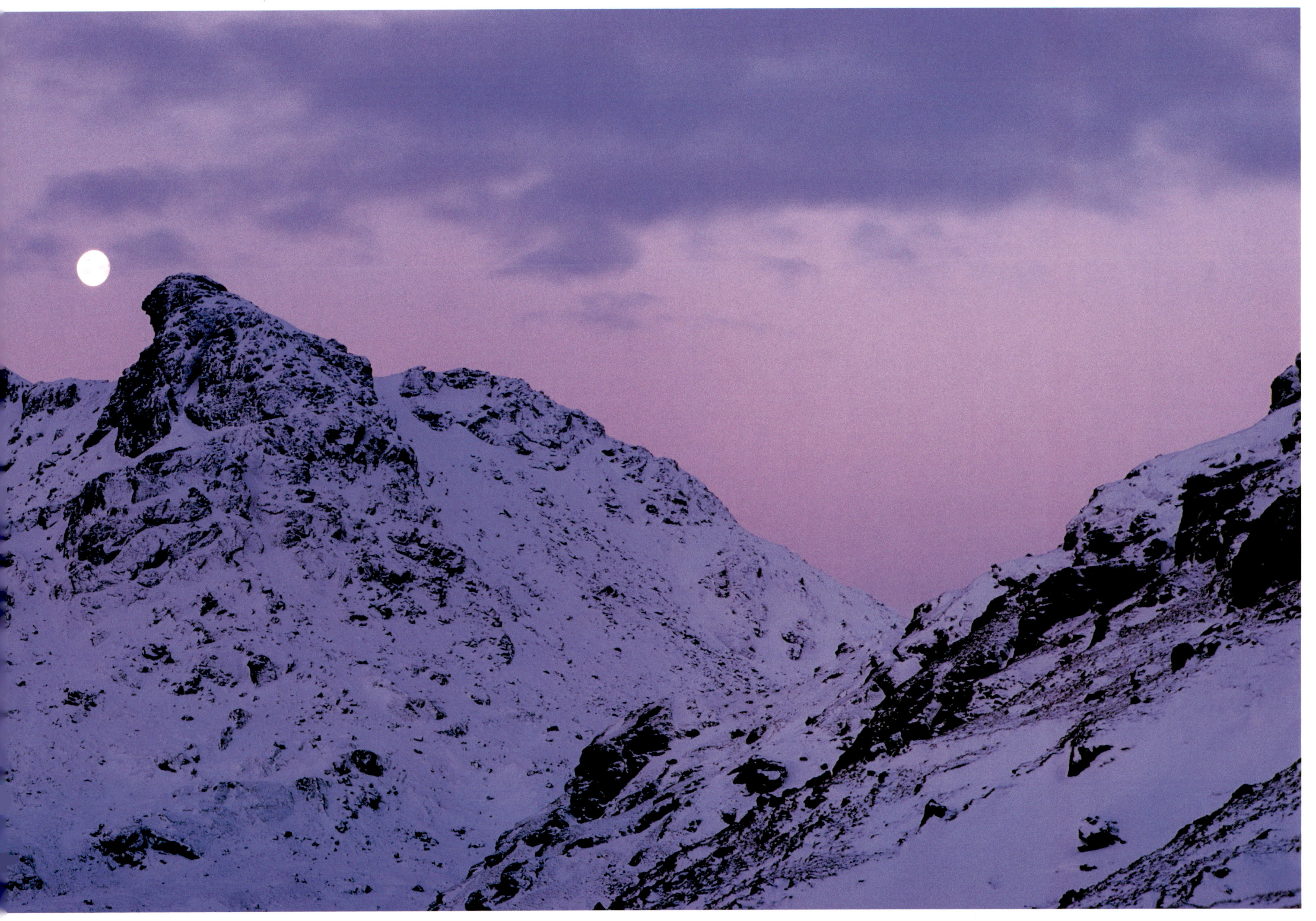

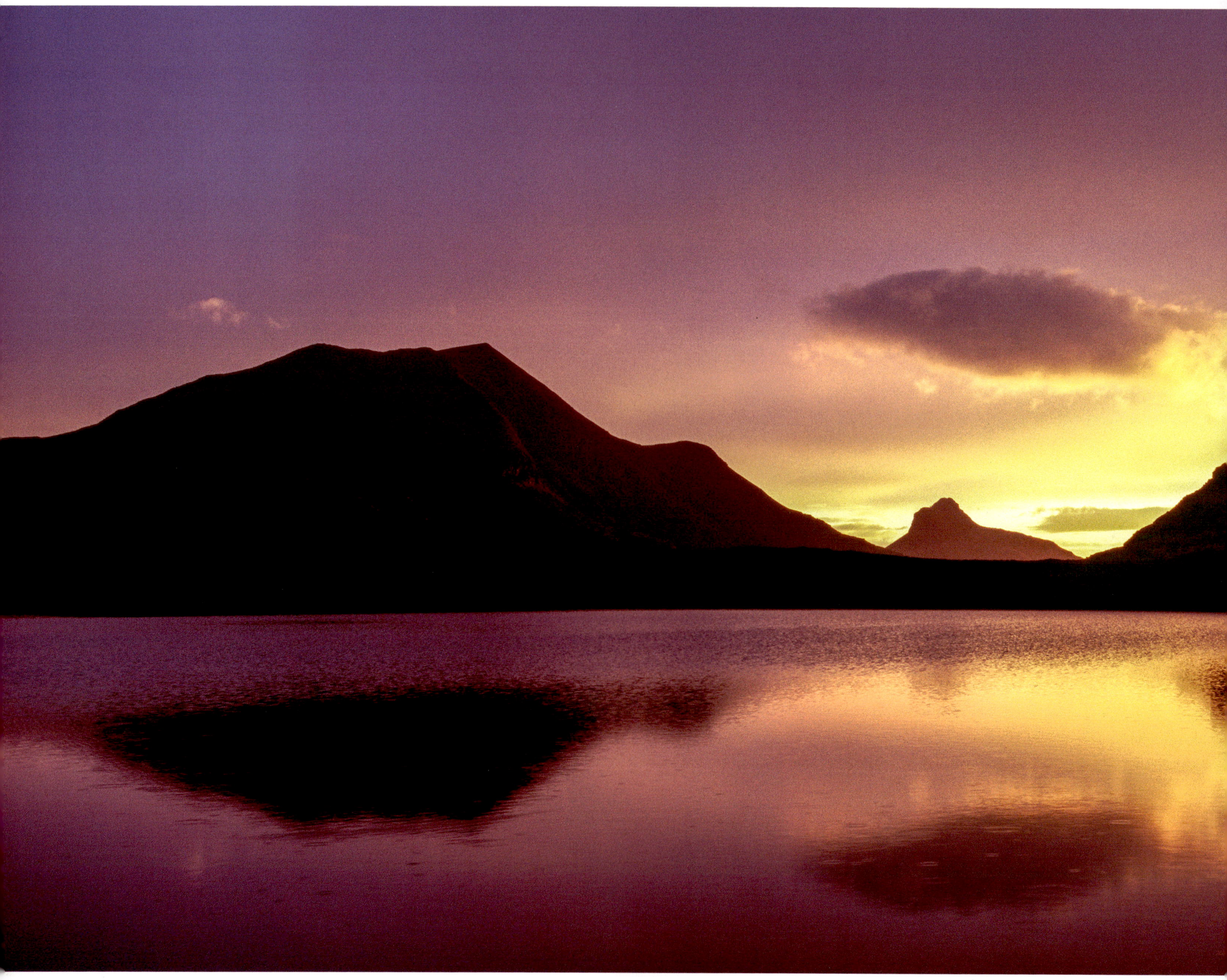

     WILD LIGHT

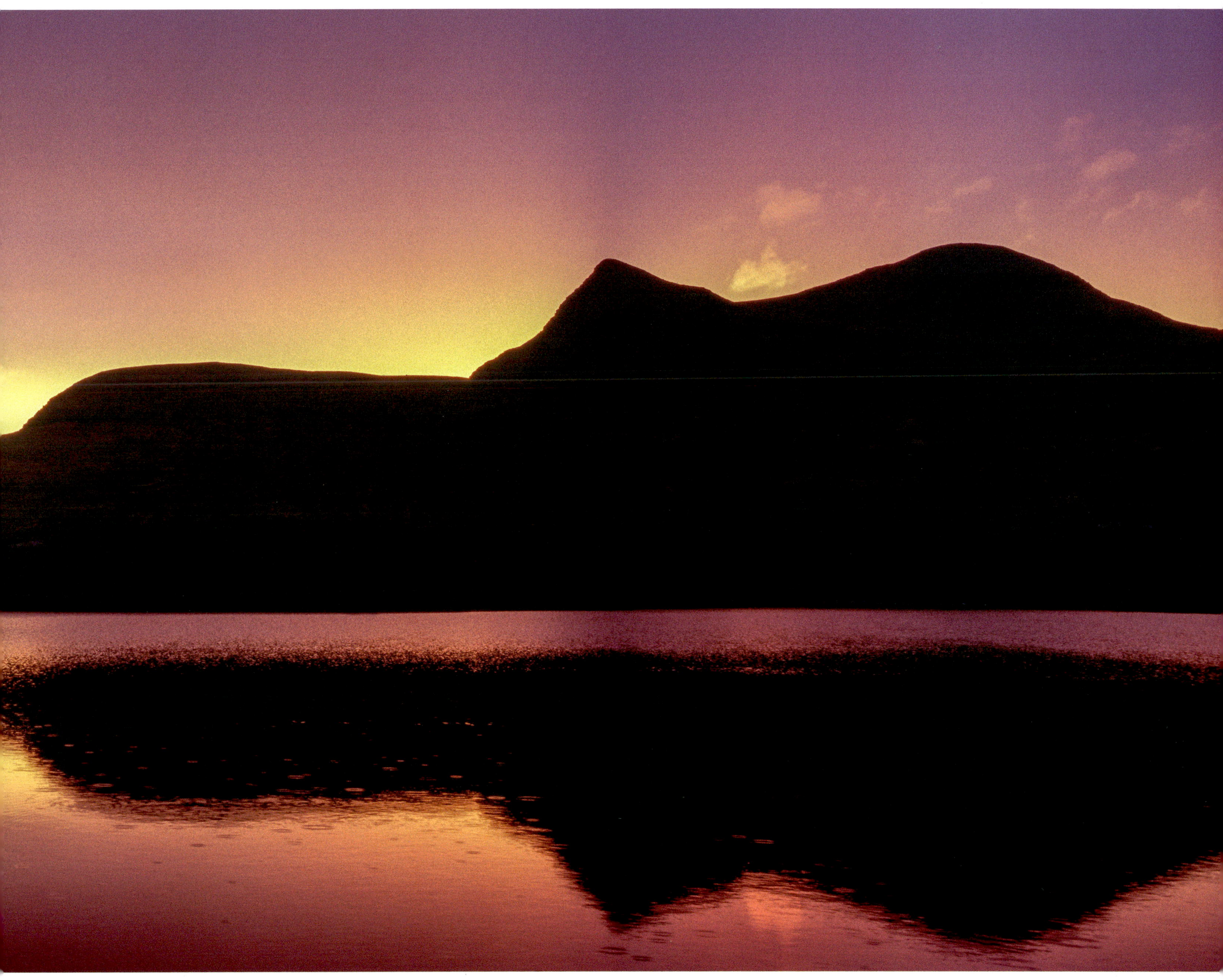

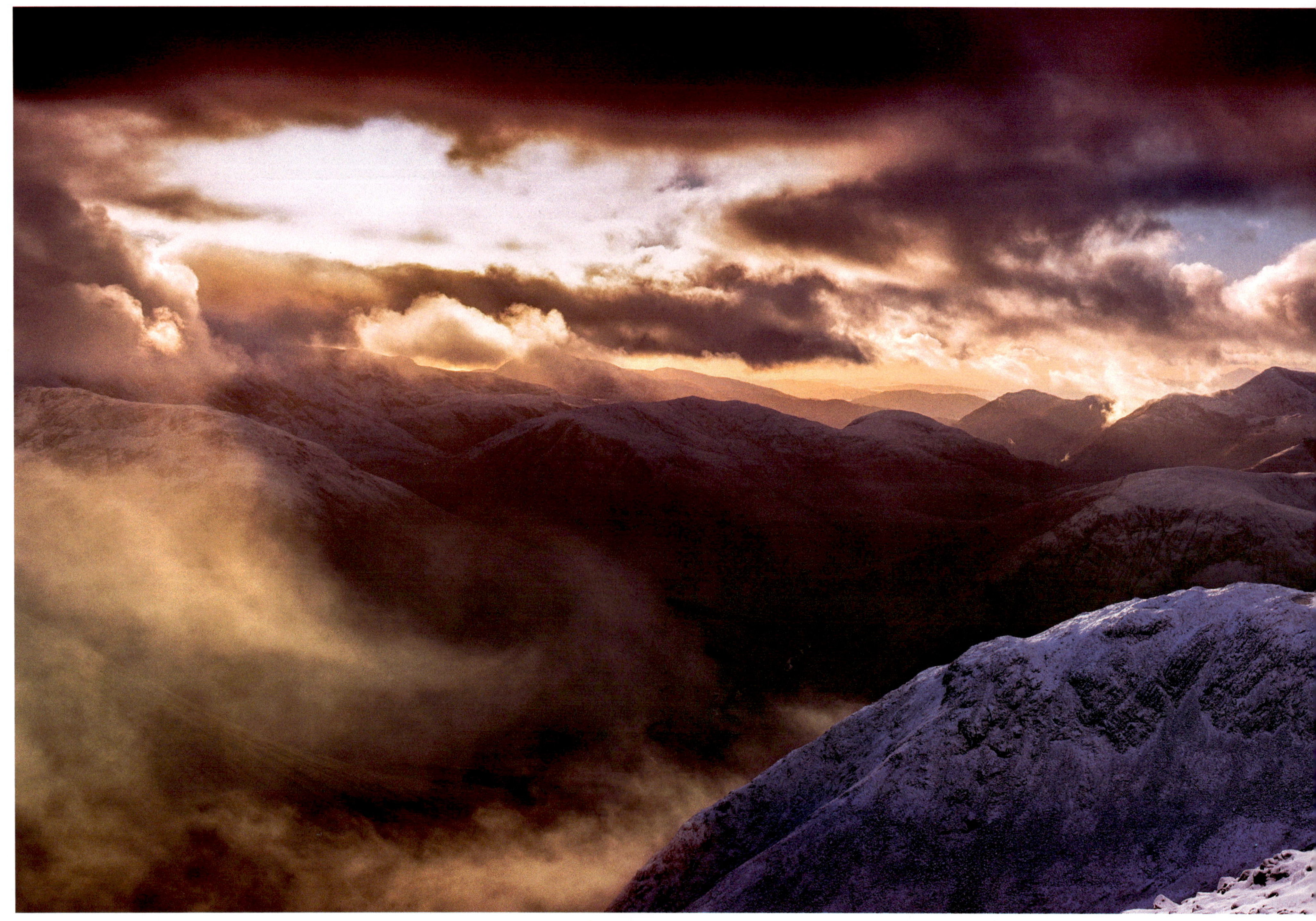

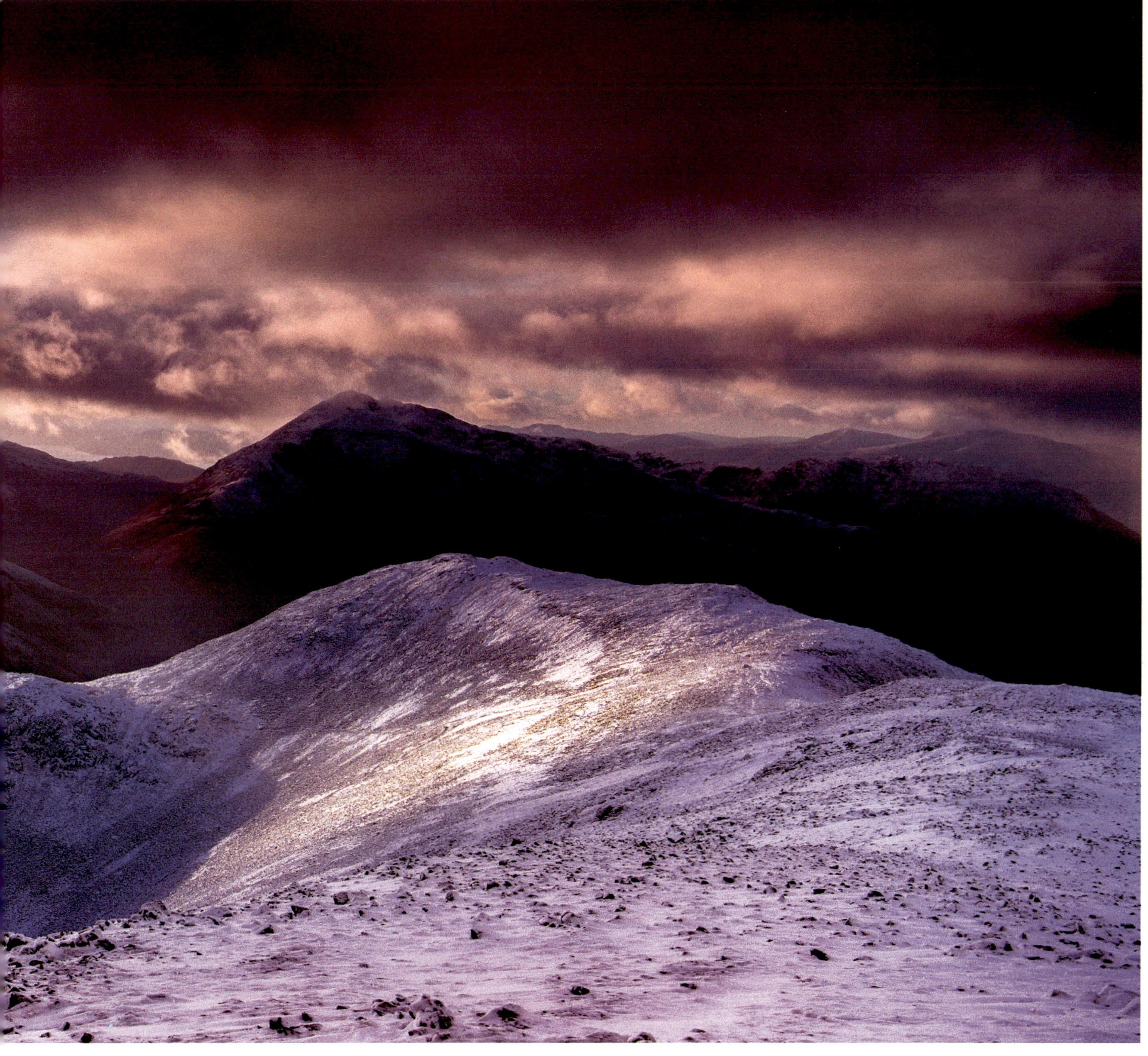

Clearing Storm, Glen Coe
December 2017

On the summit of Sgorr nam Fiannaidh the sky was busy with snow-bearing clouds being pushed along on a strong northerly wind: as one front departed another would soon approach. In between, momentary 'windows' where the light could penetrate allowed for the possibility of some real magic to happen on the mountains of Glen Coe. I watched intently in the freezing wind, waiting for the right balance between light and shade. Things were happening quickly and I managed just two frames before this moment passed and I was, once again, engulfed in cloud.

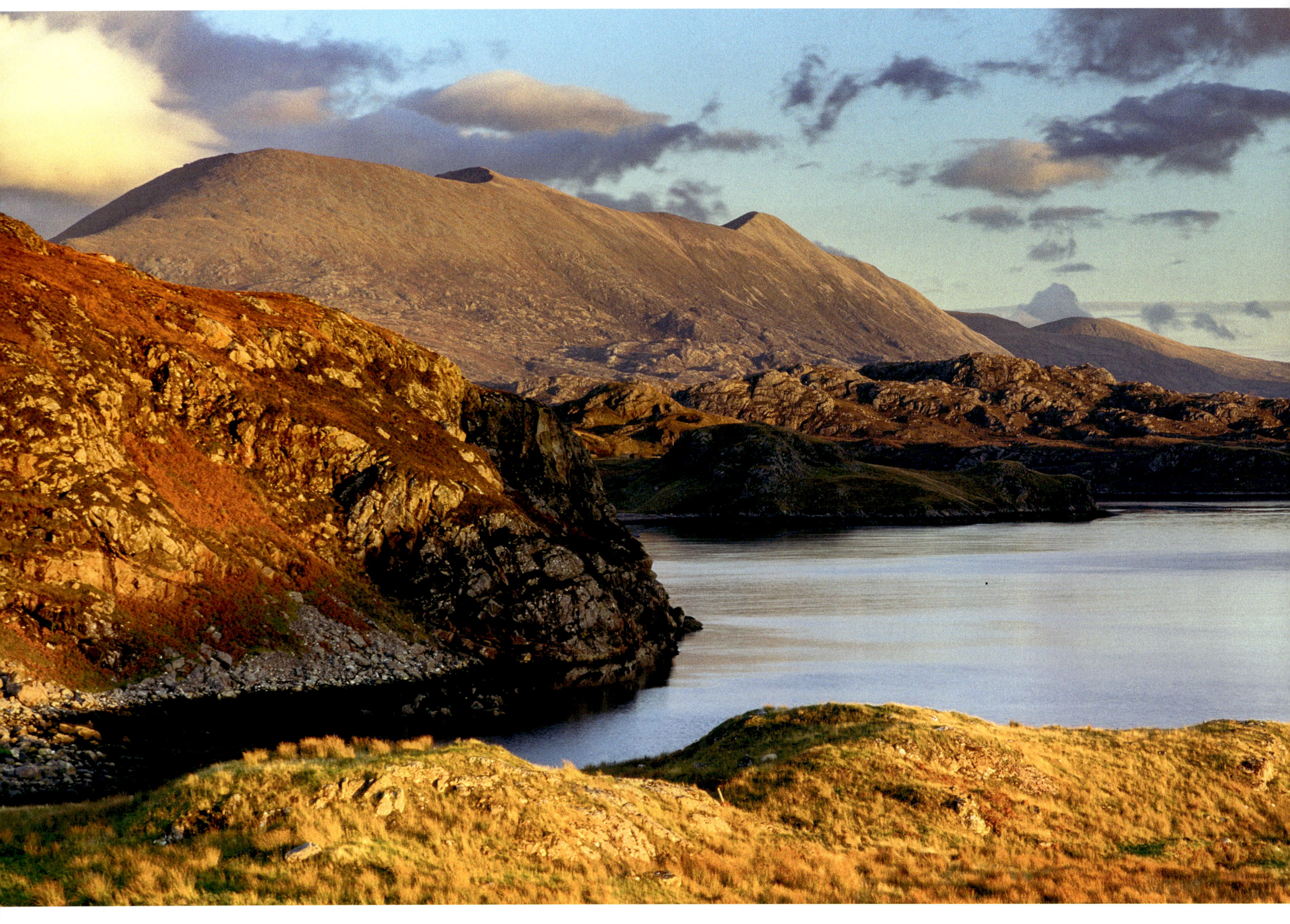

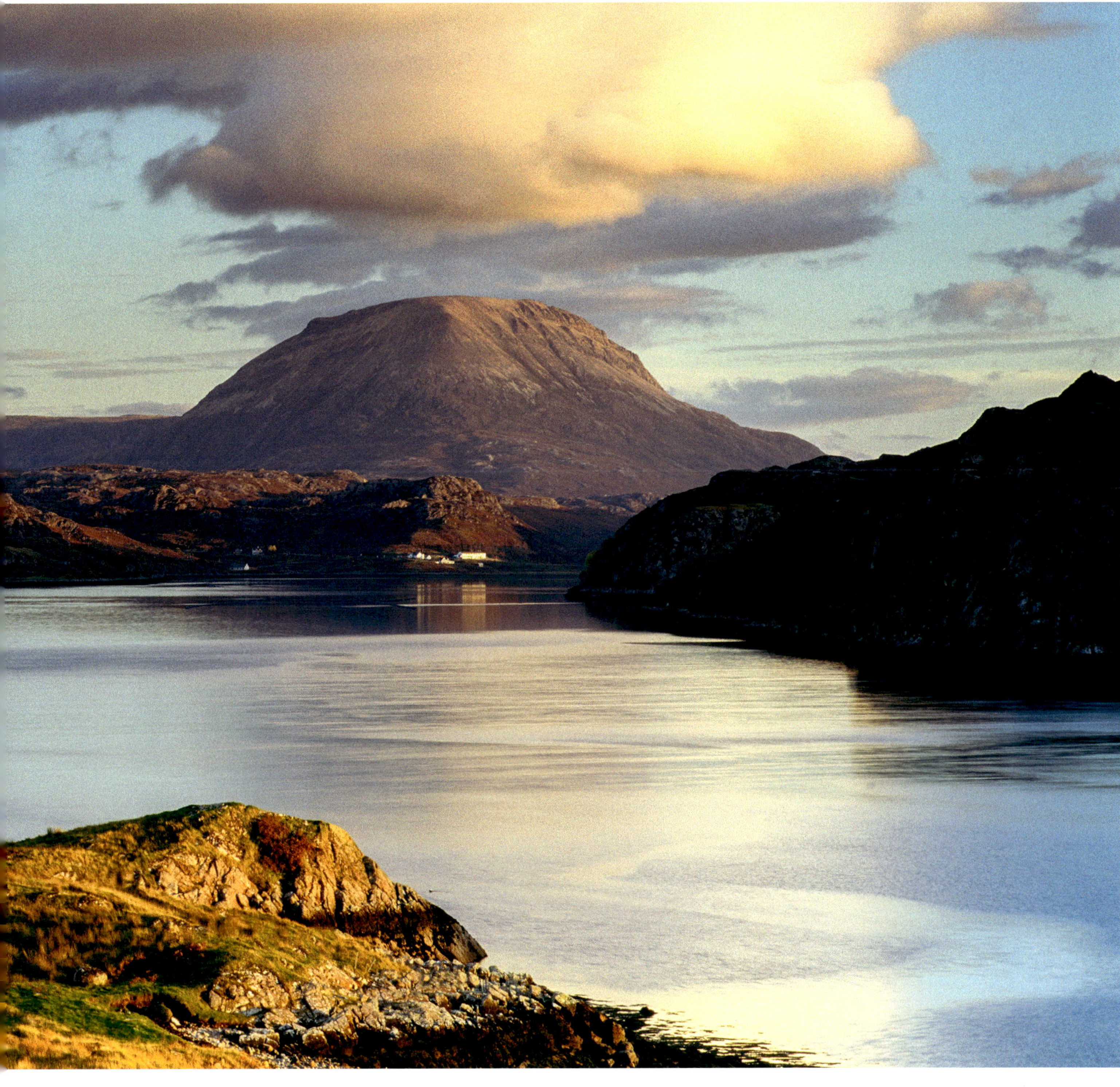

Foinaven and Arkle, Loch Inchard
October 2012

Loch Inchard is the most northerly sea loch on Scotland's west coast. Its narrow course curves for over four miles inland from the fishing port of Kinlochbervie through rugged countryside to its head at Rhiconich. Here the skyline is dominated by Foinaven and Arkle, two wonderful mountains of the north that are notoriously difficult to photograph.

North Wood, Perthshire
May 2016

The ancient woodland around Kinclaven is predominantly
mature oak with a mix of birch, Scots pine, and huge
veteran beech trees, some of which date back to the
eighteenth century. Together they form an important
natural habitat for many species of flora and fauna,
but it is the native Scottish bluebell that briefly reigns
supreme, their distinctive colour and scent usually
peaking around mid-May.

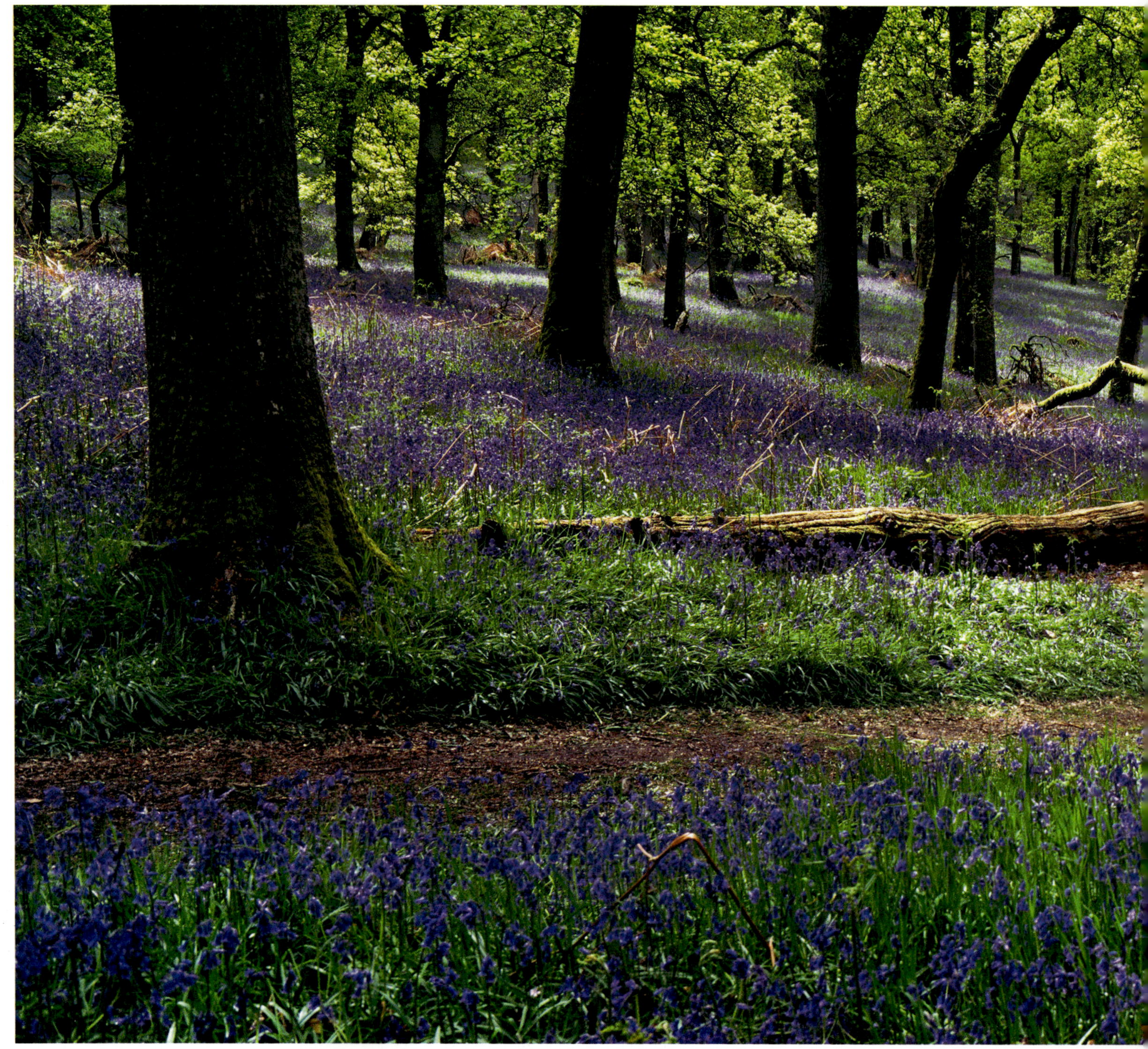

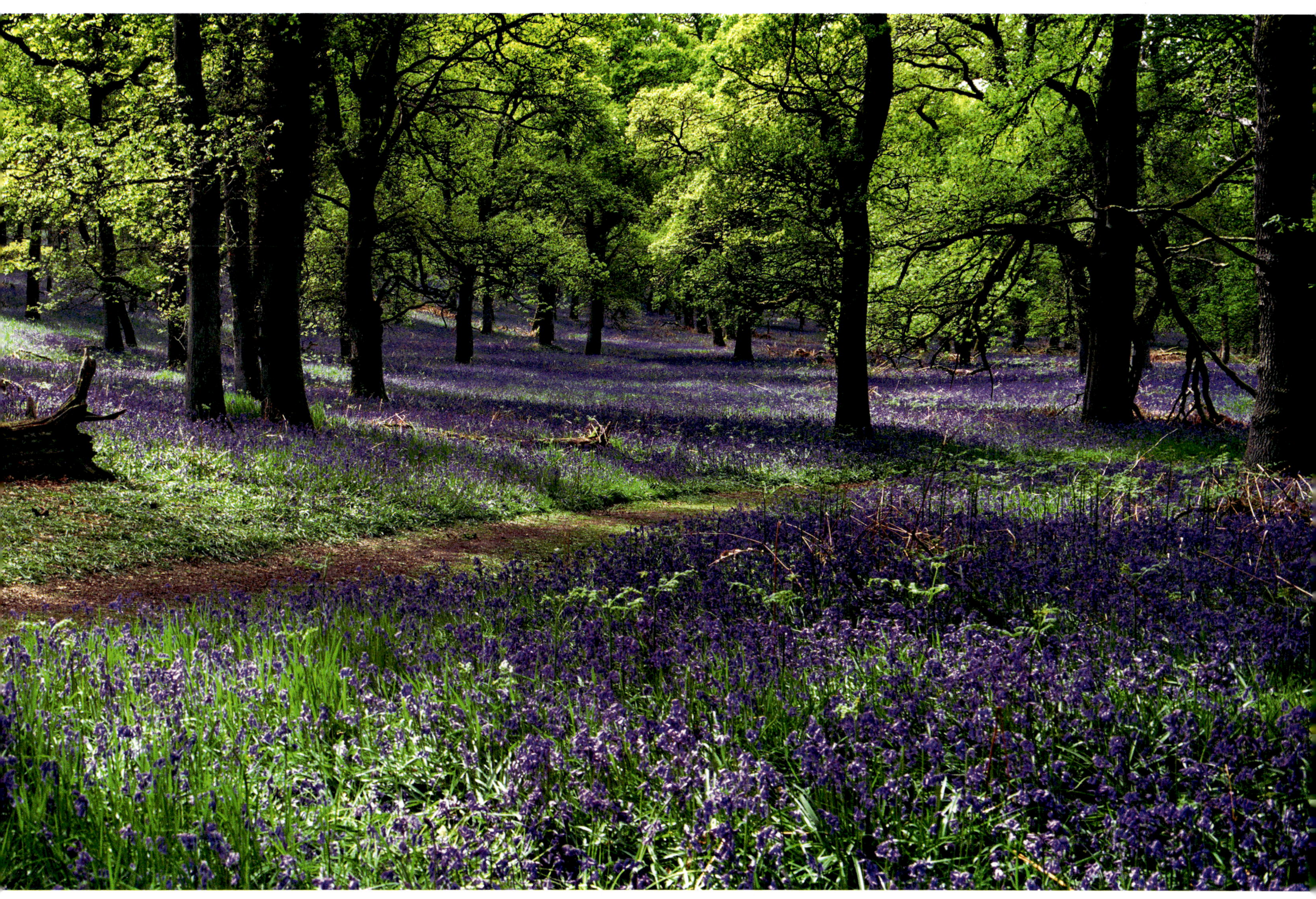

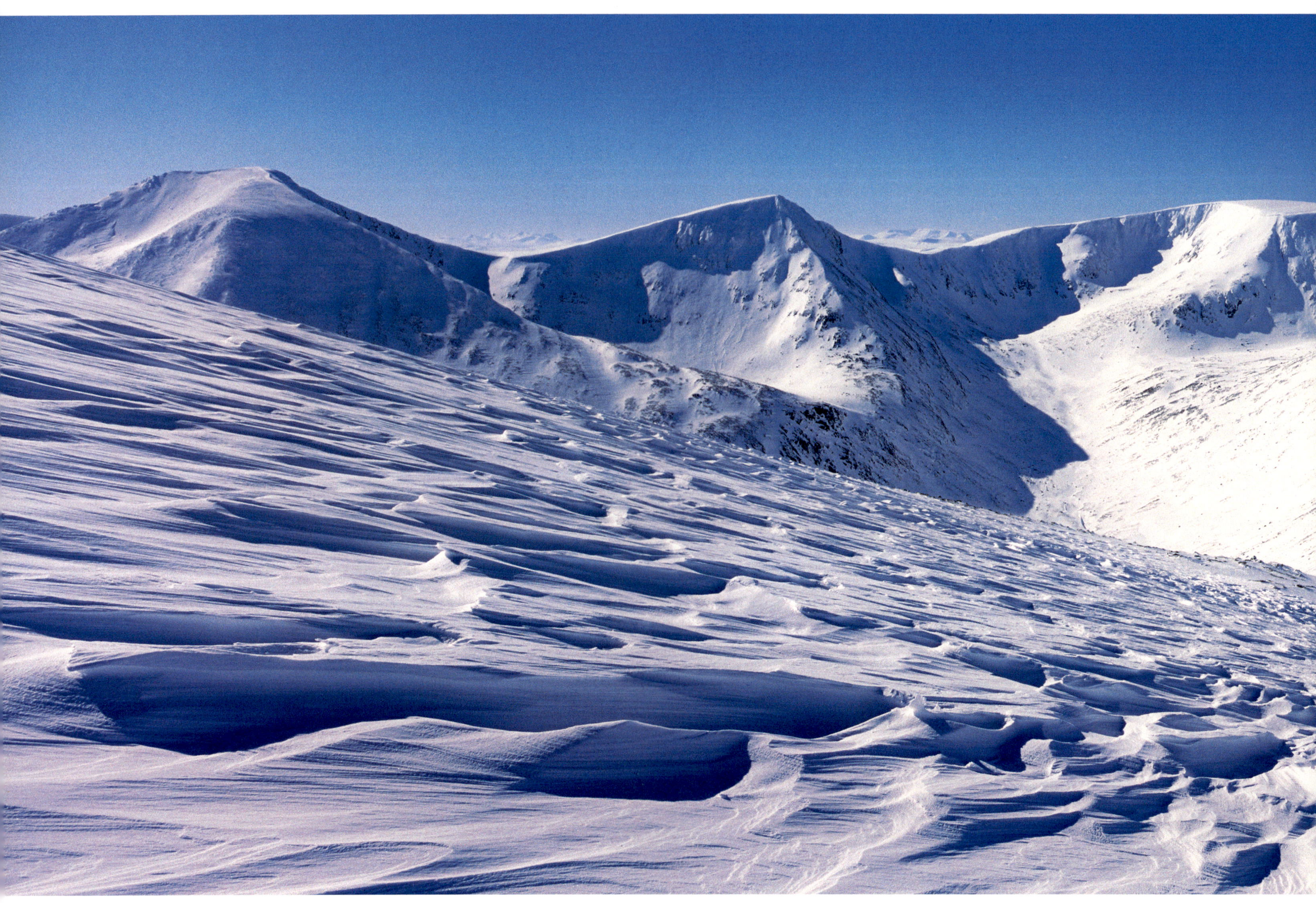

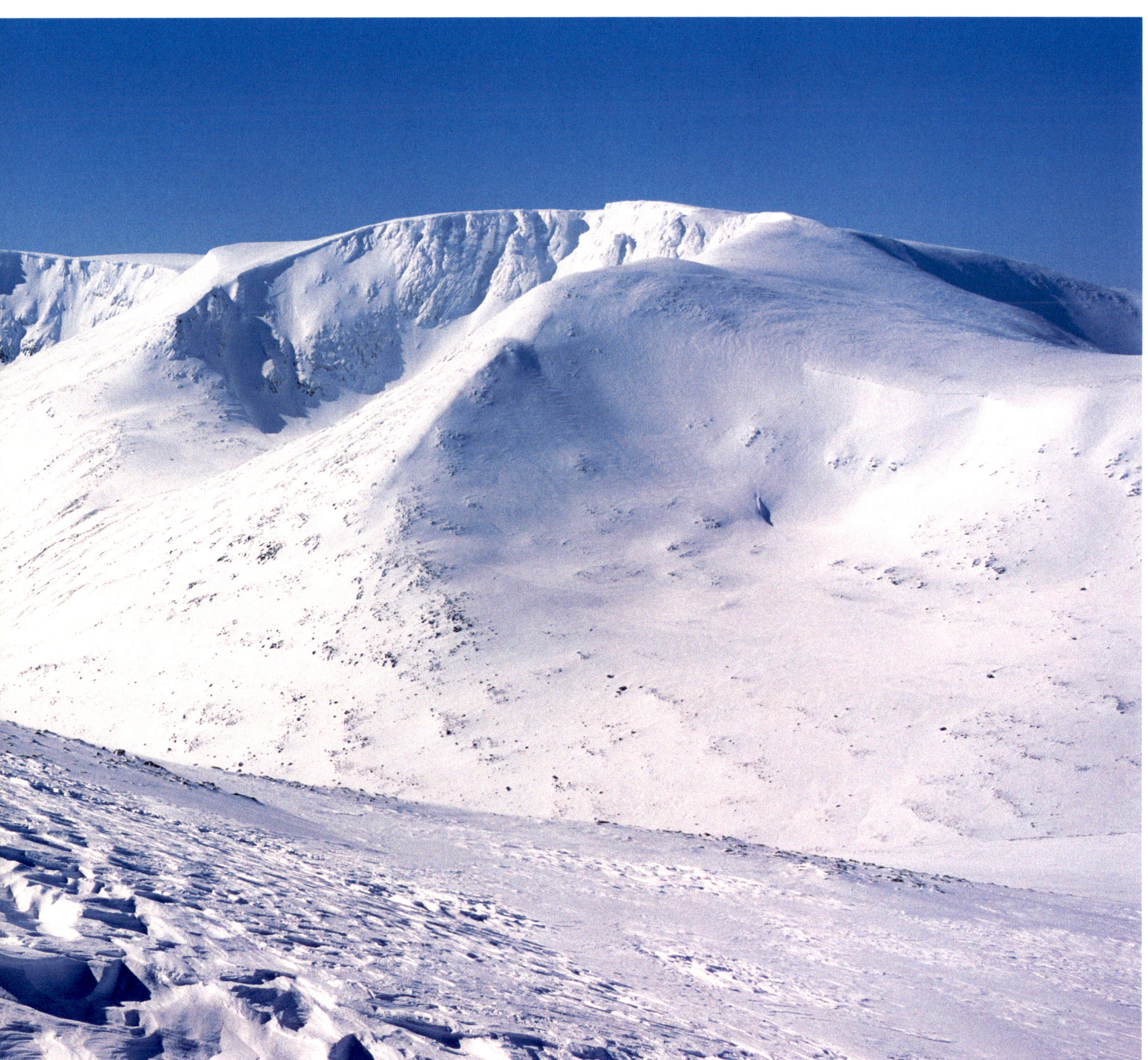

Braeriach, Cairngorms
March 2018

Making my way across the arctic mountain plateau of
the Cairngorms, I came across some wonderfully
sculptured snow formations close to the summit of
Ben Macdui. These intricate and fragile shapes are
known as sastrugi and are shaped by the tremendous
winds that relentlessly batter this wild land.

Skye and the Inner Sound
March 2017

Although this spot is easily accessed from the
high-level road that crosses the Applecross peninsula,
it was perhaps one of the more dangerous places I've
been for a photograph. It's always windy there, and the
only shelter I could find was next to a small shed at the
foot of the massive transmitter mast that crowns Sgùrr
a' Chaorachain. The rime ice that had accumulated on the
structure was being dislodged by the strong northerly,
and was falling all around me in an alarmingly random
fashion. I stood back and waited in the freezing wind
until the sun was low in the sky before quickly moving
back to my final position for the image with one eye on
the scene and the other on the mast towering above me.

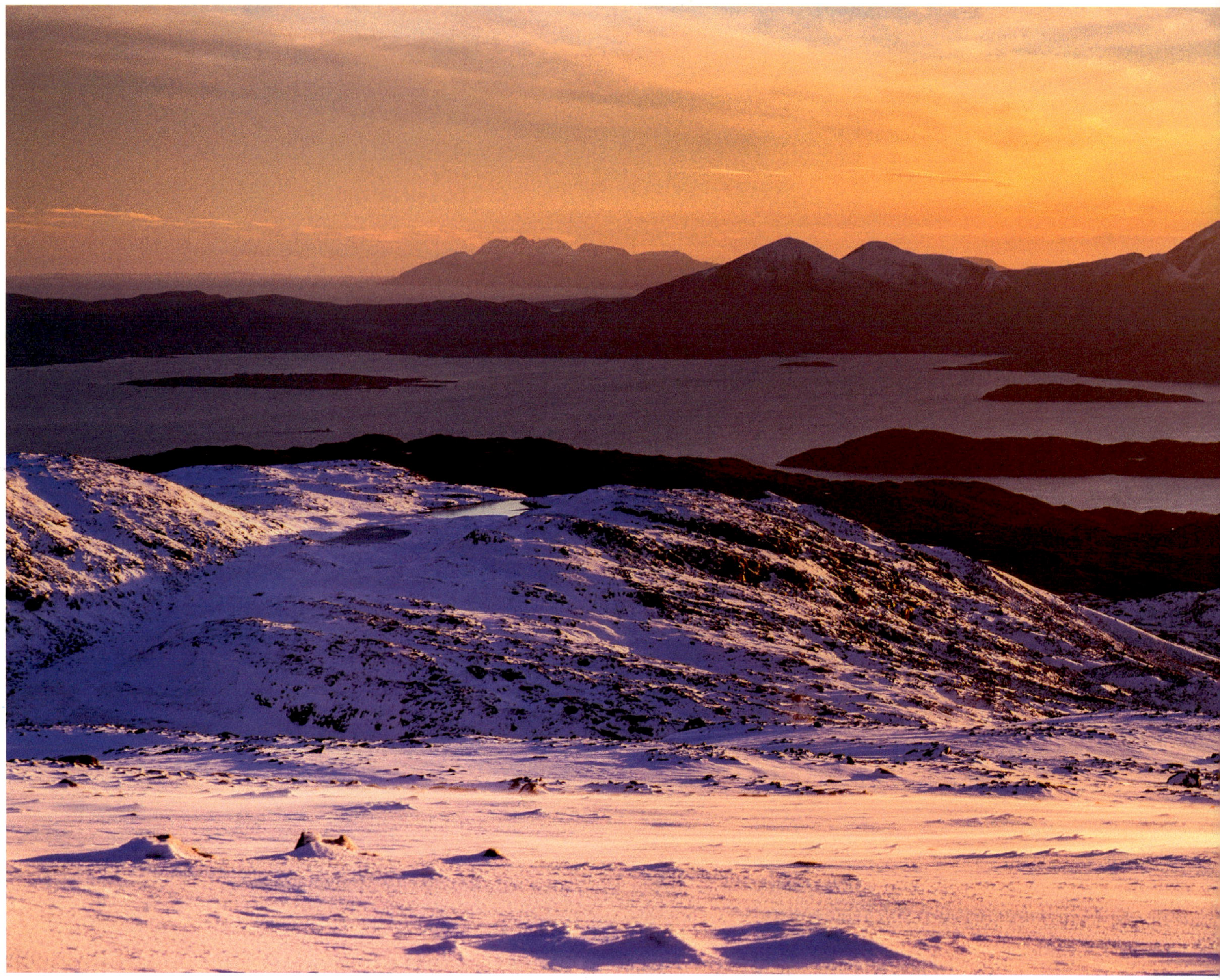

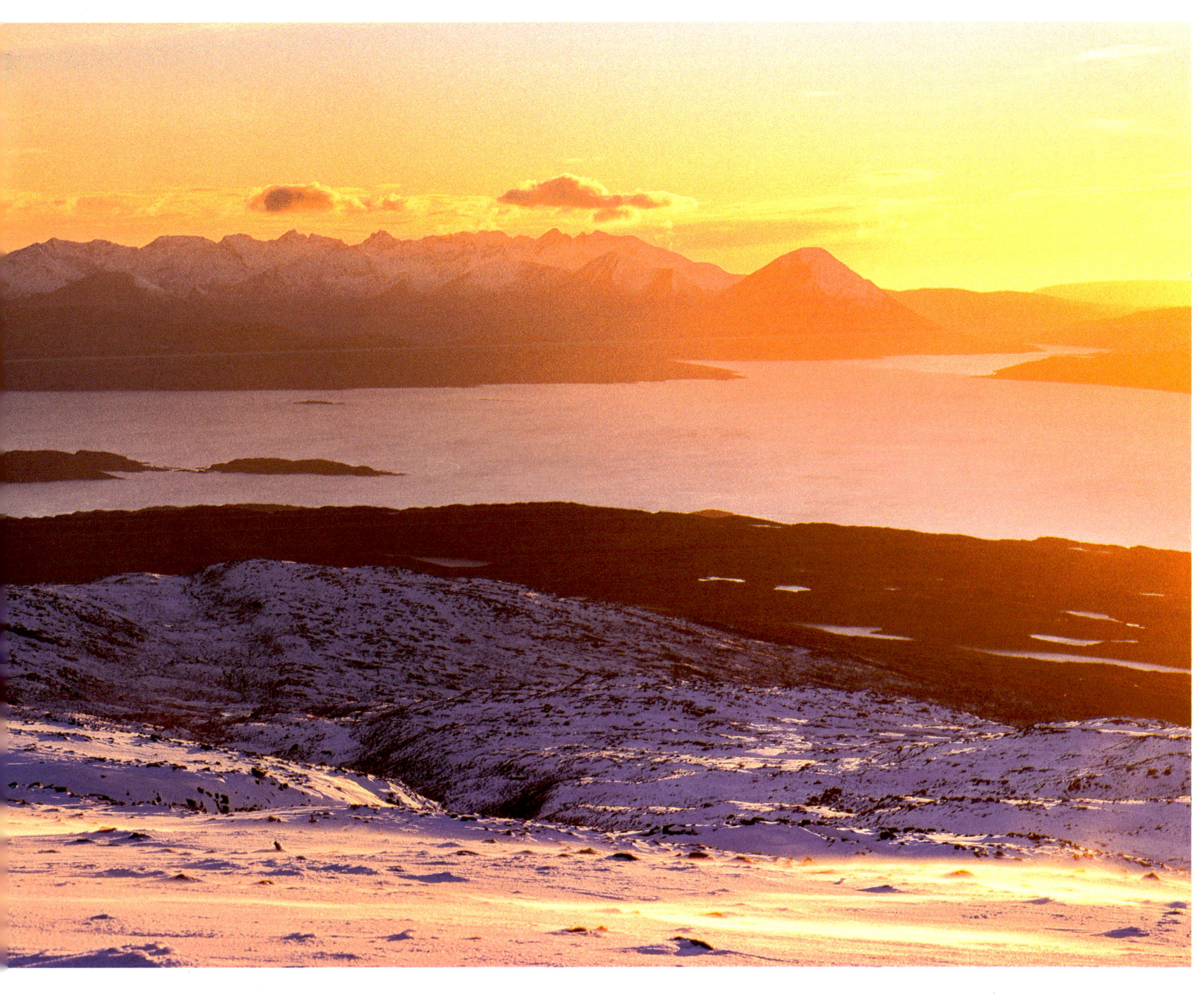

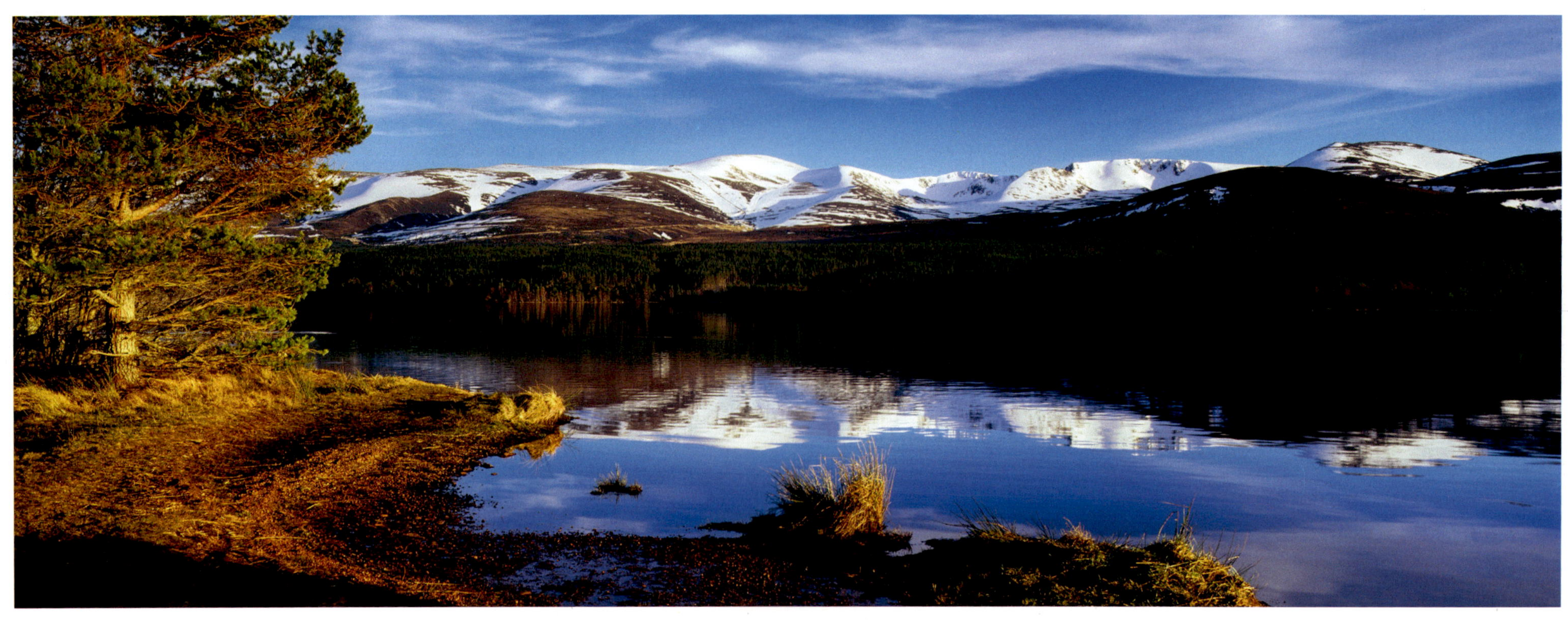

Loch Morlich, Cairngorms
March 2014

After a full day on the mountain plateau I returned
to this previously scouted location on the shores
of Loch Morlich. As the sun set I waited for the water
to settle on this classic view of the Cairngorms' famous
Northern Corries.

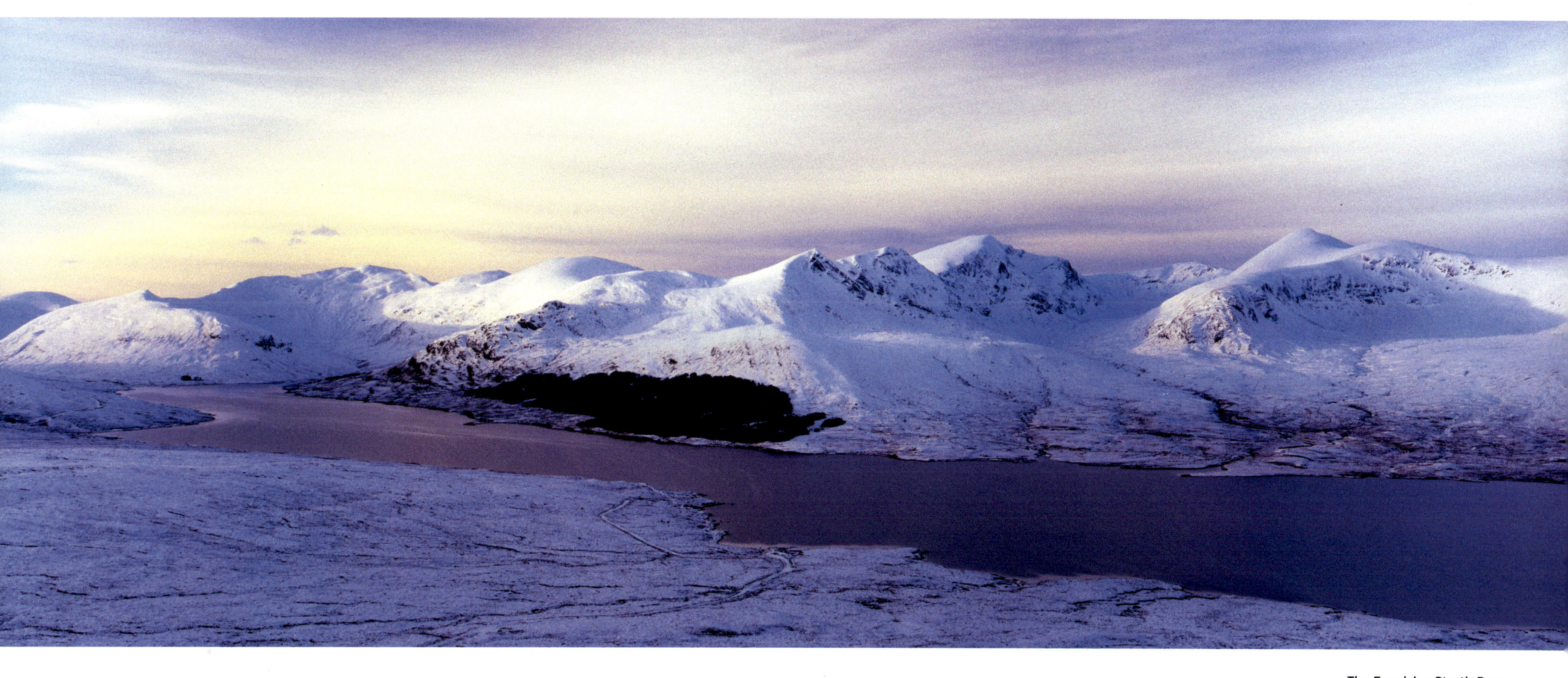

The Fannichs, Strath Bran
February 2016

High above Loch Fannich I waited for the sun to set and watched the high cirrus clouds stream across the sky on a stiff northerly wind. As time was running out, this stark frozen landscape was briefly brought to life with a final burst of dying light.

Ben Cruachan, Glen Lonan
November 2017

This often-bypassed glen is a wonderfully quiet place,
a low-lying, fertile corner of Argyll that is rich in history
and archaeological sites. The single-track road that runs
its length is known as the Road of the Kings. According
to legend, its course was used by funeral processions
carrying the bodies of Scotland's ancient kings from
Scone Palace to Iona Abbey, their final resting place.

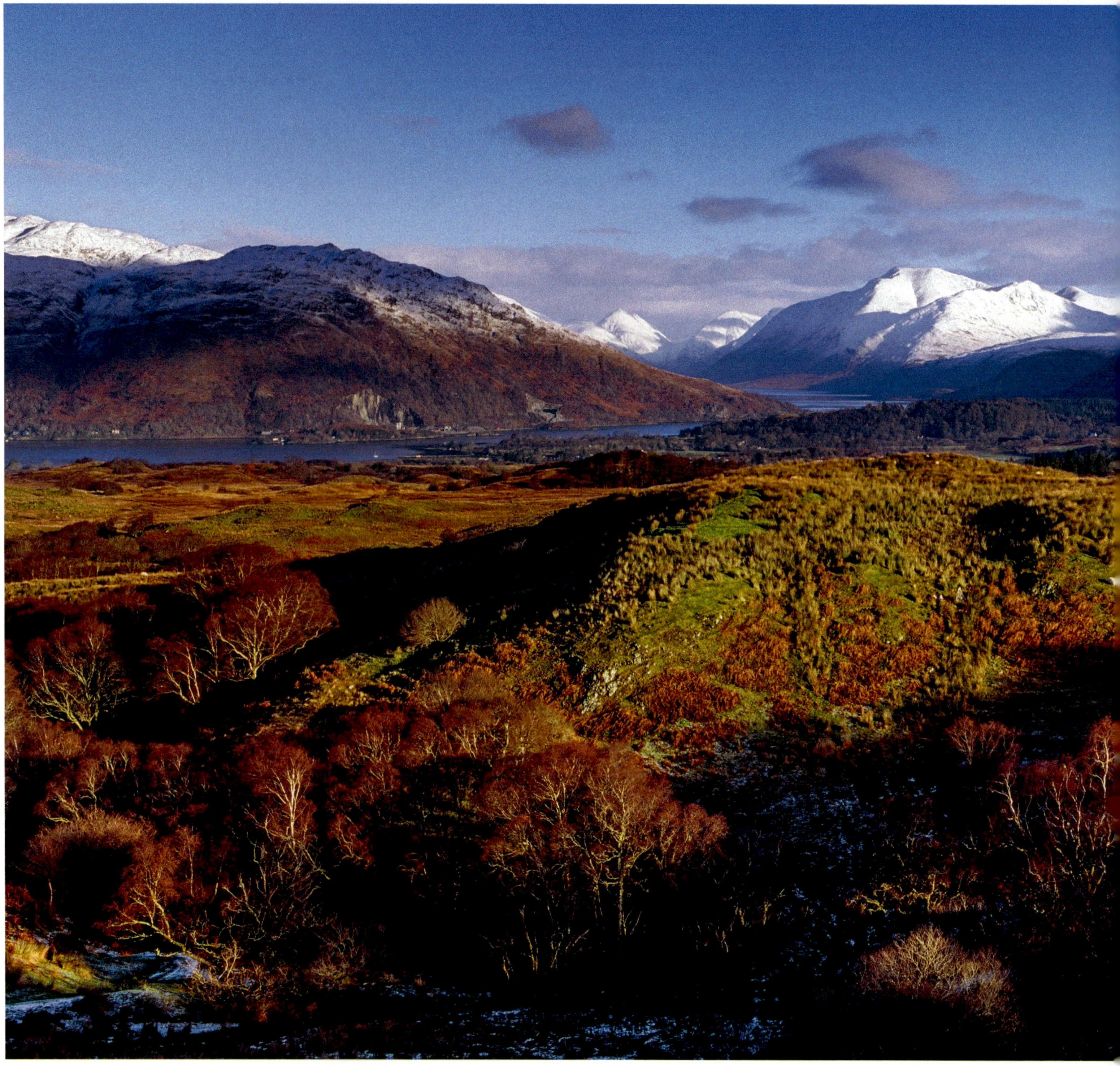

Following Page
Sunrise, Knoydart
June 2013

Midsummer sunrise from Ladhar Bheinn. A magnificent
mountain on Scotland's western seaboard, its remote
position enjoys superb views in every direction.
This image was shot practically from the front porch
of my tent pitched high above the vast Coire Dhorrcail,
my reward for the previous day's hard work.

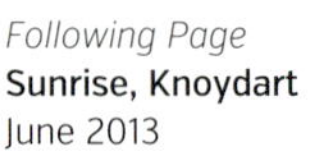

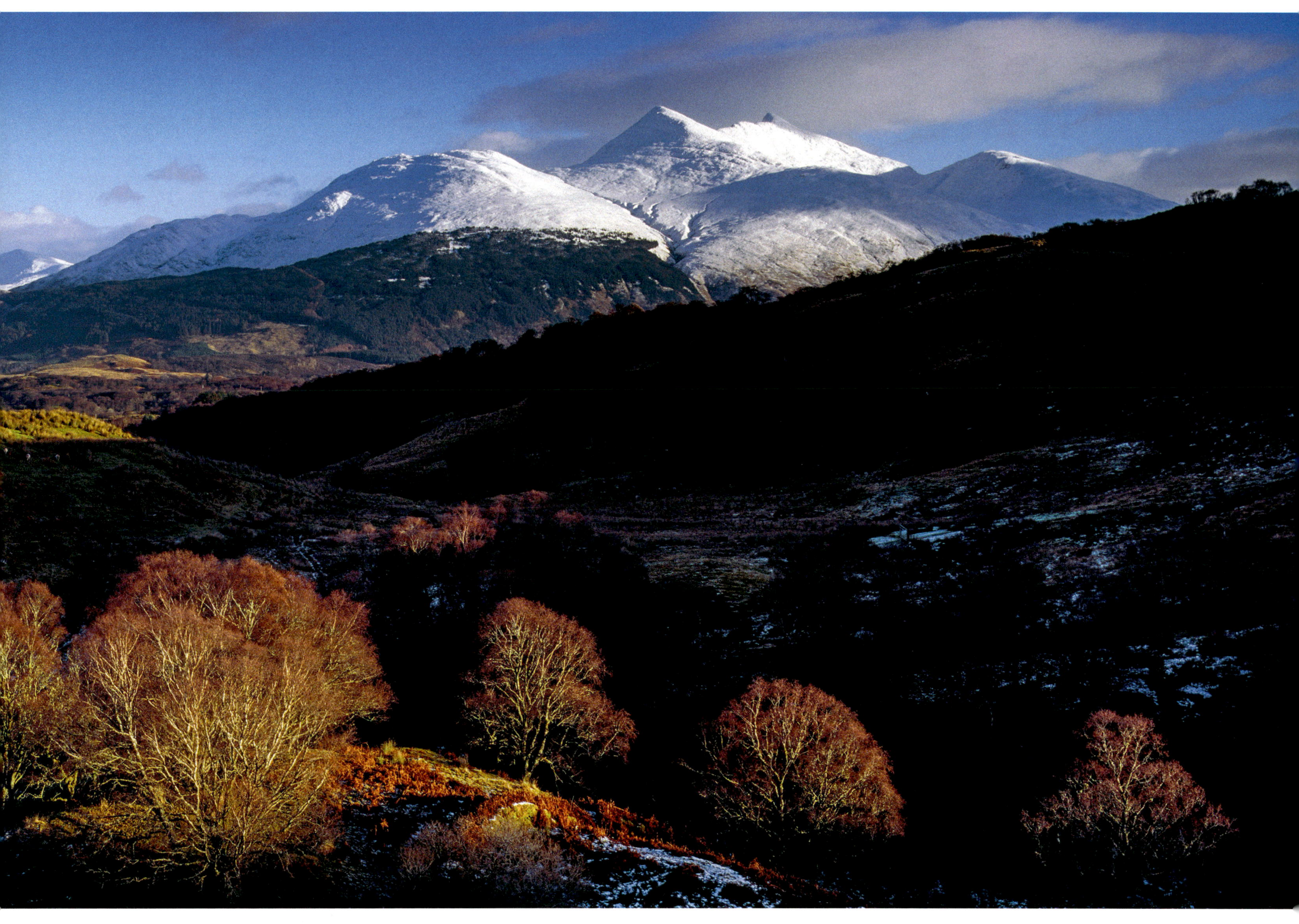

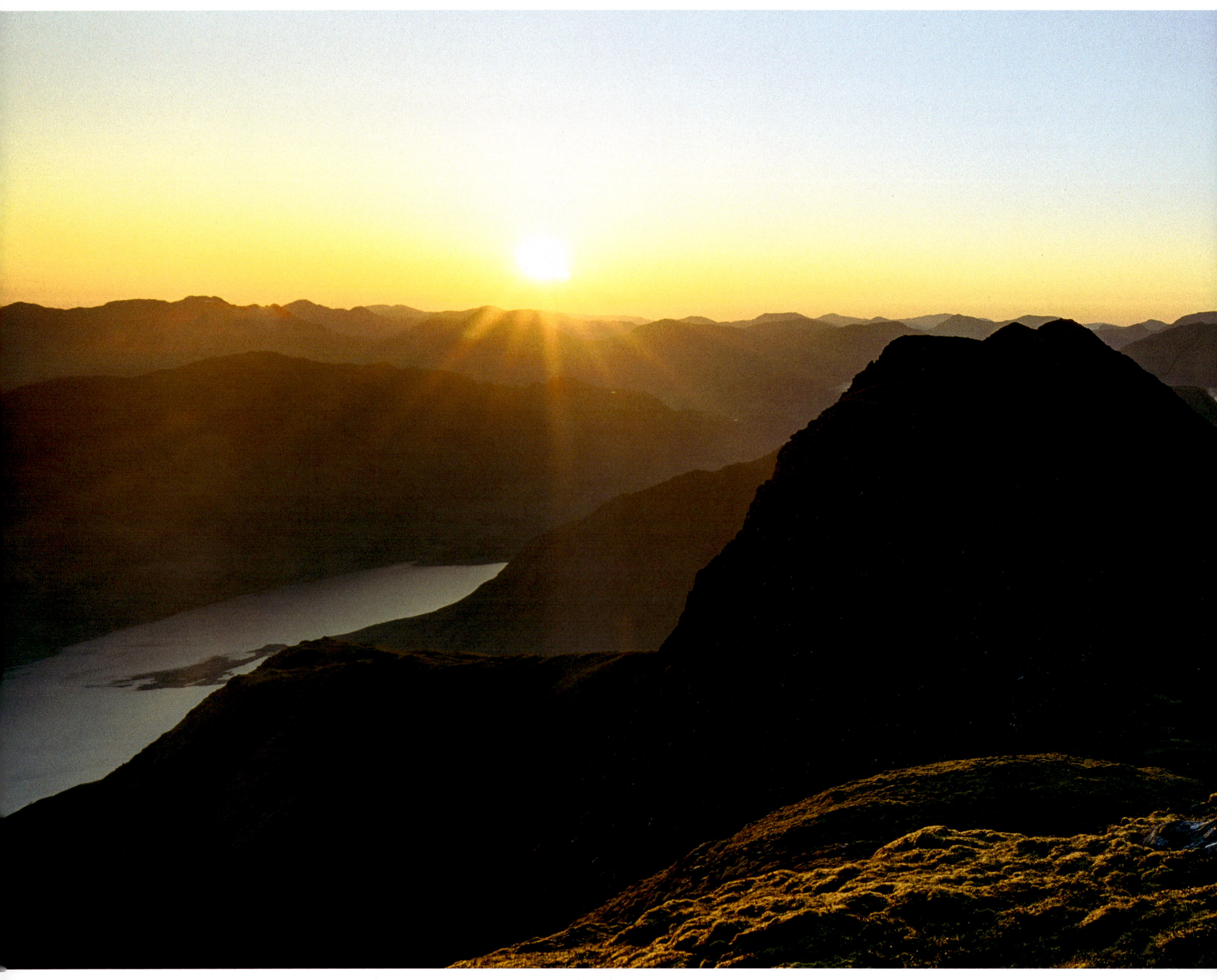

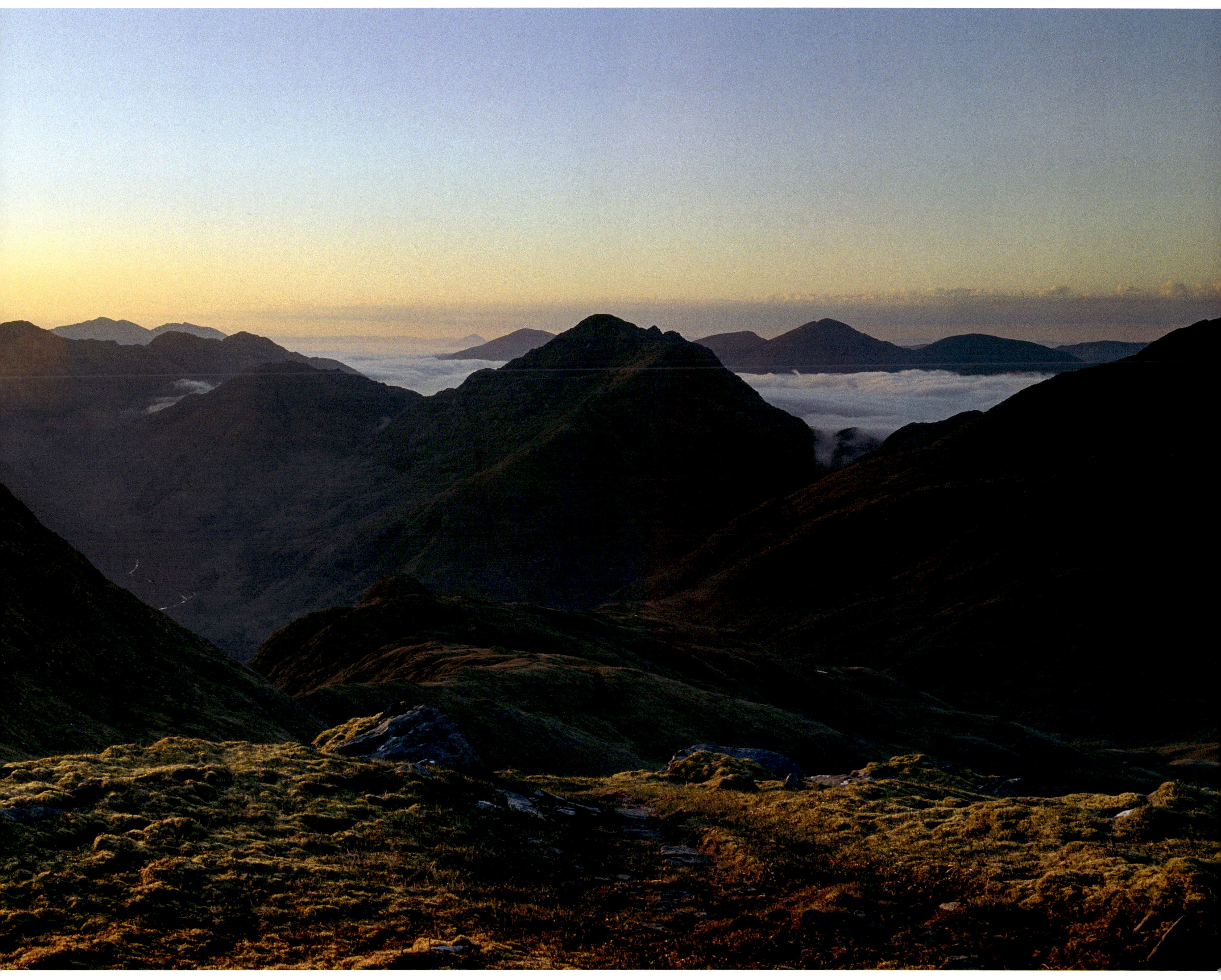

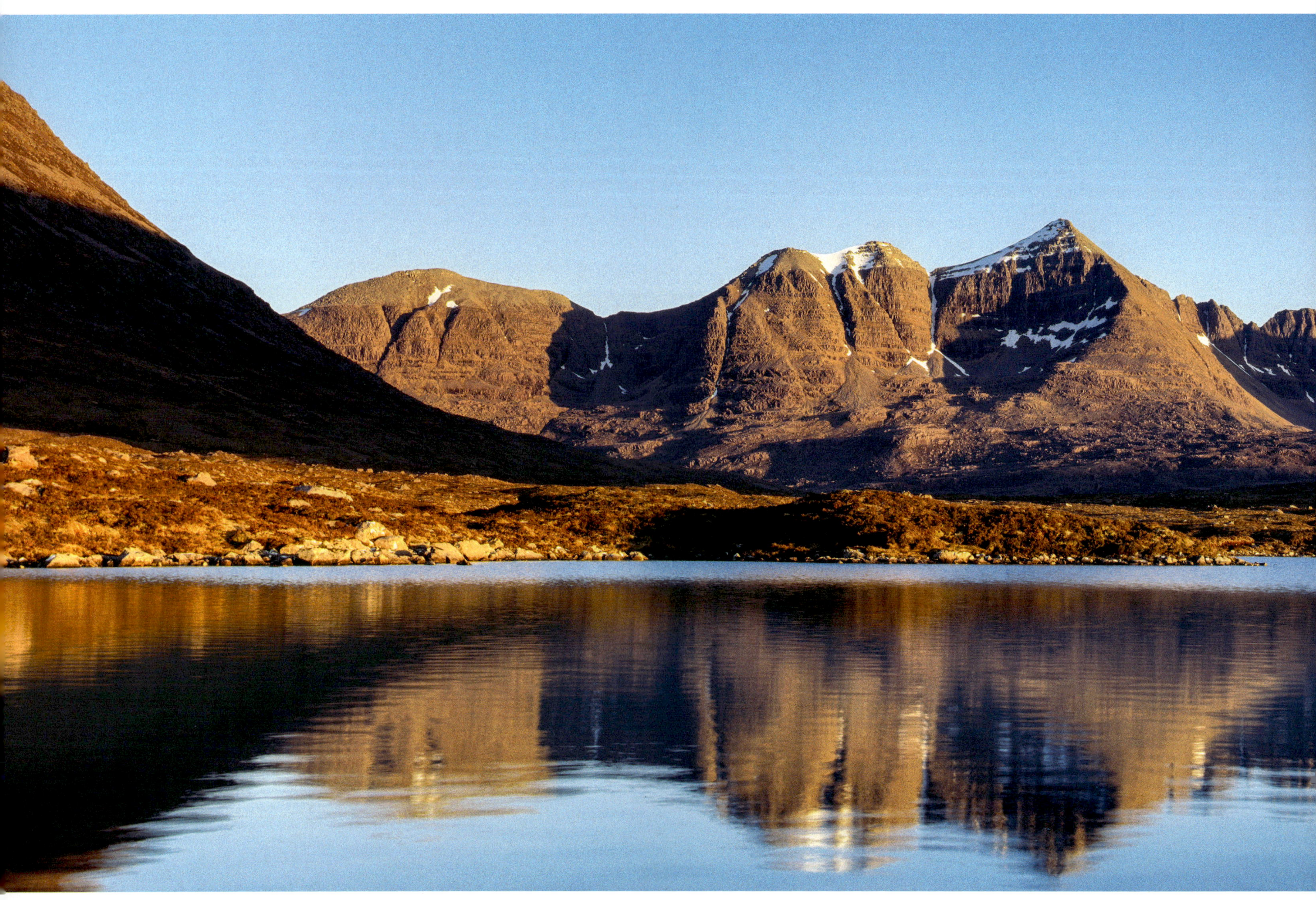

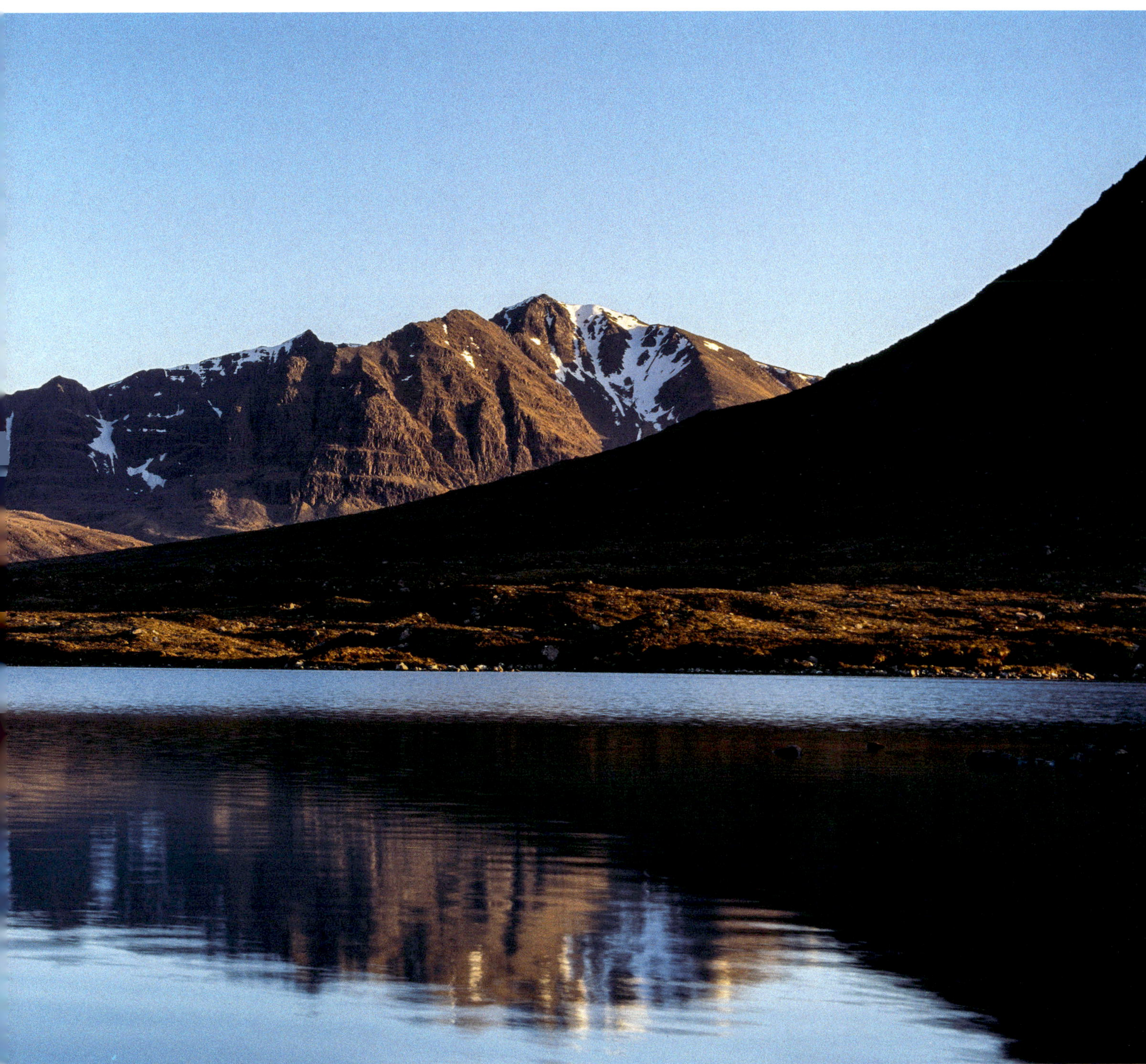

Liathach: The Grey One. Even from this aspect the appearance of impregnability is evident as the rocky terraces rise almost vertically from the treeless floor of the Torridon Forest that surrounds the mountain. During the month of April the sun sets almost directly in line with the mountain's north-facing slopes, throwing them into sharp relief in the wonderful evening light.

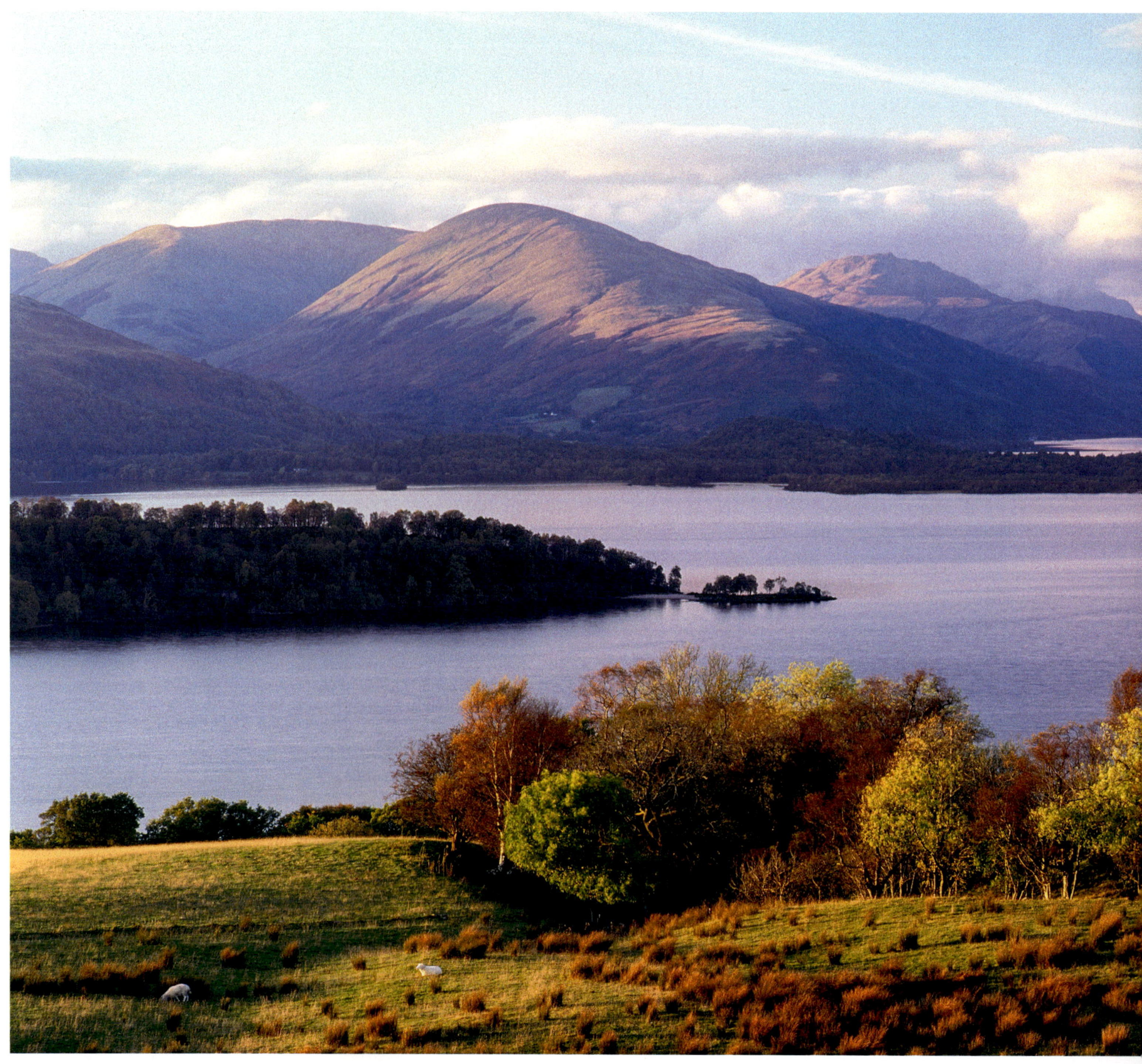

Loch Lomond, Argyll and Bute
October 2011

The vast freshwater expanse of Loch Lomond marks
an important geographical boundary in Scotland.
The islands in the loch form a visible part of the
Highland boundary fault line which stretches across
Scotland from Arran in the west to Stonehaven in
the east. This ancient fault zone is where two very
different geological terrains collided 430 million years
ago, eventually evolving into the landscape we now
know today as the Highland and Lowland regions.

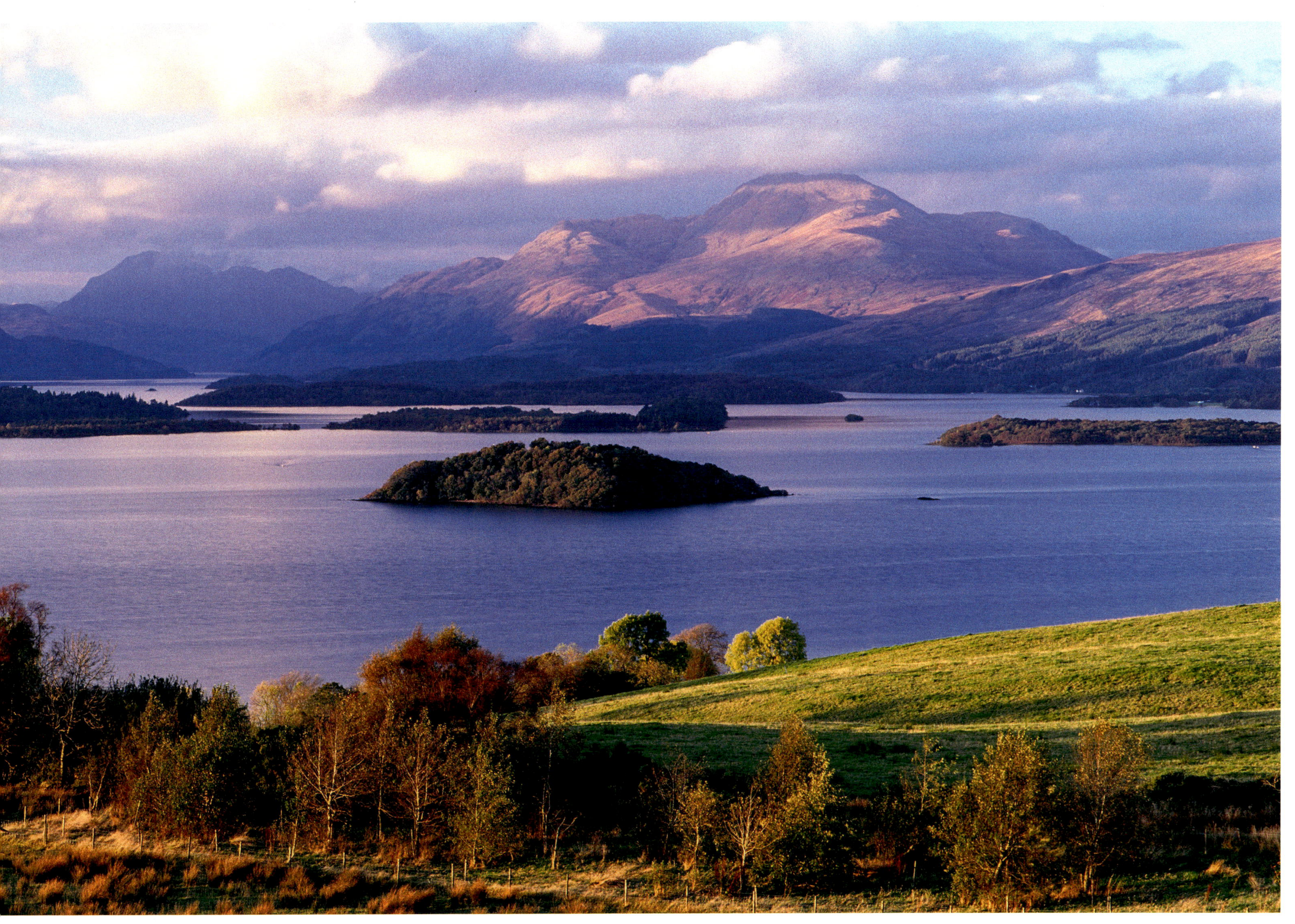

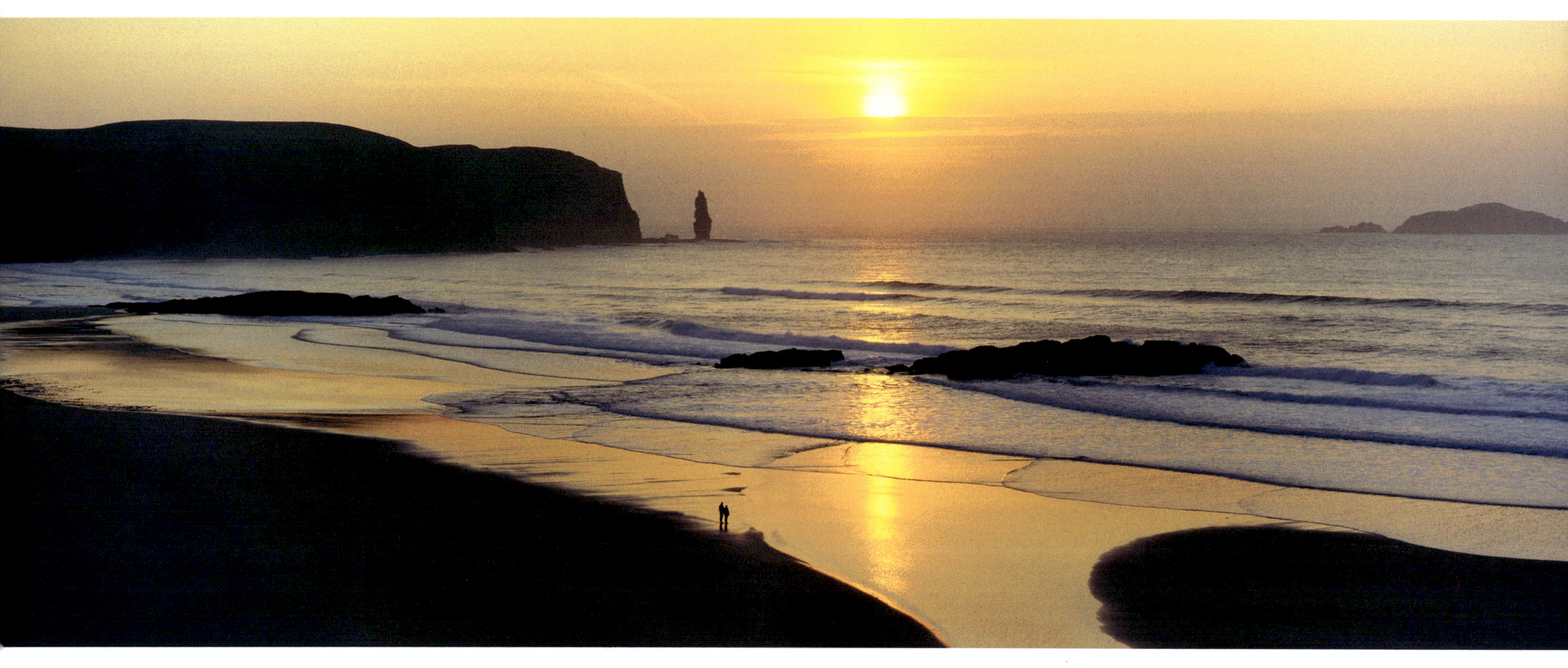

Sandwood Sundown
September 2015

Although poor visibility does not generally make for
the ideal conditions I seek, it does have the powerful
effect of diffusing the sun nicely, which allows me to
shoot directly towards it. I made my way to Sandwood
and headed for the far north-western end of the bay
where I found a high vantage point to set up my
camera, the perfect place to watch the sunset.

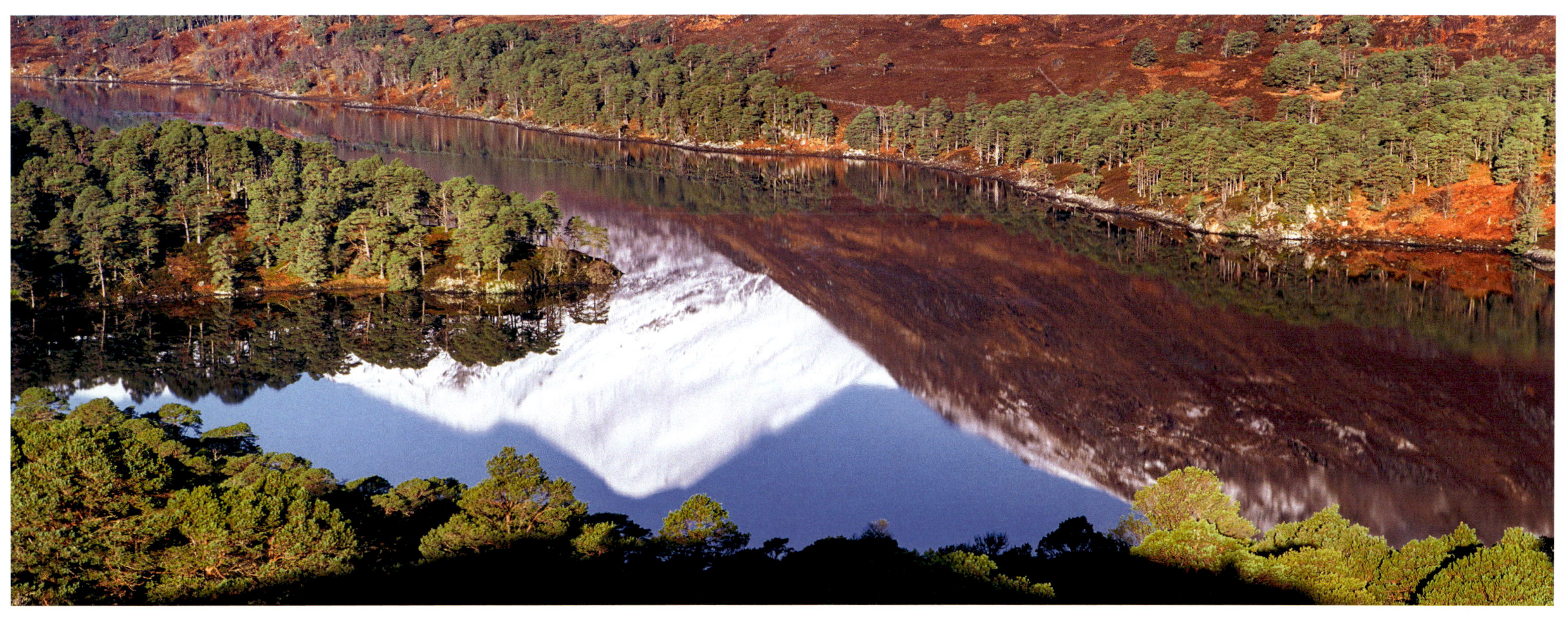

Loch Affric
March 2017

A massive high-pressure weather system had
settled directly over Scotland and brought with
it some extremely stable weather to much of
the Highlands. The vast waters of Loch Affric were
unusually still, reflecting the steep slopes of An Tudair
amongst a beautiful mosaic of Caledonian pines.

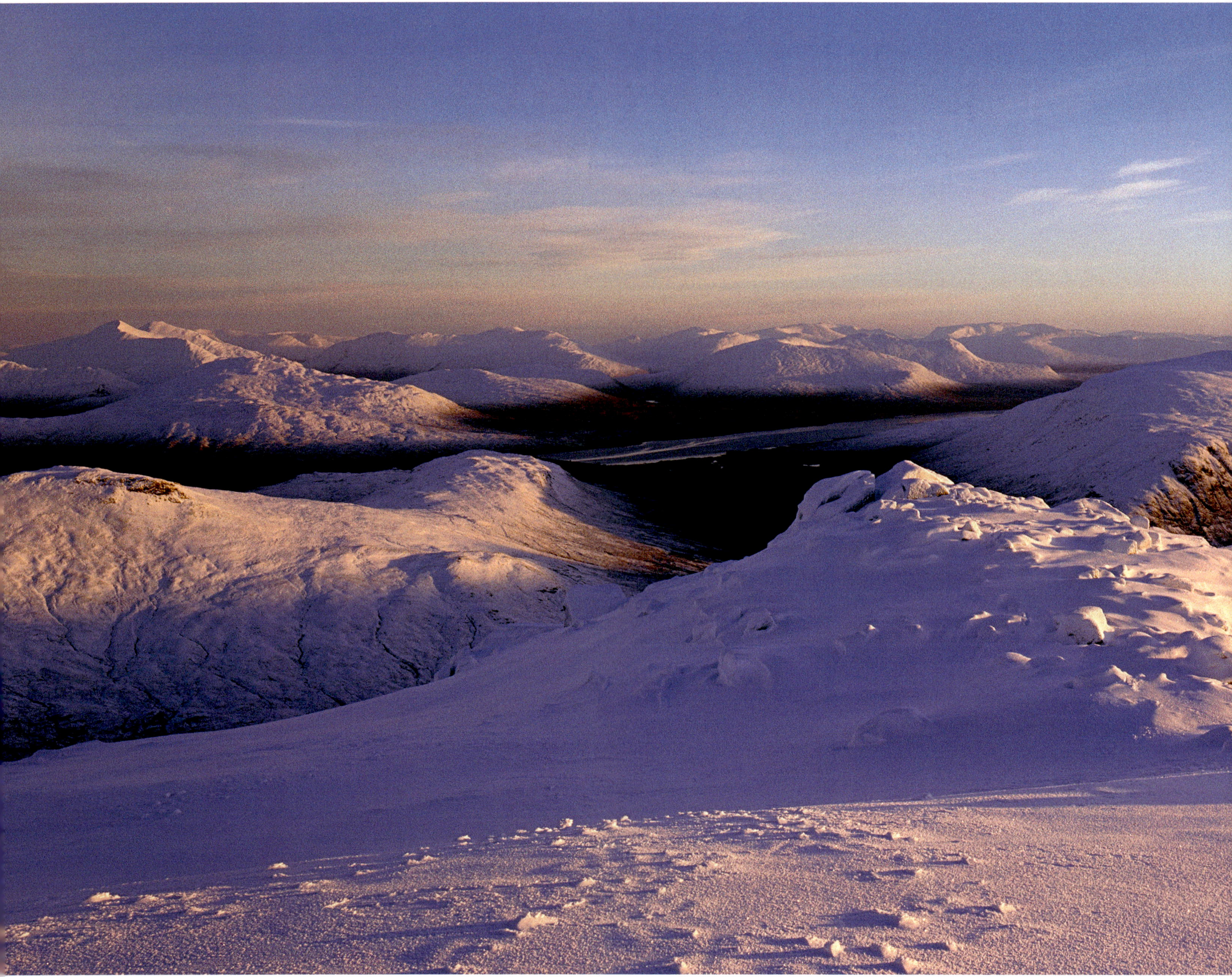

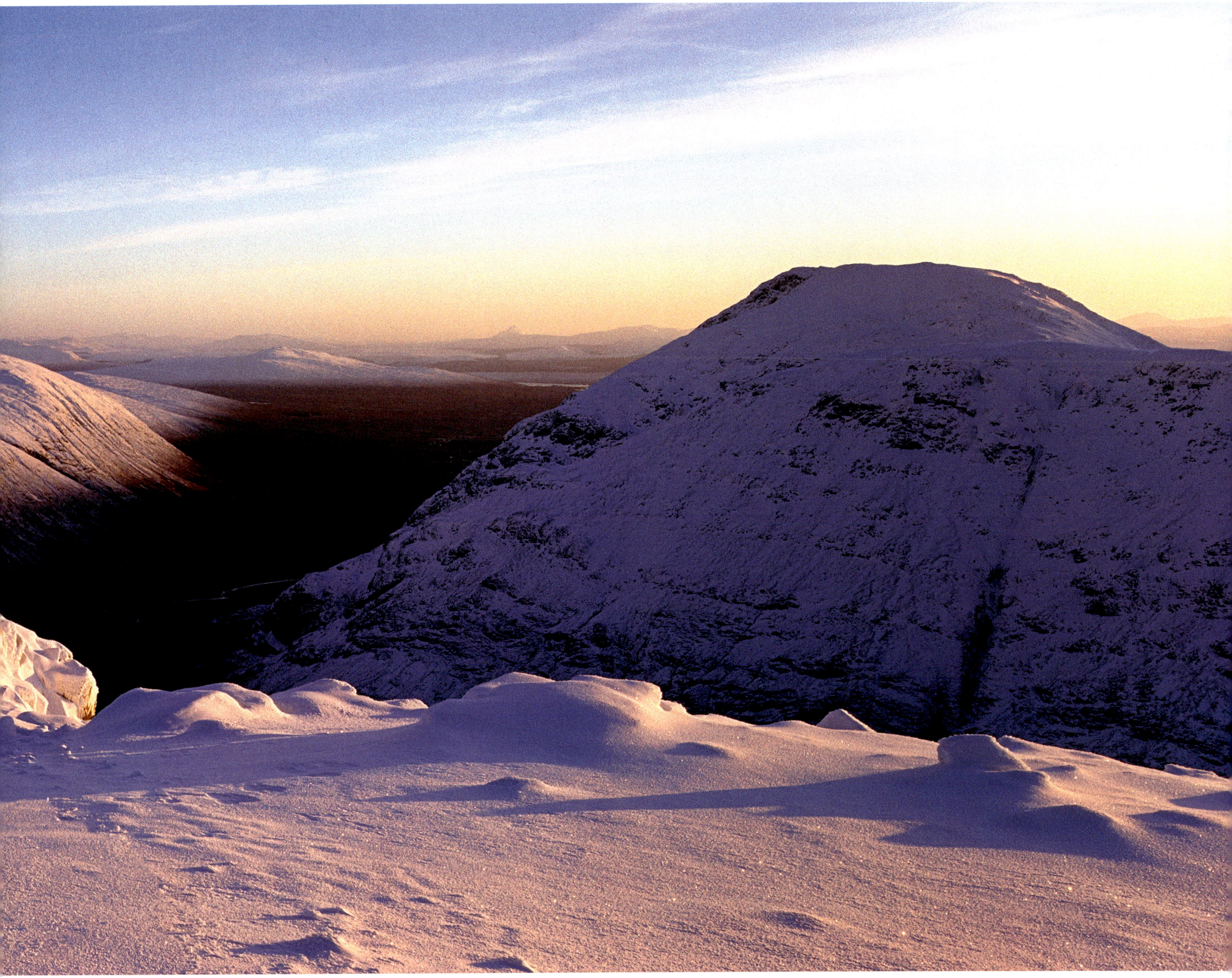

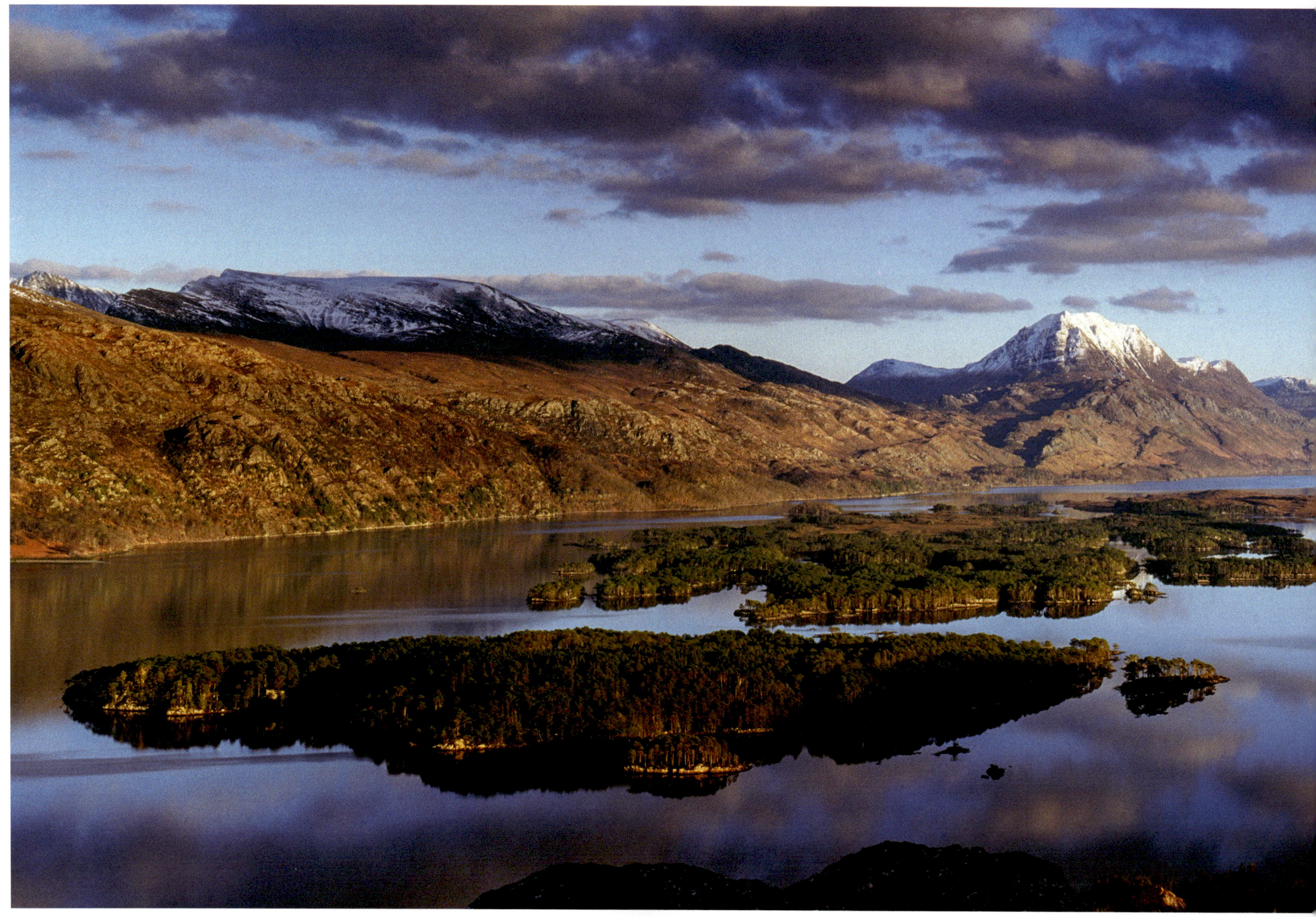

    WILD LIGHT

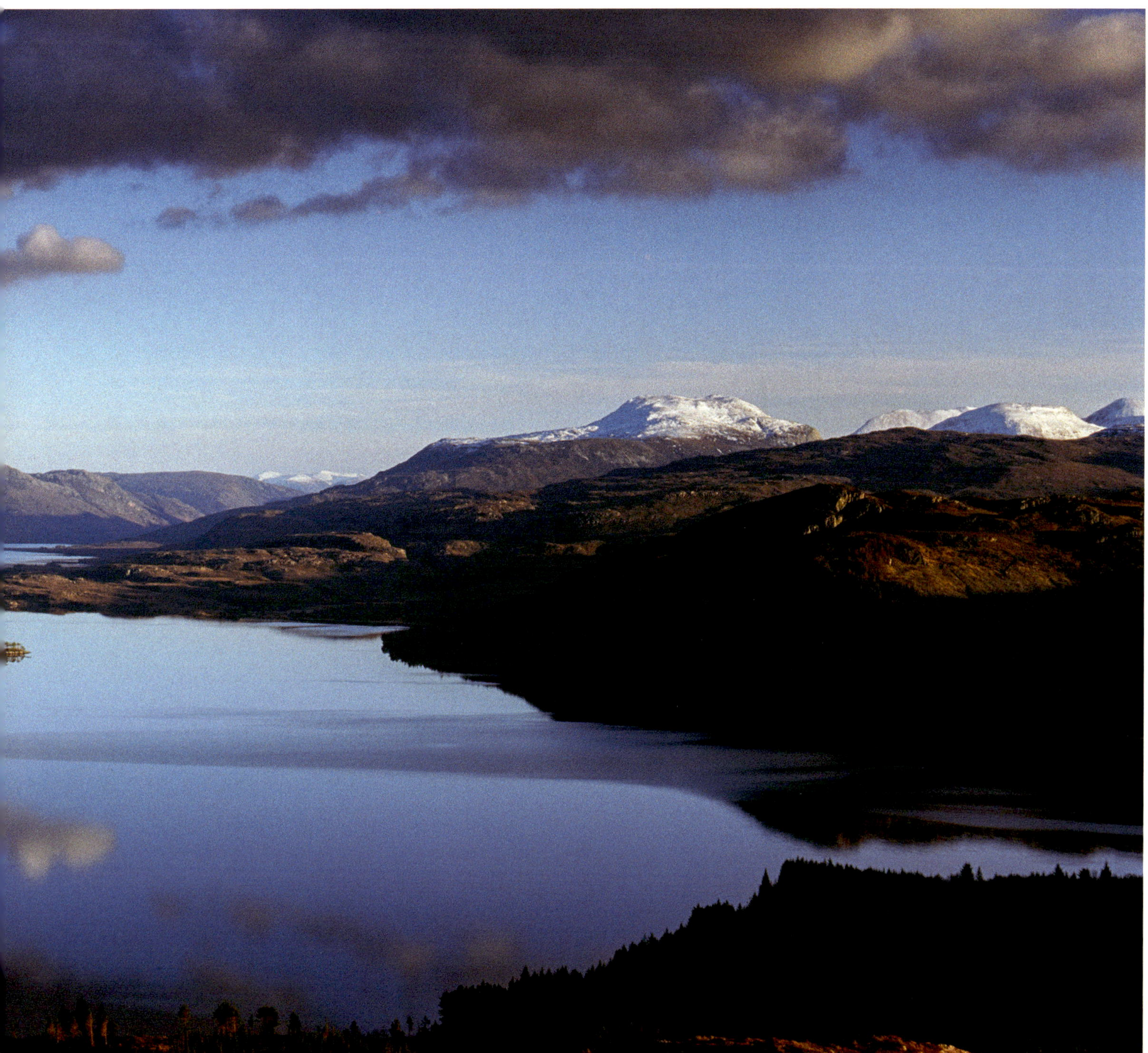

Loch Maree, Wester Ross
February 2011

Amongst the many beautiful islands of Loch Maree,
Isle Maree is perhaps one of the more interesting.
Located near to the northern shore, this tiny enclave is
home to some wonderful history spanning back to the
eighth century. Many remains can still be found today,
including a chapel, a graveyard and a holy well.

Previous Page
Mountain Sunrise, Glen Coe
January 2017

Dawn from any mountaintop is always worth the
extra effort: the added elevation means you are in
prime position to take advantage of the exquisite light
that appears soon after sunrise. Up on the summit,
having this light on the ground in front of you is
the reward for an early morning climb in the dark.
On this particular morning I had made the relatively
easy ascent of Stob Coire Raineach, a principal summit
of Buachaille Etive Beag in Glen Coe. This position
presents extraordinary views in every direction and
was the perfect spot to witness the morning light
striking the mountain tops around Rannoch Moor,
bringing the landscape slowly to life.

Sgorr na Ciche and Bidean nam Bian, Loch Leven
March 2011

The discernible contours of Sgorr na Ciche, better known
as the Pap of Glencoe, tower over the village of Glencoe
and the waters of Loch Leven. It marks the entrance
to Glen Coe itself and, thanks to its position, is one of
the best summit viewpoints within this popular area.

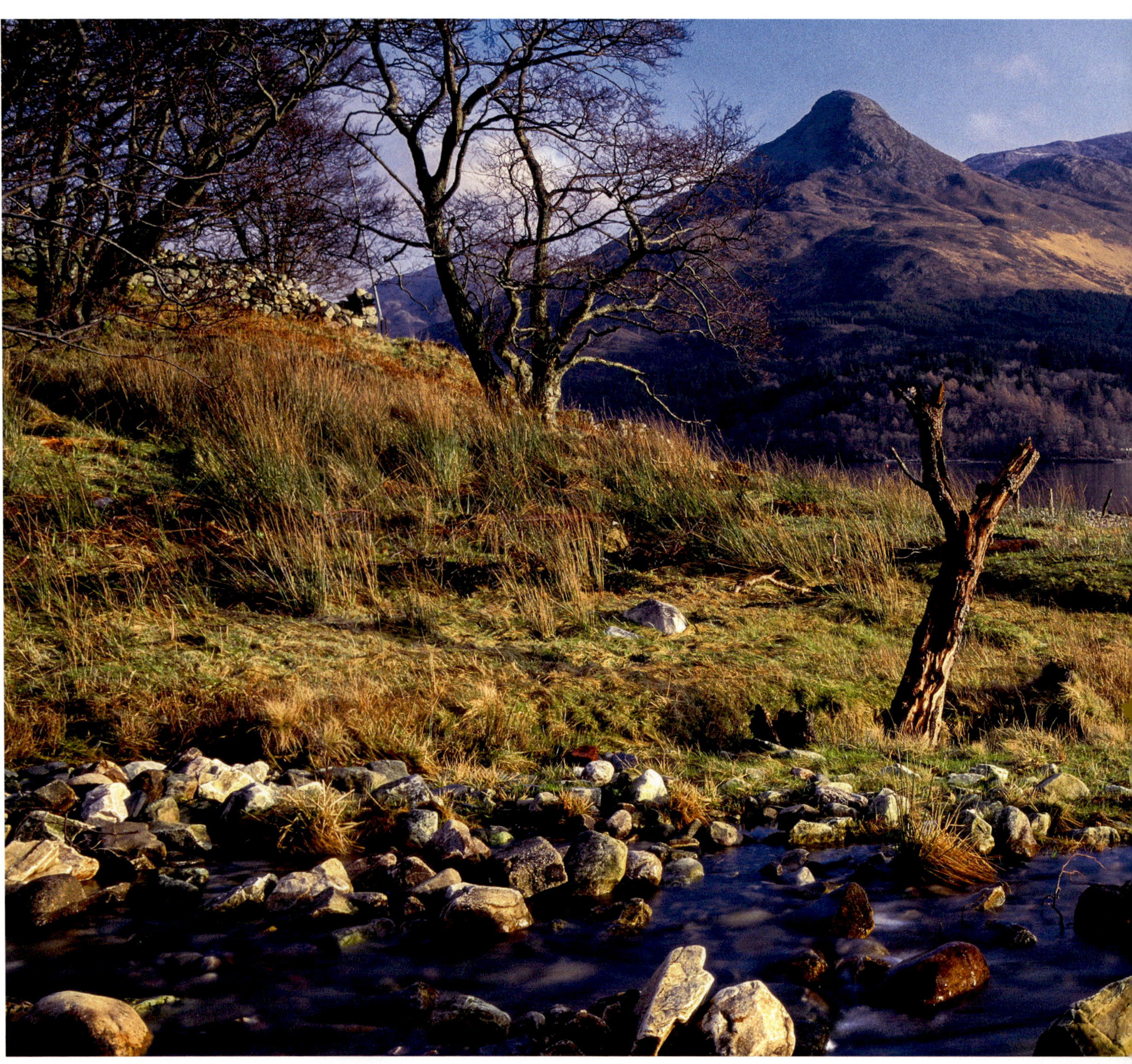

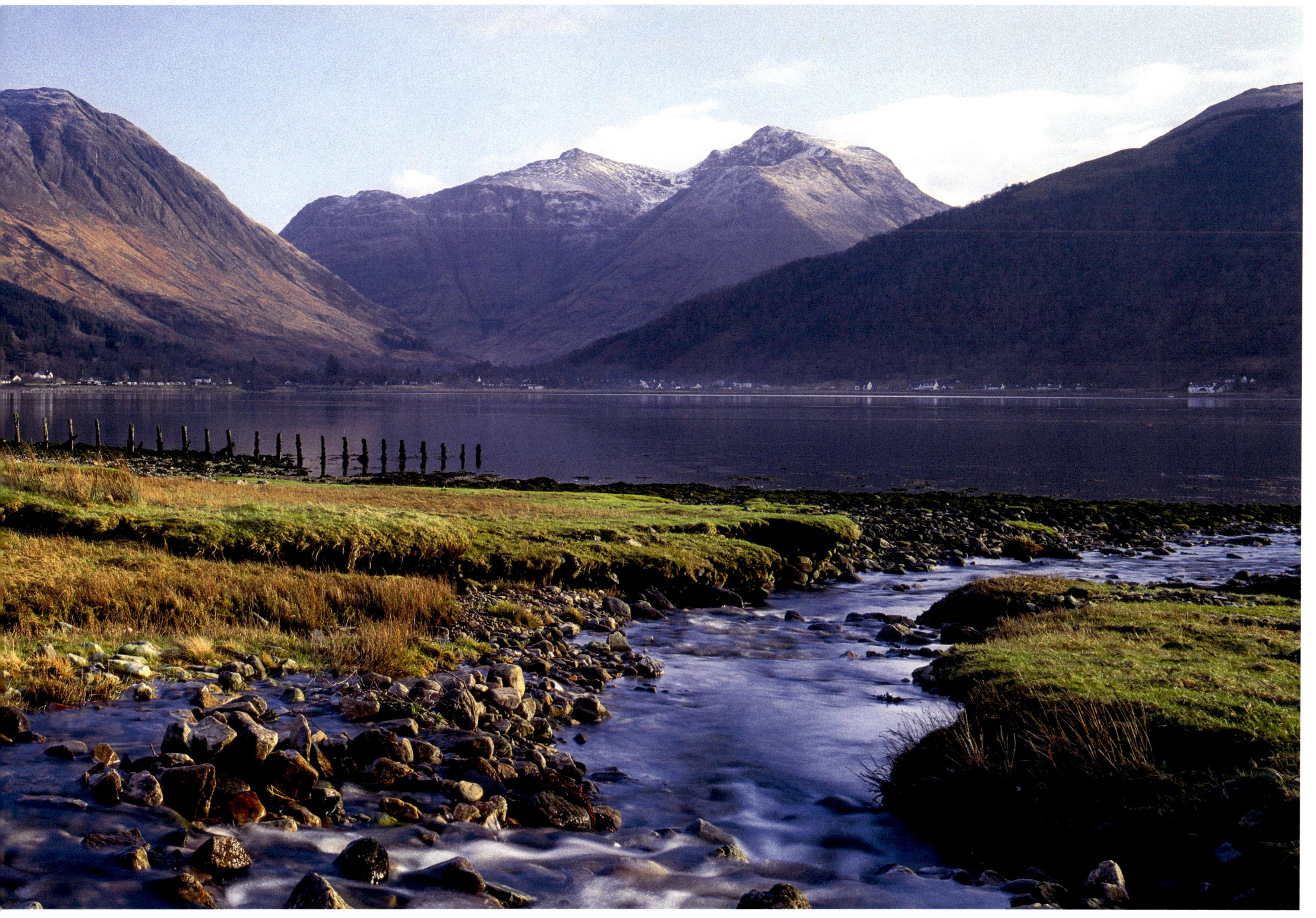

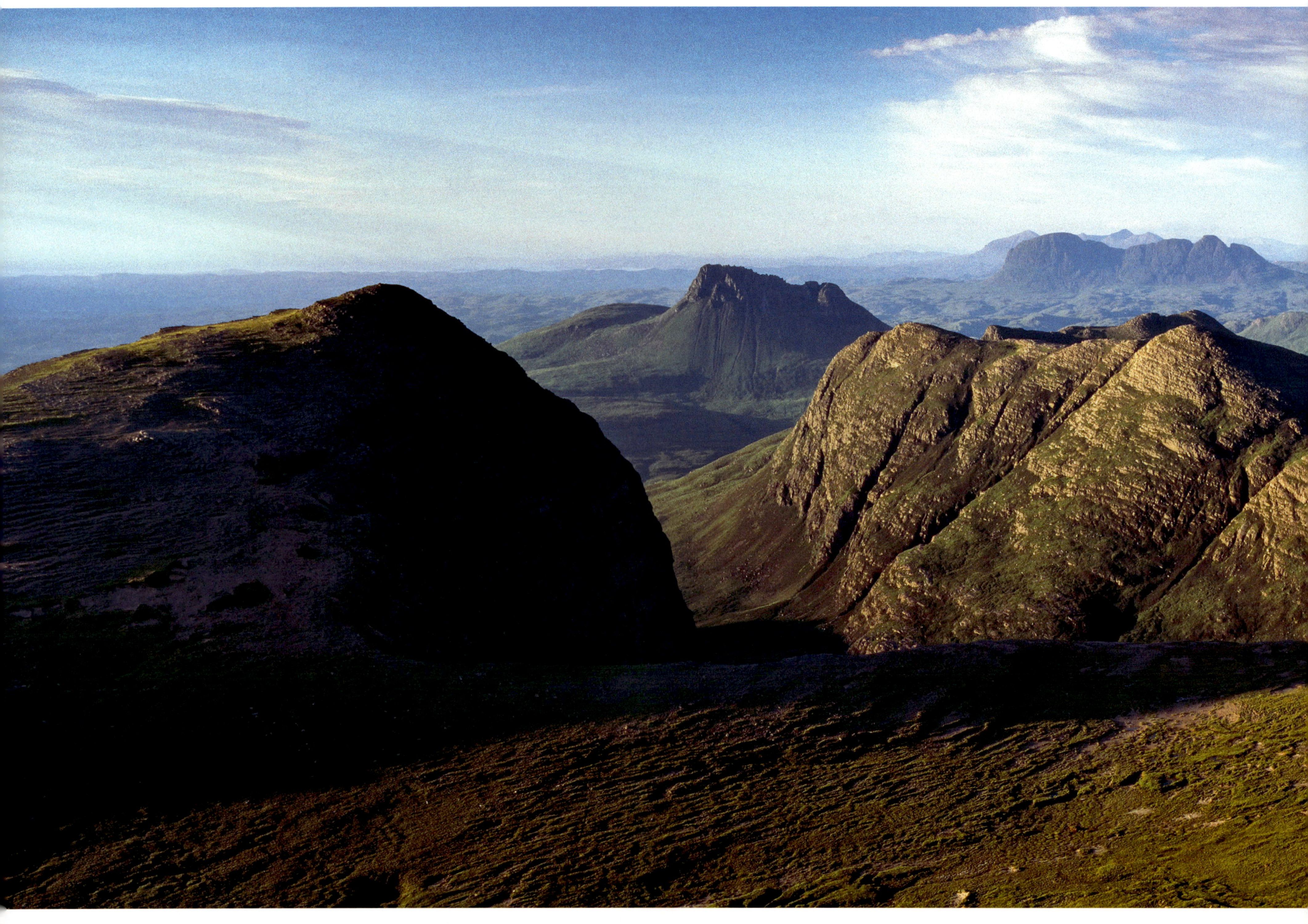

 WILD LIGHT

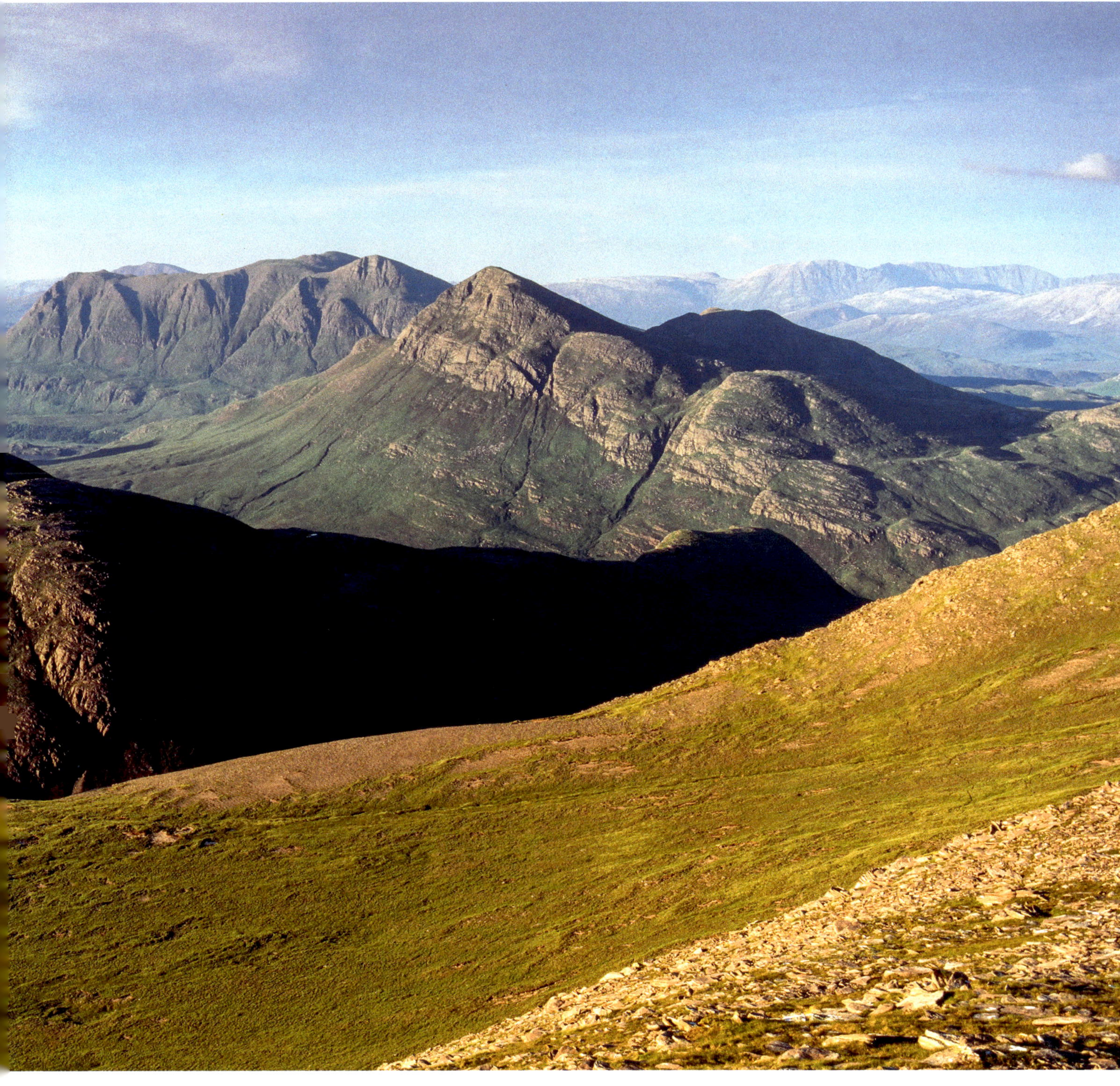

The spectacular summit of Ben More Coigach is the best place to view all of the peaks in the North West Highlands. From this elevated position, each of the individual summits are laid out in an almost perfect fashion spanning three Highland boundaries. Front to back are the summits of Sgùrr an Fhidhleir, Beinn an Eoin, Cùl Beag, Stac Pollaidh, Cùl Mòr, Suilven and Quinag, with a distant Conival and Ben More Assynt on the far horizon to the right.

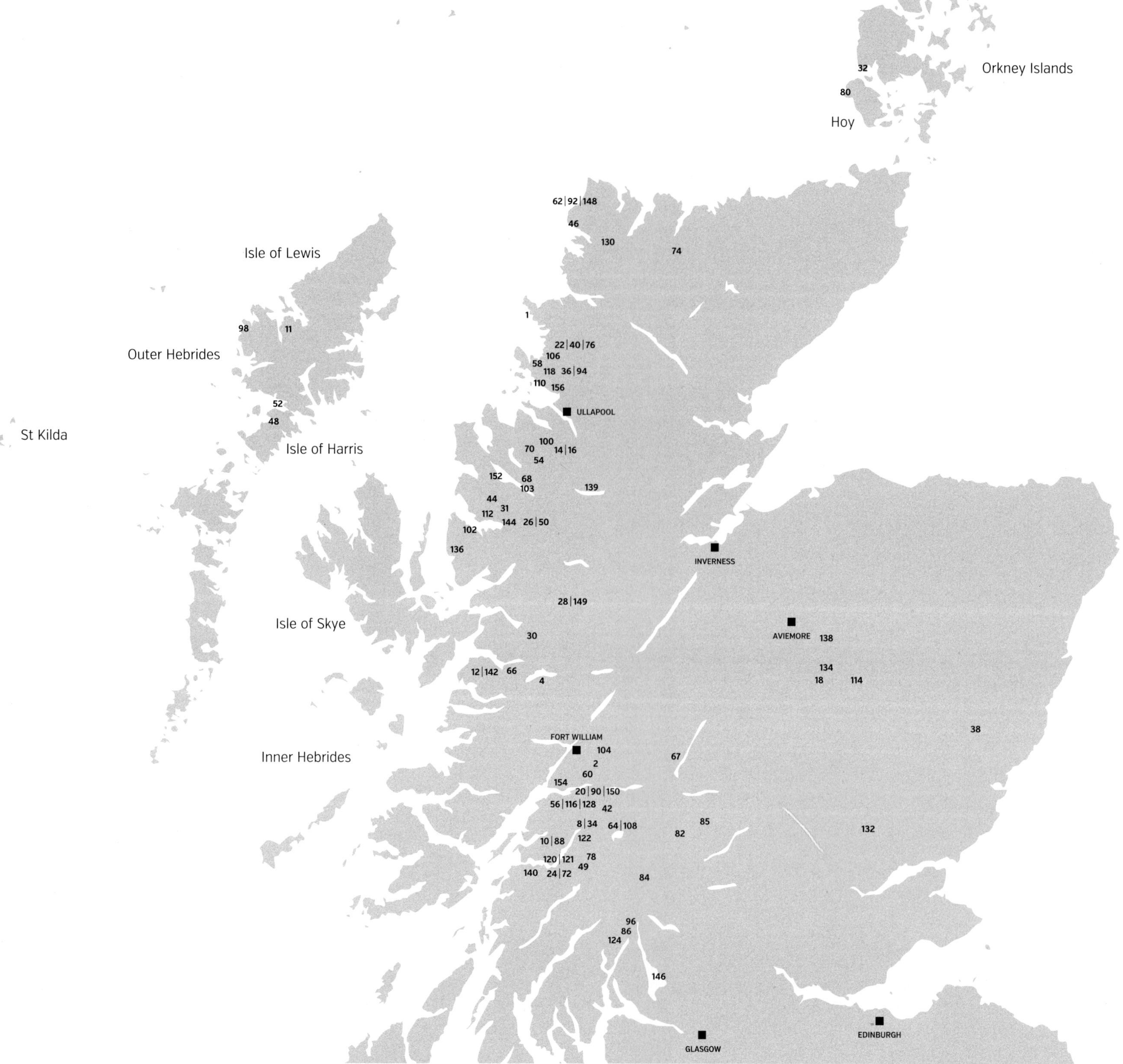

Orkney Islands
32
80
Hoy
Isle of Lewis
62 | 92 | 148
46
130
74
Outer Hebrides
98   11
1
22 | 40 | 76
106
58
118 36 | 94
110 156
St Kilda
52
48
ULLAPOOL
Isle of Harris
100
70   14 | 16
54
152   68
103
139
44
112 31
144 26 | 50
102
136
INVERNESS
28 | 149
Isle of Skye
30
AVIEMORE 138
134
18   114
12 | 142 66
4
38
FORT WILLIAM
Inner Hebrides
104
2
60
67
154
20 | 90 | 150
56 | 116 | 128 42
8 | 34 64 | 108
85
82
132
10 | 88 122
120 | 121 78
140 24 | 72 49
84
96
86
124
146
GLASGOW
EDINBURGH

MAP KEY

In book order: numbers refer to page numbers within the book.

1 Split Rock, Clachtoll	82 The River Lyon, Glen Lyon
2 The Ring of Steall, Mamores	84 The River Fillan, Stirling
4 Gairich and Sgùrr Mòr, Loch Quoich	85 Glen Lyon
8 Glen Etive	86 Loch Lomond and the Arrochar Alps
10 Loch Etive	88 Loch Etive
11 Isle of Lewis	90 Aonach Eagach, Glen Coe
12 Ladhar Bheinn, Knoydart	92 Sandwood Bay, Sutherland
14 An Teallach, Dundonnell (Winter)	94 Loch Lurgainn, Inverpolly
16 An Teallach, Dundonnell (Summer)	96 Ben Vorlich, Loch Lomond
18 The Lairig Ghru, Cairngorms	98 Mangurstadh, Isle of Lewis
20 Garbh Bheinn, Loch Leven	100 Lord Berkeley's Seat, An Teallach
22 Canisp and Suilven, Loch Druim Suardalain, Assynt	102 Loch Torridon, Wester Ross
24 Ben Cruachan, Argyll and Bute	103 Slioch, Wester Ross
26 Loch Clair, Glen Torridon	104 Sgùrr Choinnich Beag, Glen Nevis
28 Loch Affric, Glen Affric	106 Loch Sionascaig, Inverpolly
30 Kintail, West Highlands	108 Beinn an Dòthaidh and Beinn Dòrain, Loch Tulla
31 Torridon, Wester Ross	110 The Summer Isles, Coigach
32 Hoy Sound, Orkney	112 Torridon, Wester Ross
34 Glen Etive	114 Glen Luibeg, Braemar
36 Loch Lurgainn, Inverpolly	116 Bidean nam Bian, Glen Coe
38 River North Esk, Angus	118 Stac Pollaidh, Inverpolly
40 Suilven, Assynt	120 Loch Etive, Argyll and Bute
42 Rannoch Moor	121 Loch Etive, Argyll and Bute
44 Shieldaig Forest, Wester Ross	122 Lorn, West Highlands
46 Oldshoremore, Sutherland	124 The Cobbler, Arrochar
48 Luskentyre, Harris	126 Lochan an Ais, Inverpolly
49 Beinn a' Chochuill, Argyll and Bute	128 Glen Coe
50 Liathach, Glen Torridon	130 Foinaven and Arkle, Loch Inchard
52 The Sound of Taransay, Harris	132 North Wood, Perthshire
54 Beinn Dearg Mòr and An Teallach, Fisherfield	134 Braeriach, Cairngorms
56 Stob Dubh, Stob Coire Sgreamhach and Bidean nam Bian, Glen Coe	136 Isle of Skye and the Inner Sound
58 Loch Bad a' Ghaill, Inverpolly	138 Loch Morlich, Cairngorms
60 Loch Leven	139 The Fannichs, Strath Bran
62 Am Buachaille, Sandwood Bay	140 Ben Cruachan, Glen Lonan
64 Loch Tulla and Stob Ghabhar	142 Ladhar Bheinn, Knoydart
66 Glen Barrisdale, Knoydart	144 Liathach, Torridon, Wester Ross
67 Ben Alder, Badenoch	146 Loch Lomond, Argyll and Bute
68 Slioch, Wester Ross	148 Sandwood Bay, Sutherland
70 Strath na Sealga, Fisherfield	149 Loch Affric, Glen Affric
72 Stob Daimh, Ben Cruachan	150 Glen Coe
74 Ben Loyal, Sutherland	152 Loch Maree, Wester Ross
76 Suilven and Canisp, Assynt	154 Sgorr na Ciche and Bidean nam Bian, Loch Leven
78 The Southern Highlands	156 Coigach, Inverpolly and Assynt
80 The Old Man of Hoy, Orkney	

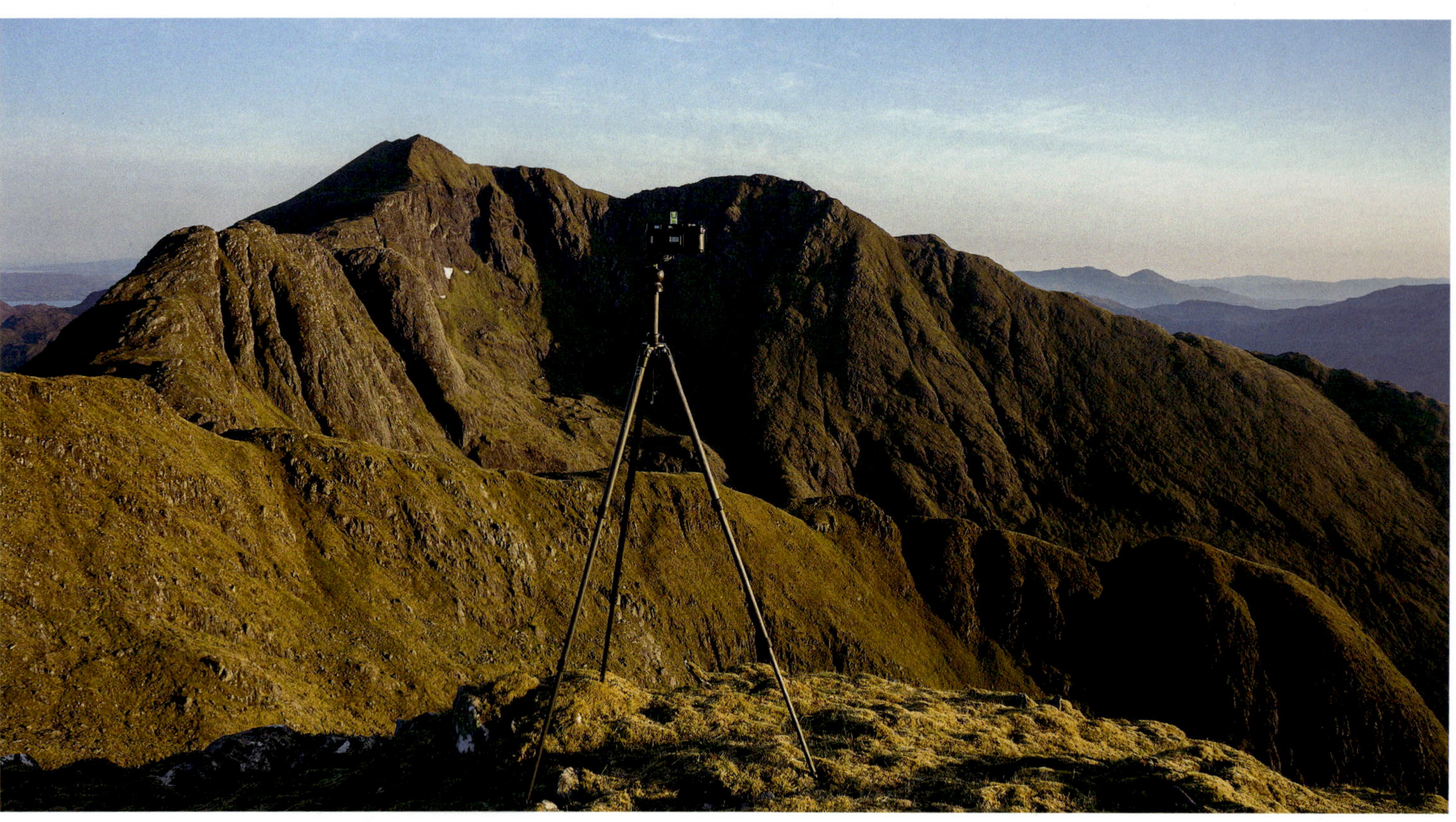

ACKNOWLEDGEMENTS

First and foremost I would like to extend my heartfelt thanks to my wife Alison for her unsurpassed help and support that has allowed me the opportunity to be away from home at ludicrously short notice. Any weather-dependent plans I had, no matter how absurd, were always prioritised and accepted without question. This flexibility was paramount for the sometimes-convoluted logistics of mountain photography, and has made my life a lot easier for when the right times came.

A special thanks also goes to my good friend Colin Marshall who has faithfully assisted and advised me on the introduction text and helped steer me through the countless decisions and intricate details that matter with such an important project. Colin's patience and attention to detail have helped immeasurably with the production of this book and I deeply appreciate the time and effort invested by him over the years.

Honourable mentions are also extended to Ian Scovell at *www.ianscovell.com* and Tim Parkin at *www.drumscanning.co.uk* for their professional film scanning. Working with film comes with many challenges and I wish to thank them both for their in-depth knowledge and expertise in the dark art of digital replication and for getting my images beautifully duplicated on screen.

I would also like to offer my personal thanks to John Coefield, Jane Beagley and all those at Vertebrate Publishing for their commitment to and investment in my photography and this project as a whole. It means a huge amount to me and I feel privileged to be allowed this platform from which to showcase my images.

Finally, my thanks to all those who have helped me indirectly. David Morrison, Gerry McAllister, James Blest, Ian Rodney, Bridget McCann, Douglas Griffin and my mum and dad.